A Volume in
Contemporary Perspectives in
Early Childhood Education

Contemporary Perspectives on Play in Early
Childhood Education

Library of Congress Cataloging-in-Publication Data

Contemporary perspectives on play in early childhood education / edited
by Olivia N. Saracho and Bernard Spodek.
    p. cm. – (Contemporary perspectives in early childhood
education)
  ISBN 1-930608-31-4 – ISBN 1-930608-30-6 (pbk.)
  1. Play. 2. Early childhood education. I. Saracho, Olivia N. II.
Spodek, Bernard. III. Series.
  LB1139.35.P55 C66 2002 *2003*
  155.4'18–dc21
                         2002015501

Printed in the United States of America

Contemporary Perspectives on Play in Early Childhood Education

Edited by

Olivia N. Saracho
University of Maryland

and

Bernard Spodek
University of Illinois

INFORMATION AGE
PUBLISHING

80 Mason Street
Greenwich, Connecticut 06830

CONTEMPORARY PERSPECTIVES
IN EARLY CHILDHOOD EDUCATION
Advisory Committee

Consulting Editors

CONTENTS

INTRODUCTION
Historical Antecedents of Early Childhood Educational Play

Olivia N. Saracho and Bernard Spodek

Throughout much of history children's play has received little attention. However, recently it has gained considerable attention and important concerns about play in young children have emerged.

Play has been a part of early childhood programs since the initial kindergarten developed by Friedreich Froebel more than 150 years ago. The Froebelian kindergarten curriculum included the manipulation of *Gifts*, the application of craft activities or *Occupations*, and the children's participation in the *Mother's Plays and Songs*. Spodek and Saracho (1994) provide a description of Froebel's gifts. Children were not free to express themselves through the different forms of play, although the activities were manipulative and many were abstracted from children's free play. The natural play of German peasant children was carefully observed and became the foundation of this kindergarten activity. Friedrich Froebel identified the essential elements of the play and abstracted and systematized what he considered to be the essential elements to guarantee that they would be available to all children. While play in the Froebel kindergarten was highly teacher directed, a freer form of play was found in the Macmillan Nursery

Contemporary Perspectives on Play in Early Childhood Education
A Volume in: Contemporary Perspectives in Early Childhood Education, pages vii–xv.
Copyright © 2003 by Information Age Publishing, Inc.
All rights of reproduction in any form reserved.
ISBN: 1-930608-31-4 (cloth), 1-930608-30-6 (paper)

School and in the reform kindergarten that was reconstructed in the progressive education era.

Activity was also an essential part of the early childhood curriculum designed by Maria Montessori. When she developed her educational method, she also drew the essential elements from children's natural play activities, reconstructed them, and systematized them in an instructional method. Activities in the early childhood curricula of Friedreich Froebel and Maria Montessori were designed to accomplish very different instructional goals. Froebel's purpose was to help children acquire the spiritual meanings symbolized by the materials and the activities. In contrast, Montessori's purpose was to help children obtain a better understanding of the properties of objects and acquire specific skills by manipulating the objects. In both cases, the aspects of the activity regarded as educational were abstracted and various features of play were deleted from the educational technique.

In the first quarter of the twentieth century, the emergence of the reform kindergarten movement and the modern nursery-school movement precipitated the acceptance of children's organic play as a vehicle for learning. These educational approaches supported and nurtured children's natural play activities as being educationally meaningful in their own right. However, neither of these innovative educational systems considered play to be the only way for children to learn. The increased concerns about educational play and its effects in young children's education stimulated numerous studies that have used varying methodologies to explore the effects of young children's play.

EDUCATIONAL CONCERNS: PRÉCIS

With increased concerns about young children's education in early childhood programs, alternative approaches to educating them have developed. Researchers have focused on a variety of current concerns that have emerged, including the interaction between children and adults and between children and their peers. This volume provides an overview of some of these concerns.

This volume presents a review and critical analysis of the research and theoretical knowledge on the educational play of young children. The chapters reflect a range of philosophies on various aspects of children's play. Each chapter includes

1. a review of research and theory,
2. implications for practice, and
3. a comprehensive set of references that directs the reader to further study in an important aspect of play covered.

In the first chapter, "Understanding Play and Its Theories," Olivia N. Saracho and Bernard Spodek describe the historical developments related to the theories that assist individuals to understand play and justify young children's play. Classical and modern theories as well as contemporary theories allow the reader to understand the contemporary rhetoric on children's play and philosophies presented in the volume within the intellectual context within which they have been generated.

In Chapter 2, "Spontaneous Play in the 21st Century," Fergus Peter Hughes defines children's play as a spontaneous activity that promotes their intellectual, language/literacy, and social·development. Children's play is seen as being influenced by their particular sociocultural context and the characteristics of their environment. It is dependent on this context and these characteristics for support. Hughes believes that the social and cultural conditions that support spontaneous play are less in evidence today than they were in the past, because of the increasing complexity and specialization in children's play materials, the increasing organization in children's games, and the growing tendency to characterize rough-and-tumble play as symptomatic of pathology.

During the past 25 years, studies have explored characteristics of play in early childhood, the conditions under which it occurs, and its relationships to the development and learning of young children. Building upon the existing knowledge base that has been developed over these years, researchers are now delving more deeply into questions concerning how play (especially pretense play) fosters a range of cognitive processes. Experimental and observational research on mental representation (theory of mind) has linked development of theory of mind to pretense. Another area of research that has links to play, especially to social pretense, is that of development of humor. Doris Bergen, in Chapter 3, "Theories of Pretense, Mental Representation, and Humor Development: Answers and Questions," reviews some of the theoretical issues and research findings from the pretense/theory of mind and pretense/humor studies and raises questions about the potential relationship between theory of mind and humor development. She makes a case for studying the characteristics of humor expressed by young children in their social pretense to shed light on the course of both pretense and theory of mind development.

In some Western countries, play has become an integral part of the school's curriculum. The main reason for this is that early childhood education now is seen to encompass both the preschool years and the early years of primary school, from the age of 0, up to 8 or 9 years. In Norway and other Scandinavian countries two educational traditions are being integrated in the curriculum according to new reforms, the tradition of preschool education, and the tradition of primary school education. Against this background a change in the teacher's role in relation to children's play is necessary, although it represents a challenge. The modification of the teacher's role can be seen as a tendency in other countries as well, however, not to the same extent as in the Scandinavian countries.

Research on children's play in relation to the teachers' role in learning and in developing a sense of competence in the classroom is presented in Chapter 4, "Play in School—The Teacher Role: Reforms and Recent Research" by Ole Friedrich Lillemyer. This chapter is based on studies conducted in Europe, the United States, New Zealand, and Australia. Lillemyer assumes that teachers look at play both as an inspiration and a challenge. He uses the concept of "scaffolding" as an effective way of helping children enhance and extend their knowledge in terms of the teacher's role in play. Lillemyer believes that teachers seem to support and emphasize choice for the children even if the teacher determines the classroom activities. This requires adults to intervene to encourage young children to explore available choices during play sessions. This indicates that adult involvement in play and children's development of independence are not mutually exclusive. Lillemyer encourages the reader to look at two conceptions of play: learning through play and the value of play as such. The research studies presented in this chapter disclose the differences in the extent to which play really is an integral part of the curriculum: these strongly differ from one country to another. Even in countries like Norway, where play has a rather strong position in the curriculum guidelines, the children do not seem to expect much free learning to take place in school (e.g., learning that occurs when children choose among alternatives and make decisions about what and how in the activities). Nevertheless, a strong emphasis on play actually offers varied forms of learning as far as student autonomy is concerned. Lillemyer highlights what research indicates to be the change of the teacher's role. Some of these changes are presented and discussed in his chapter from the perspective of the relationship between child care and school, which contributes to a change in the teacher's role in children's play in the future.

Lillemyer maintains that the inclusion of play in the first years of school implies development towards a new and broader concept of school learning. He views learning as processes providing an increased capacity to comprehend, experience, feel, reflect, and act. Hence, he believes that a new and broader concept of school learning has to include both the acquisition of knowledge and skills, as well as the applications of knowledge, as it is seen in experimentation and creativity. Furthermore, learning affects the whole personality of the children and in turn the personality also affects their learning.

In understanding children's learning, many studies have focused on their personal characteristics. Researchers conclude that individual personality factors affect the children's learning performance, because they influence their cognitive functioning. Functional components of cognitive processes affect the individuals' mental, personality, and social behaviors. Modes of cognitive functioning that become evident in an individual's perceptual and intellectual experiences in a highly consistent and pervasive manner makeup an individuals' cognitive style, which refers to the consistent mode in which individuals process information. Cognitive style characterizes the individuals' responses to a variety of situations. It includes stable attitudes, preferences, or habitual strategies that distinguish the individual styles of perceiving, remembering, thinking, and solving problems. Researchers believe that there is a relationship between cognitive style and social interaction. Studies that examine the relationship between preschool children's social orientation and cognitive style have focus on children's play, what Saracho (1986) refers to as a form of social behavior. Olivia N. Saracho, in her chapter, "Young Children's Play and Cognitive Style," reviews studies that explore this relationship in reference to the field dependence, independence dimension of cognitive style and its characteristics in young children's social behaviors (e.g., social interaction, social orientation, cognitive-social play). She recommends that teachers use play to assist young children in becoming flexible in their cognitive functioning. This relationship will continue to be examined diversely in future research.

David H. Uttal discusses a different aspect of cognitive development in young children in relation to play and the study of mathematics. He looks at the way that children understand the symbols they use. Symbolic play is typically used in teaching young children. The use of hands-on activities to support children's learning, based on the concept that children's manipulation of symbolic materials, leads to a greater understanding of the concepts underlying these symbols and their manipulation. In Chapter 6, "The Relation Between Play and Symbolic Thought: The Case of Mathematics Manipulatives," Uttal uses the term play to refer to structured activities in which teachers (or parents) guide the children's play activities where teachers often plan activities and choose particular playthings with the goal of facilitating children's development or learning. His chapter focuses on a quintessential example of this type of structured play, the use of manipulatives to teach mathematics. He treats the term manipulatives in a general way, using it to refer to any physical system of objects that is (a) intended to help young children learn mathematical concepts, and (b) do not require that children use or comprehend written representations of the same concepts. Manipulatives are concrete objects (rods, blocks, etc.) that are designed to represent quantities and are used to facilitate children's mathematical development. There are formal manipulative systems, such as Dienes Blocks and Cuisenaire Rods that are designed specifically to teach mathematics. But teachers also use many informal types of manipulatives, which can include household objects (paper clips, coins, etc.) and even pieces of candy or cereal. In addition, manipulatives have moved into the digital age. For example, there are now several digital libraries of manipulatives. Computer scientists have created systems that combine the features of traditional hand—held manipulatives with advanced electronic technologies. These "digital manipulatives" indicate electronically when children have combined the manipulatives in the correct or expected way. For example, manipulatives representing the "tens" units in an addition problem may turn red and those representing the "ones" units may turn blue. Obviously there are real and important differences in the types of manipulatives that young children are asked to use. It seems likely that different forms of manipulatives affect children's mathematical thinking in different ways. However, most manipulative systems share a common characteristic; each is intended to represent mathematical information in a form that is tractable and does not require the use of written representations. Uttal focuses on this substitution for written representations, and the consequences of this substitution. The focus of this chapter is on the difficulties and opportunities that arise from the use of manipulatives in early mathematics education. He addresses the specific question of why children seem to have so much difficulty relating physical (concrete or manipulative) representations. He begins by documenting the problem that children have in relating manipulatives to written representations. Next, he situates the problem of understanding the relation between manipulative-based representations and written representations within cognitive research on children's understanding of symbolic and representational relations. This literature provides insights into the special challenges that children face when they are asked to relate one system of representation (e.g., manipulatives), to another (e.g., written representations). Finally, he concludes with specific recommendations regarding how teachers can best help children to understand and use manipulatives.

Manipulatives are used extensively in early education. Their use is encouraged for children of all ability levels, including not only typical preschoolers but also gifted children and those with developmental disabilities. The fundamental assumption that drives the enthusiasm regarding manipulatives is that young children understand mathematical concepts and relations in fundamentally different ways than older children and adults do. Young children's conception of mathematics is more concrete and tied to manipulations and transformations that can be performed manually. The theoretical basis for this belief is derived from the writings of Bruner (1966), Piaget (1964), and others. Each of these scholars stressed, in different ways, the importance of concreteness and concrete objects on the development of children's concepts. Educators and developmental theorists alike have assumed that concrete is inherently appropriate; abstract is inherently not appropriate at the beginning, at least for young learners. Manipulatives are thought to be particularly appropriate for young children because they encourage learning through natural exploration and play. In this view, manipulatives allow children to learn through play or at least in a playful manner. Despite the enthusiasm for the use of manipulatives, serious questions have been raised about their efficacy. Both meta-analyses and intensive, longitudinal studies of children's mathematical development have failed to confirm that using manipulatives conveys a clear and consistent advantage in young children's learning of mathematics (Chao, Stigler, & Woodward, 2000). Young children often fail to make a connection between concepts that they learn from manipulatives and written representations of the same or similar concepts. For example, a child might learn about the base-ten system through the use of Dienes Blocks, but the same child might gain no advantage in mastering the written representation of the base-10 system. Similarly, children might learn basic principles of addition from manipulatives but then fail to see a connection to the + sign.

In Chapter 7, "Play and Early Development and Education: The Instantiation of Parental Belief Systems," Jaipaul L. Roopnarine, Meera Shin, Kwanghee Jung and Ziarat Hossain review studies on parental beliefs concerning the importance of play in the children's development and early childhood curriculum in relation to the tremendous intra-cultural and inter-cultural variations in belief models about the value of play. They provide some theoretical propositions on how parental belief systems are formulated and an overview of research on parental cultural models about play. Roopnarine and his associates conclude that parental beliefs seem to fall along a continuum: parents in some societies embrace play as the *sin qua non* of early childhood socialization experiences, while in other societies they seem less impressed by its possibility for contributing to childhood development. They discuss the implications of the diverse parental beliefs within the classic didactic instruction versus play-based constructivist model of early childhood education. They then make a plea to examine parental beliefs about play in early childhood education using the *trajectory principle.*

Several theorists have the notion that play activity has the potential to promote both cognitive and social competence in children. For example, young children and toddlers who engage in sophisticated pretend play (e.g., using a crayon as a phone) are often brighter than children who engage in less complex forms of play as well as preschoolers who engage in play that involves elaborate sociodramatic themes (e.g., "Let's play Star Wars!") are more socially competent and better liked than their counterparts that do not initiate such behavior. In Chapter 8, "Social Play in Children: An Attachment Perspective," Gary L. Creasey and Patricia Jarvis report that some experts believe that training children to play in more competent ways may encourage more acceptance within the peer group, while other experts suggest that encouraging parents and children to play together may serve as a vehicle to improve relationships in the family system. Their chapter examines why ethological attachment theory provides an important perspective to consider for professionals interested in children's play. They believe that integrating this perspective with other popular theories on children's play—such as Vygotsky's—may encourage more diverse thinking about potential antecedents and consequences of this important activity. Creasey and Jarvis provide an overview of ethological attachment theory and highlight the role of play within this perspective. Next, they discuss why consideration of attachment theory may have important implications for theoretical approaches to children's play. Following this discussion, they turn to research that support's Bowlby's contention that attachment relationships form a major foundation for the development of exploration and play in children. Finally, they consider why such theory and research might have important implications for intervention efforts involving children's play.

Chapter 10,"The Teening of Early Childhood" by Francine Smolucha specifically addresses a concern for the teening of preschoolers. During the past 20 years, teen clothing and music have been marketed for preschoolers. Pretend play has also been "teened" as evidenced by the preponderance of sexy teenage dolls and violent Superhero action figures marketed for 3-year-old girls and boys, respectively. This is part of a larger trend, the teening of childhood, which has been discussed in the popular press but not in academia. She suggests that play researchers investigate whether there has been a change in children's play culture in the United States of America during the last 30 years. Smolucha claims that teachers and caregivers need strategies for guiding pretend play in positive directions. They need to consider the possibility that the media culture of postmodern America has fundamentally changed the psychosocial stages of child development. According to Aries (1954/1963) 19th century European concepts of a sheltered childhood and an adolescent identity crisis are historical/cultural constructs peculiar to that era. With the advent of television, and the media culture that followed, distinctions between childhood, adolescence, and adulthood are being blurred. Children witness traumatic events that have occurred thousands of miles away, such as the terrorist attack on September 11, 2001 on the World Trade Center, at the same time as adults. Media technology (including television and video games) and pretend play are tools that can be used to promote either healthy or dysfunctional behaviors. Smolucha's presents a field report using her experience as a researcher who has spent the last five years as a participant observer of contemporary American preschool culture. She also has surveyed and interviewed over 400 parents and a dozen preschool teachers. She reviews the research literature on pretend play in relation to the teening of preschool play.

The final chapter in this volume, "Preserving Play with Diversification and Distinction" by Olivia N. Saracho and Bernard Spodek, focuses on summarizing what theories and research regarding play have contributed over the years and provides a justification for spontaneous and naturalistic educational play in early childhood programs. The theories of play suggest that young children's behavior should be voluntary, enjoyable, and pleasurable in order for children's activities to be considered play. Children should have the motivation to engage in play for long periods of time, socialize with one another within their own world, pursue information, interact with their surroundings, and learn through play. Children maintain their play if it provides a pleasing experience and allows them, in their own way, to interact with peers within their world. According to Spodek and Saracho (1994), the value of play is that it encourages children to inquire about and understand role dimensions and interaction patterns, which will assist them in understanding their social world and build a realistic sense of *self*. Play provides children with an information seeking process (personal response), a means to interact with their environment (response to the social environment), and a way of learning how to learn (Saracho & Spodek, 1995). Saracho and Spodek make a plea for teachers to assume the important role of implementing children's play that has educational value, is natural, is spontaneous, and conserves its qualities as play. The children's consistency and interest in engaging in their play as well as its efficiency to achieve the early childhood program's educational goals are the best criteria in determining the value of play.

Collectively these chapters provide an expansive notion of the contemporary status of knowledge that recognizes and accepts children's play in a variety of forms. They offer recommendations to researchers in examining children's play and pinpoint the implications of the current status of knowledge for teachers and others who work directly or indirectly with young children. The content that is communicated in this volume ought to open new frontiers for those in early childhood education that for countless eras has immortalized play as a learning medium for young children.

REFERENCES

Aries, Philippe. (1954/1963). *Centuries of childhood.* Penguin Books.

Bruner, J. S. (1966). *Toward a theory of instruction.* Cambridge, MA: Bilknap.

Chao, S. J., Stigler, J., Woodward, J. A. (2000). The effects of physical materials on kindergartners' learning of number concepts. *Cognition and Instruction, 18,* 285-316.

Piaget, J. (1964). *The child's conception of the world.* London: Routledge & K. Paul.

Saracho, O. N. (1986). Play and young children's learning. In B. Spodek (Ed.), *Today's kindergarten: Exploring the knowledge base, expanding the curriculum,* (pp. 91-109). New York: Teachers College Press.

Saracho, O. N., & Spodek, B. (1995). Children's play and early childhood education: Insights from history and theory. *Journal of Education, 177*(3), 129-148.

Spodek, B., & Saracho, O. N. (1994). *Right from the start: Teaching children ages three to eight.* Boston: Allyn & Bacon.

CHAPTER 1

UNDERSTANDING PLAY AND ITS THEORIES

Olivia N. Saracho and Bernard Spodek

Play primarily affords juveniles practice toward the exercise of later skills
—Smith, 1982, p. 166

Understanding play has been difficult because of its many definitions. This understanding becomes more complex because the role of play in the early childhood education curriculum has been in constant flux since the 19th century. Children's play is depicted in several ancient writings, although each civilization has had a different view of play. In Ancient Greece, adults were gentle with children and gave them affection (French, 1977). In contrast, early Western civilizations neglected play and provided vague information about children's play.

The concept of play has always been part of early childhood education al programs since their early development. The current theory of play as a vehicle for learning and development in the early years, originated in the Progressive Era. Although both Froebel and Montessori saw children's activities as a means to achieve learning. Progressive early childhood edu-

Contemporary Perspectives on Play in Early Childhood Education
A Volume in: Contemporary Perspectives in Early Childhood Education, pages 1–19.
Copyright © 2003 by Information Age Publishing, Inc.
All rights of reproduction in any form reserved.
ISBN: 1-930608-31-4 (cloth), 1-930608-30-6 (paper)

cators differentiated between play and other children's performance. In their view, children's play resulted from the children's free and inherent motivation. Play was action performed for its own sake; in contrast, work was an activity done for external reward or requirement. Since children's play is a serious activity, it must be integrated as an important part of in the early childhood education curriculum (Spodek & Saracho, 1997).

The Progressive theory of play continues to underlie contemporary early childhood programs, where equipment and materials are provided to support play in classrooms. For example, almost all classrooms for three-to five-year-old children have a dramatic play area that includes miniature representations of kitchen equipment (e.g., play pots, pans, dishes), household furniture, dolls, cleaning equipment, plastic food, and other comparable items. Children use these miniature representations to dramatize their home life. Materials may also represent other familiar areas of adult life such as a supermarket, a doctor's office, or a garage for repairing cars. Children construct busses, airplanes, or trains and assume the role of drivers, pilots, or engineers. They may transport toy vehicles through streets, superhighways, or rivers that they build with blocks to portray particular settings. Teachers observe how children play to sustain and encourage it by introducing new ideas and materials or recommending elaborations to the children's activities (Saracho, 1991).

Children's activity was considered an important element in early childhood education even before the Progressive era. Froebel, the creator of the earliest kindergarten, refers to play as an educational aim. The kindergarten curriculum was composed of *Gifts, Occupations,* and *Mother's Plays and Songs*. The *gifts* were sets of objects (e.g., wooden and woolen balls, wooden blocks). *Occupations* represented arts-and-crafts activities (e.g., paper weaving; paper folding, cutting, sewing). *Mother's Plays and Songs* were songs and games. The activities and materials in Froebel's curriculum symbolized his basic concepts about the unity of the individual, God, and nature that Froebel wanted children to acquire. Froebel (1887) used the terms *freedom* and *play* in describing his program, his activities were less free and less a form of play that we would consider today. His kindergarten activities were prescriptive, giving children precise directions on how to utilize the materials. Although the activities were manipulative and derived from free play, children did not immerse themselves in free, expressive forms of play. The lack of spontaneity in Froebel's activities cannot be regarded as play today (Saracho, 1991).

At the beginning of the twentieth century, Maria Montessori developed a different early childhood curriculum, the Montessori Method (Montessori, 1965, 1973). Maria Montessori (1870-1952) culled her perception of the essential elements of her method from the natural play activities of children. She designed materials and observed children play with them freely in the classroom. She reassembled and systematized these play elements, discouraging children's free play with the Montessori materials (Montessori, 1965). Children were allowed to manipulate the Montessori materials but in prescribed ways. These manipulative activities were considered work instead of play.

Although both the Froebelian kindergarten and Montessori methods used observations of the play activities of children in developing their program, their educational methods on children's play differed, because of their different perspective on the nature of knowledge. Froebel, an idealist, utilized the materials and the activities of his kindergarten in assisting children to understand abstract ideas and spiritual meanings they represented. Montessori, an empiricist, utilized her method to assist children to become aware of their qualities by manipulating them. Children formulated knowledge by collecting and systematizing their sensory impressions to formulate knowledge. Both approaches regarded activities as educational even though several of the attributes of play were ignored.

Both of these early childhood curricula were based on observations of children's play, although each curriculum developer differed in their inferences about the play observations and diagnosed activities accordingly for their curriculum. Inasmuch as the curriculum activities were based on children's play, the activities themselves were not play.

It was with the work of John Dewey (1859-1952) that early childhood educators developed their modern conception of play as education. Dewey rejected Froebel's view of play. He separated his views of children's play activities from those that had been established in colonial times, when adults cautioned children "to avoid the frivolity of play," and advised them to become more work-oriented as they grew up (Hartley & Goldenson, 1963, p. 1). Dewey's conviction of how child learn was the cornerstone for the contemporary perspective on the educational use of children's play. In the laboratory school at the University of Chicago that he established, he included "sub-primary" class instead of a kindergarten. Dewey believed in an education of young children that integrated their daily experiences in the community. He believed that education was embedded in the social life of the community and that children made these experiences educational by reconstructing their experiences. Using play to reconstruct their experiences, could gain meaning from them and a higher levels of awareness and action (Dewey, 1900). Teachers provided an atmosphere that would support the children's mental and moral growth through play (Dewey, 1916).

The growing interest concerning the educational consequences of early childhood programs initiated many investigations on the effects of young children's play. A review of the theories of play and strategies on how to promote educational play can help understand play.

PLAY THEORIES

Scholars have searched for an understanding on the nature of children's play behavior. Over the years, many theories have evolved, often related to the many that have been proposed.

These are a sample of these definitions:

Seashore: Free self-expression for the pleasure of expression.

Froebel: The natural unfolding of the germinal leaves of childhood.

Hall: The motor habits and spirit of the past persisting in the present.

Groos: Instinctive practice, without serious intent, of activities which will later be essential to life.

Dewey: Activities not consciously performed for the sake of any result beyond themselves.

Schiller: The aimless expenditure of exuberant energy.

Spenser: Superfluous actions taking place instinctively in the absence of real actions . . . . Activity performed for the immediate gratification derived without regard for ulterior benefits.

Lazarus: Activity in itself free, aimless, amusing, or diverting.

Shand: A type of play directed at the maintenance of joy.

Dulles: An instinctive form of self-expression and emotional escape value.

Curti: Highly motivated activity, which, as free from conflicts, is usually, though not always, pleasurable (Mitchell & Mason, 1948, pp. 103-104).

Each definition noted above suggests a different understanding and interpretation of children's play. Such differences explain the variations from theory to theory. Two categories of play theories have been identified: (1) *classical theories* from the 19th and early 20th centuries and (2) *modern theories* emerged after 1920 (Mellou, 1994).

Classical Theories

Classical theories describe the reason and functions of play. They are

1. Surplus Energy,
2. Recreational or Relaxation,
3. Practice or Pre-exercise, and
4. Recapitulation theories.

The Surplus Energy Theory can be found in the Aristotelian philosophy of catharsis. Much later Friedreich Schiller (1759-1805), the eighteenth century German poet, historian, and philosopher, also postulated the surplus energy theory. He believed that play was an "aimless expenditure of exuberant energy." This theory suggests that play helps to eliminate any organism of "excess energy" that is left over after meeting basic survival needs. This theory of play assumes that animals create more energy than they need to survive. According to the surplus energy theory, all living things (humans as well as other animals) generate ample energy to fulfill their survival needs; whatever extra (surplus) energy exists is removed through play. All human and nonhuman animals need to eliminate any surplus energy.

Herbert Spenser (1820-1903), the British philosopher, adopted a separate version of the Surplus Energy Theory. At a very early age, the organism has an intractable yearning to play; therefore, Spenser perceived play as a superfluous activity. He associated this surplus energy theory of play in the context of evolution: Higher species animals play more than lower species ones. The younger of the higher order species take advantage of the surplus energy theory, because they depend on their parents for prolonged periods of time in their lives. They use less energy for survival (e.g., meeting the organism's fundamental needs); therefore they have more energy for play.

A 20th century psychologist, Berlyne (1969) integrated Spenser's thoughts on surplus energy theory into his arousal theory. He believed that the sensory mechanism was responsible for the existence of play. According to Rubin (1982), Schiller described play as related to "surplus energy," whereas Spenser referred to it as a "superfluous activity." These philosophers did not think play was necessary for human development. Instead they considered it to be a mechanism that assists the organism to balance its energy. On the other hand, Berlyne thought play provided an important purpose in human development and was essential for cognitive development.

Recreational or Relaxation Theory, as stated by Moritz Lazarus (1883), the German poet, describes play as an activity that individuals use to replenish energy. If play is the opposite of work, it restores the energy that was consumed during work. Play is created as a recreational activity (Lazarus, 1883) or as a behavior pattern that surfaces from a necessity to relax (Patrick, 1916). Recreational or Relaxation theory can be seen as the reverse of surplus energy theory (Lazarus, 1883).

Practice or Pre-exercise Theory, developed by Karl Groos (1896, 1901), identifies a myriad of customs and purposes of children's play in adult games, rituals, and competitions. Groos (1901) developed a categorical system that consisted of experimental play (games with rules), socioeconomic play (rough-and-tumble play), and imitative, social, and family games (dramatic play). Play motivates children to imitate and practice adult roles that prepare children for adulthood and their future. For instance, children enact parental roles in dramatic play. Children are practicing roles that they will assume as adults in the future. Several modern developmental theorists (e.g., Bruner, 1976; Sylva, Bruner, & Genova, 1974) support Groos' Practice or Pre-exercise Theory. This theory is currently supported by constructivist theories where play is considered to develop the children's intellectual performance (Piaget, 1951, 1962).

Recapitulation Theory, developed by G. Stanley Hall (1844-1924), an American psychologist, suggests that the individual's development reestablishes the species' development. Hall (1906) based his recapitulation theory on Charles Darwin's theory of evolution. Hall (1906) hypothesized that each human being originates at the embryo stage and proceeds through evolutionary stages that are similar to those of the human species. In this process children dramatize the human race's developmental stages (e.g., animal, savage, tribal member) in their play. In these stages, play offers a catharsis that liberates children from any primitive instincts that are unsuitable for current society.

The classical theories of play can be matched into pairs: (1) *Surplus Energy Theory* with *Recreational/Relaxation Theory* and (2) *Practice/Pre-exercise Theory* with *Recapitulation Theory*. Each pair can be seen as consisting of opposing theories on how play consumes energy or harnesses instincts. The Surplus Energy and Recreational/Relaxation theories describe how play controls energy. One theory distributes excess energy, whereas the other restores the shortage of energy. Both the Practice/Pre-exercise and Recapitulation theories explain play and its attachment to instincts. One theory familiarizes children with adult life as they rehearse the roles in adulthood; whereas the other assists children to relieve themselves of dysfunctional instincts of earlier stages.

The classical theories are grounded in philosophical convictions rather than empirical research (Ellis, 1973); therefore, these theories are considered to be profoundly inadequate. They also lack the current theoretical knowledge of energy, instinct, evolution, and development (Johnson, Christie, & Yawkey, 1999). Nevertheless, they are the cornerstones for the modern theories of play (Rubin, 1982) that are discussed in the following sections.

Modern Theories of Play

Modern theories of play provide an understanding of its essential role in children's development. Typically, the modern theories of play yield an understanding of play by justifying the strength of the theoretical concepts and by supporting it with empirical research. Modern theories view play as a system that fosters cognition or symbolization. Such theories consist of

Psychoanalytic, Arousal Modulation, Metacommunicative, and *Cognitive theories* (Mellou, 1994).

Psychoanalytic Theory, developed by Sigmund Freud and his followers, was derived from clinical practice where individuals described their earlier development and were assisted to handle the suppressed conflicts that occurred at their earlier stages of development and were hidden in their subconscious.

Freud hypothesized that play performed a special function in children's emotional development. Since it enables children to relieve themselves of negative emotions and replace them with more positive ones, play achieves a cathartic effect. This catharsis facilitates children's ability to deal with the consequences of negative feelings and traumas. Consequently, children play to disengage themselves of any negative feelings brought on by traumatic experiences or personal confrontations and allows them to develop a better emotional equilibrium.

Freud (1938) noted that children use play as a tool to overcome their own hidden thoughts related to their perceived actions. Children's active involvement or inactive observation dominates their internalized thought processes and their conscious physical movements. Activity, the second role of play, is associated with the individual's socio-emotional development. Anguish influences the individuals' social relationships or interpersonal dialogues. Play activities and explorations help the children better understand distressing events and search for alternative meaning that embrace pleasurable feelings and forego unpleasant ones. Play assists children to construe an event and link symbolic properties of people and objects in the present and past. Hence, play helps children to communicate their feelings (Wehman & Abramson, 1976).

Freud explored the unconscious. The knowledge he gained from his investigation helped him postulate a series of stages of psychosexual development through which all individuals must undergo. They include the *oral stage* (zero to one year) which is the center of sensual stimulation and pleasure, the *anal stage* (one to three years) which is focal pleasure in withholding or eliminating feces, the *phallic stage* (three to six years) where identification of parents occurs, the stage of latency (six to 12 years) which focuses on industriousness and suppression of sexual interest, and the *genital stage* (12 years and up) which develops mature sexual interests.

Several theorists have modified Freud's psychoanalytic theory based on their separate interpretations. Each theorist interprets a different function of play in human development. Psychoanalysts relate play to wish fulfillment, anxiety, and ego processes (Takhvar, 1988). Erikson (1963), one of Freud's disciples, contributed to personality development theory. Erikson modified Freud's stages of psychosexual development, creating a system of stages of psychosocial development that start at birth and proceed throughout the individual's life (Erikson, 1950). According to Erikson, children play to enact the past, the present, and the future. These play dramatizations assist children to settle any conflicts they encounter at each specific developmental stage.

Peller (1952), another of Freud's followers, suggested that children's imitations of life during play are precipitated by their basic emotional feelings, including love, admiration, fear, and aggression. Both Erikson and Peller believed that the structure of play influences the individual' s psychosocial or psychosexual development.

Psychoanalysts hypothesize that children employ fantasy play events to dramatize adult roles. This gives them a sense of competence that enables them to handle actual predicaments. Children enact personally distressing experiences, overcoming the pain, as they are able to understand it during the play setting. Their ability to manage the situation can also assist children to manage the affective components of positive life events (Murphy, 1956). For instance, a child may becomes sick and need to be rushed to a hospital. This event can leave some negative emotional impressions, since the child suddenly has to leave his warm and reassuring environment to be taken to unfamiliar surroundings with people that he/she does not know. Adding to the child's pain and suffering from the illness, he/she may experience emotional trauma. After the child's health has been regained, he/she may reenact the experiences during the illness through hospital play. While Freud believes that play serves as catharsis; Murphy feels that the child's dramatic play provides a better understanding of the experiences, allowing the child to cope with the emotional consequences of that experience as the child controls the play situation. The child acts out fearful situations in order to be able to cope with them. Thus, play provides a mechanism that assists children to manage the world, understand it, and cope with its problems.

A clinical application of the psychoanalytic theory of play is play therapy, a treatment that is employed with children who have emotional problems. Through play therapy children are able to naturally express themselves and enact emotions of tension, fear, and insecurity. A therapist provides children with toys that help to draw out the children's emotions through play. Therapists observe children during play to gain insight about the children's problems and provide opportunities that assist children to deal with their problems. Play therapy helps children to manage their emotions and obtain security (Axline, 1974).

Arousal Seeking/ Modulation Theory, developed by Berlyne (1969), describes how play lets the organism find sources of arousal to capture certain information. Berlyne (1969) speculated that a need or drive is found in the children's central nervous system that keeps arousal at an optimum level. Too much stimulation (e.g., seeing a strange object) increases arousal to distressingly high levels, steering children to participate in activities that reduce stimulation (e.g., looking at an object to become familiar with it). Lack of stimulation reduces arousal to lower levels, creating monotony. The organism then strives to seek more stimulation, which Berlyne calls "diverse exploration." Searching for activity diminishes the incentive for arousal.

A second arousal-seeking theory, proposed by Ellis (1973), refers to play as a stimulus-seeking activity that offers children with opportunities to manipulate objects and actions in innovative and unusual ways. Ellis (1973) hypothesizes that play increases the levels of both stimulation and arousal. He recommends that individuals continuously aim for sensory adaptation. It has been found that sensory input remains fixed when individuals only concentrate for a short period of time. They explore an assortment of supplementary sources of information to attain more simulation. However, an overabundance of information prompts them to ignore stimulation by overlooking some of the information sources. Individuals think best when conditions offer a wealth of novelty, uncertainty, and complexity. Through play children reach their fullest potential when children are reinforced with the stimulation they need.

Metacommunicative Theory, developed by Bateson (1955), states that the children's play is based on interactions when they engage in make-believe play. Children let their counterparts know that the play episodes are not real; they are only reproductions of life. As a result, through play children learn to behave simultaneously on two levels: (1) make-believe function of objects and actions and (2) authenticity of life (e.g., real identities of players and real function of objects and actions).

Bateson's Metacommunicative theory also asserts that play texts and experiences are continuously developed based on their contexts, including the play environment. Play is the metacommunicative context to the text of reality that gives birth to the cultural and personal resemblance of the individual, implying that play and fantasy are important for the children's cognitive development. Bateson's theory has motivated researchers to study the relationship between play and cognition. Wolf and Grollman (1982) found a developmental age trend in the narrative qualities during children's play changes. Schwartzman (1978) revealed that the children's social status changes their play. The perceptual association between text and context is comparable to the association between communication and metacommunication (Takhvar, 1988).

Cognitive Theories of Play

Child development theorists and researchers have explored the relationship between play and cognitive development. Jean Piaget and Lev S. Vygotsky are the two leading theorists who have contributed knowledge about this relationship. Their ideas are presented here.

Jean Piaget (1896-1980) states that children acquire knowledge through the dual processes of assimilation and accommodation. In assimilation, children gain information from their experiences in the external reality. Then they assimilate or integrate such information into existing mental structures. For accommodation, children modify their mental structures as they compare new information that does not match with the information that they already know. Usually, such controversy forces function in harmony to achieve a state of balance or equilibrium. For spontaneous play, assimilation considers primacy over accommodation, that is, children accommodate the world into their mental structures. Children utilize their present mental schemes and movement patterns to settle their existing problems as they imagine that the world is different. In reality they are not able to cease reality such as how events actually occur. Consequently, children need to accommodate the incoming information (Fein & Schwartz, 1982).

Piaget's (1962) theory includes three stages of play:

1.   sensory-motor play,
2.   symbolic play, and
3.   games with rules.

Such stages portray representations of play that occur in a sequence. When individuals proceed through the stages, their mental structures gradually blend into later stages. Children also progress through these stages in a conforming sequence. Playing games with rules consistently follow symbolic play whereas symbolic play follows sensory-motor play.

In the first stage of play, children's repetitive actions concentrate on physical activity, where accommodation is proclaimed. In the second stage, make-believe or symbolic play emerges, which usually starts at the age of 18-months-old and ends at the age of seven when symbolic activities alter their pattern. Consequently, children's play influences their literacy development. Symbolic play exists regardless of whether the real object being represented is present or absent. Any object can represent and possess the characteristics of the original piece. For instance, a wooden box can portray a car or truck.

Piaget's final stage of play, games with rules, is founded on social protocols and interactions. It evolves during Piaget's concrete operational stage at the age of 6 or 7 years. Activities in games with rules require at least two children, such as checkers, chess, and card games. When games take over, sensorimotor play and symbolic play decrease throughout the individuals' lives.

According to Piaget, modifications in his stages of cognitive development establish the grounds for alterations in the stages of play. Piaget's belief that play develops the individuals' cognitive development is challenged by Vygotsky.

Lev S. Vygotsky (1896-1934), the Russian psychologist, states that play affects more than the children's cognitive development. According to

Vygotsky (1962), symbolic or dramatic play fosters the children's abstract thinking. Make-believe play aids them in their interpretations of the objects they portray in their dramatic play. Thus, initially the correct representation of the objects is critical; in the later stages of development the representation of the objects becomes irrelevant. Initially, the play materials should resemble their representation. Afterward, the play materials can vary from their actual representation. Vygotsky characterizes play as the children's creation of make-believe incidents of real life problems.

Vygotsky's assumption of make-believe reflects Goethe and Schiller's 19th century beliefs, when the "world of childhood" started to be accepted and the children's play started to be associated with adult experiences. In Germany, both Goethe and Schiller appreciated the imaginary components in children's play and their implications of their behavior as adults. Goethe assumed that his relationship with his mother motivated him to envision and narrate stories. Schiller's surplus energy theory on the nature of play made an influential effect on modern theories (Mellou, 1994). Vygotsky's theory added to Piaget's theory that the children's play experiences stimulated their cognitive development in the social context of culture where the cultural aspects of cognitive development occur.

CONTEMPORARY THEORIES

A number of contemporary scholars have provided a rich rationale for considering an individual differences approach in today's society. Although each scholar's approach varies, the total result is undoubtedly beneficial for research on pretending, perspective taking, and mental states. Currently scholars are beginning to consider some convergence in relation to selected characteristics about play and some provocative queries about its impact in current society.

The individual differences mode has a checkered heritage in developmental psychology. Although it is valued, its competitive domain-general theories associated with age or phase criticize and eschew it. Nonetheless, more compelling is the issue on the value of examining individual differences. "Often we are left wondering about two nagging questions: One of these might be called 'what-else-is new?' questions; the other the 'so-what?' question' (Kavanaugh 2001, p. 256).

"What else is new?" is shorthand for several all-powerful third factor (e.g., intelligence, age) that extends the theoretical emphasis of any bivariate association. Frequently, there is no constant association besides age or intelligence. The goal of studies on individual differences is to provide an extended, assessment criterion of its performance. A debatable version of the "what-else-is-new?" and the "so what?" questions must be considered in an individual differences process (Kavanaugh 2001). The following sections discuss theories of mind and culture as examples of an individual differences process.

Theory of mind

In the social process that occurs during play, children communicate and learn from others including understanding each others' point of view. Contemporary theories concentrate on the effect of the social context on the children's interactions that has an impact on their pretend play. Numerous researchers confirm the prominence of the social context in children's play including theory of mind.

The issue of how children understand pretending is particularly intriguing. Pretense is an activity that young children engage in for many of their waking hours, and yet until recently very little research has examined how children understand it (Lillard, 2001). Kavanaugh and Engel (1998) suggest that by age two and a half children are correctly able to interpret other's pretense actions, for example, knowing that if someone has poured pretend water on teddy, then teddy is "wet." In addition, in recent years there has been a good deal of attention focused on children's understanding of the mental properties of pretense. When people pretend, they project a mentally represented situation onto a real one (Lillard, 1998). For example, someone pretending a stick is a horse projects his/her mental representation of what horses look and act like and projects that onto the stick. This is a crucial component of pretense; if an individual were to ride on a stick without mentally representing it as a horse, that individual might be sorely mistaken or confused but that individual would not be pretending it was a horse. For example, when an individual pretends, such individual practices entertaining two representations of the same situation: an object is both a horse and a stick (Amsel & Smalley, 2000; Lillard, 1998, 2001).

Recently, researchers have focused on children's understanding of the mind within the cognitive development domain and its methods, extending this focus to the social development domain as well. Since understanding the mind is basic to human interaction, individuals elicit from their knowledge of the mind in the majority of their social engagements, such as whether something was heard, the reason for being surprised, or ways to motivate someone to work harder. A theory of mind relates to such social knowledge, because (1) mental states constitute theoretical constructs, although several philosophers (e.g., Stich, 1983) challenge their existence and (2) knowledge about minds assumes the form of a theory when it causes specific ontological differences, contains a causal-explanatory framework, and describes its constructs in relation to other constructs in the theory (e.g. surprise is described in regard to belief). Knowledge has been compelling to human support in social circles. Currently in developmental psychology it has been essential in understanding young children's responses to a false belief task. Researchers have initiated studies to interpret how children understand the mind. They have examined a range of topics such as children's understanding of emotion, thinking, perception, and desire. Pretend play is also part of the realm on children's theory of mind.

Theoretical and practical foundations that interface pretend play and theory of mind depend on understanding mental representation. Several studies support the practical foundations, because they demonstrate the relationship between pretending and social understanding. A fundamental premise is that this relationship develops when pretend play enhances social reasoning such as children's pretend play develops theories of mind. It is assumed that the relationship of pretense play contributes to social understanding.

Research suggests that pretend play may promote mentalistic understanding. Lillard (1998) defines mental representation as a mental model of some person or concept—its "re-presentation" inside the mind. Mental representations are biased since one individual's mental representation of something can differ from another's. This subjectivity is an important feature of minds. The individuals' interactions with the world are grounded on their biased mental models of the way the world is instead of the explicit knowledge of reality. For example, politicians may establish two conflicting representations of their platform on a single issue. They can convince one cluster of people that they support a particular law, while convincing a different cluster of people that they oppose it. Understanding representational variety, both between individuals and within the same individual over time, is essential to social knowledge, which is perceived as being the essence of a theory of mind. Understanding is essential in concluding the deceitful conviction undertaking and the fundamental understanding that everybody has their own truths. Social cognitive theorists usually attribute these double meanings to pretending and theory of mind, because both abilities seem to depend on understanding mental representational variation. Pretense definitely engages employing mental representations. When individuals pretend, they expect their internal, mental representation of some real instance or object (Lillard, 1998).

The conclusions of the studies on theory of mind indicate some fundamental problems in understanding the mental aspects of pretense. Even very young children think about pretending as a mental state. When they pretend merely as outermost manifestations, like actions, pretend play continues to be linked to a theory of mind. Pretenders mediate their pretend roles, thereby contending and harmonizing different conceptualizations and aspirations. Inside the pretend matrix, children rehearse perceiving one object or circumstance in two contradictory means at once, and envisioning one object to portray another. They also consider their peers' point of view during pretend role-play. Since the substance of pretense is frequently emotional and confronting, pretending offers children the opportunity to experience managing such situations. The children's pretense play can offer an understanding of the children's theory of mind. Pretend play indicates the way children imitate their worlds as well as the way they think about internal states and the social order. It can also present information relating to the children's predominant problems, reactions to specific occurrences, and current functioning. It suggests the children's performance and guidelines to assist children in advancing their understanding. Thus, pretending can present information that can be utilized to adjust ones predictions and in instructing children about minds and subjectivity (Lillard, 1998).

Culture

Modern conventions of culture view it as a habitat of common behavioral interpretations and associations, which are symbolically deciphered, communicated, and passed on from one generation to another through diverse means. Environmental knowledge must be understood to appreciate, identify with, and accept human behavior and societies. Coexistent humans have learned, deciphered, and transgenerationally transmitted almost all behavior, belief systems, everlasting media (e.g., writing, sculpture), cultural elements, common meanings, and interceding environmental human interactions and its resources. The knowledge from the environments needs to be learned and emitted to understand ancient societies (Roberts, 2001).

Culture is transformed and grounded in individuals through a rich evolutionary history. As such the cause of any advanced phenomena like language is ambiguously associated to a specific aspect of evolution or any unitary motive. Language initiates the presence of culture, although culture provides its own description, conceiving outrageous circles (Roberts, 2001). The assumptions that underlie cultural development consist of the following:

> Change is seen as a process that is *natural* to both biological and social entities; social change is viewed as *immanent* (i.e., proceeding from forces within the entity); change is *continuous* and *directional*; therefore, it manifests itself in an orderly sequence of *stages*, which move cumulatively and linearly from one given point to another point; change is *necessary* because it is "natural;" change corresponds to *differentiation* and proceeds in a pattern from the homogeneous to the heterogeneous; and finally, change proceeds from *uniform* causes (Nisbet, 1969, p. 12).

In the 19th century anthropologists were concerned with the "science of man" and originated the notions of biological (Darwin) and social (Spencer) evolution. Schwartzman (1978) believes that the theory of social evolution was established based on the metaphor that considered cultures to be biological organisms that displayed analogous systems of "growth" and "development." According to Potts (1996) "culture makes man makes culture" (p. 182). Culture is based on changes in noncultural phenomena (e.g., biological, social, ecological) that anatomically affect contemporary human beings and the disposition of human information systems, especially the appearance of symbolic behavior. According to Roberts (2001), bodily ornaments, statues, musical instruments, regional stylism, and painting defines symbolic culture.

Considering children as delegates in a transactional state with their environments, childhood can provide a feasible procreative origin for evolution that can be reached and developed. Recurrently in paleanthropology, children are referred to in relation to the struggle that is indispensable in caring for them or as docile storage of knowledge segments. Opie and Opie (1959) indicate that children are the guardians of rich cultural heritage. "Any consideration of the role of children in human evolution would be incomplete without emphasis on one of the most important aspects of childhood, indeed human behavior, at which children are the experts: play" (Roberts, 2001, p. 106).

Perceptions of play are intimately related to one's culture. In the West, our understanding of play has been most significantly influenced by shared attitudes about what play is not. Western theories of play suggest a pursuit for principles. Theoretical concerns consistently extended to play have effectively challenged the value of play for learning and cognition. Most theorists and researchers have neglected to contribute to a comprehensive theory of play that seriously integrates the endless substances of culture. This is lamentable in the recognition of diversity in culturally continuous and discontinuous play contexts. The divergent make-up of societies throughout the world (e.g., industrialized pluralistic, industrialized homogeneous, post-colonial, hunting-gathering, etc.) would make it a difficult undertaking (Roberts, 2001). Schwartzman (1978) assumes that current studies of play suffer from too much definitional familiarity, even if studies have different theories and findings.

The works of Bruner (1976), Rogoff (1990), Vygotsky (1978), and others offer an understanding of the individuals' development through their sociocultural interactions. Since it is untimely to chart a theory of culture and play, Roopnarine, Lasker, Sacks, and Stores (1998) offer the following guidelines in investigating children's play across cultures:

- Biosocial factors, both somatic and reproductive, influence parent-child participation

- Differences also exist in the psychology of the importance of play whether it is in the peer group or parent-child system.
- Finally, in preindustrial societies education occurs in formal and informal settings... Theories of play must account for the myriad of ways in which play is used for learning social and adaptive skills that are essential for successfully negotiating the demands of the individual's socio-cultural world. The socio-ecological contexts that represent the work-play mixture are antithetical to most Western frameworks regarding children's play (pp. 197-198).

As the world merges through travel and trade, agricultural lands and rain forests decrease (e.g., among the Aka, Efe, and Yanomamo), industrial and residential buildings overthrow space once allotted to play (e.g. Taiwan), technological devices substitute for traditional toys (e.g., United States and Japan), and educational goals are better expressed in the developing countries. This has guided apparent reforms for both the context and nature of young children's play across cultures. For example, educational goals in Africa have been converted to more formal ones, making work and play more explicit. As a result, children may have less time to informally observe, learn, and accommodate their knowledge of their environment and roles within it through work and play. The preschool concepts in western countries (e.g., Taiwan, Japan) have focused on constructive and symbolic play in educational settings (Roopnarine, Lasker, Sacks, & Stores 1998). Pan's (1994) study of Taiwanese children's play activities indicates that preschool children favor slides and swings and transportation toys over more traditional objects (e.g., kites, paper folding). Takeuchi (1994) reports that in Japan over the last 10 years there has been an accelerated increase in video games. Nowadays Japanese children prefer to look at television, read comic books, and play with video games than in traditional Japanese games.

Several cultures have seen play spaces shrink. The destruction of the rain forests in Africa and South America caused families and children to accelerate their extrication as the environments of the Aka, Efe and other hunting-gathering societies became hazardous. Play materials from the bordering areas acutely restricted the play activities, although such event extend to survival societies. In the industrialized world, play spaces have degenerated in large cities (Pan, 1994) while faddish technological tools have replaced conventional games. The repercussion of faddish play materials (video-games, power-rangers) on children's imaginative and aggressive dispositions is mainly camouflaged (Roopnarine, Lasker, Sacks, & Stores 1998).

The above stated facts and the perception of "Western" cultural beliefs affect the circulation of distinctive manufactured toys worldwide. It is rare to find billboards with advertisements of Barbie Dolls and other play materials that are culturally relevant to the United States in South Asia, South

America, and the West Indies. Still the choice for toys in these countries are related to the cultural values of the postindustrialized societies, because such societies challenge and sometimes dismiss native toys and play practices in their countries. They believe that play objects from the industrialized world are superior. Presently educators from abroad and the United States are focusing on the revival of ethnic dignity, early childhood professionals need to explore this concern more cautiously (Roopnarine, Lasker, Sacks, & Stores 1998).

SUMMARY

Traditionally, theories of play have been related to what play is in regards to all humans or all animals. Modern theories were created to view play form the perspective of human development, positing how play enhances the development of young children. Contemporary theories have looked as play in relation to how children make sense of the world and how they come to understand the nature of understanding, thereby creating a theory of mind. Contemporary scholars have also looked at play in relation to culture. They originally identified the differences in the way children in different cultures play. More recently, with increased international commerce and communication, children's play has become more global with modern societies impacting more traditional societies both on how children play and in what they play with.

REFERENCES

(Amsel, E)., & Smalley, J. D. (2000). Beyond really and truly: Children's counterfactual thinking about pretend and possible worlds. In E. Riggs & P. Mitchell (Eds.) *Reasoning and the Mind* (pp. 12-147). Hove, UK: Psychology Press.

Axline, V. M. (1974). *Play therapy.* New York: Ballentine Books.

Bateson, G. (1955). A theory of play and fantasy. *Psychological Abstracts Research Report, 2,* 39-51.

Berlyne, D. (1969). Laughter, humor, and play. In G. Lindsey & E. Aronson (Eds.) *Handbook of social psychology,* Vol. 3 (2nd ed.), (pp. 795-852). Reading, MA: Addison Wesley.

Bruner, J. (1976). *Play: Its role in development and evolution.* New York: Basic Books.

Dewey, J. (1900). Froebel's educational principles, *Elementary School Record, 1,* 143-145.

Dewey, J. (1916). *Democracy and education.* Carbondale, IL: Southern Illinois University Press.

Ellis, M. (1973). *Why people play.* Englewood Cliffs, NJ: Prentice-Hall.

Erikson, E. H. (1950). *Childhood and society.* New York: Norton.

Fein, G. G., & Schwartz, P. M. (1982). Developmental theories in early education. In B. Spodek (Ed.), *Handbook of research in early childhood education* (pp. 82-104). New York: Free Press.

French, V. (1977). History of the child's influence: Ancient Mediterranean Civilizations. In R. Q. Bell & L. V. Harper (Eds.), *Child effects on adults.* Hillsdale, NJ: Erlbaum.

Freud, S. (1938). *The basic writing of Sigmund Freud* (Ed. A.A. Brill). New York: Modern Library.

Froebel, F. (1887). *The education of man.* New York: Appleton-Century.

Groos, K. (1985). The play of animals: Play and instinct. In J. S. Bruner, A. Jolly, K. Sylva (Eds.) *Play: Its role in development and evolution.* Bergenfield, NJ: Penguin Books (originally published in 1896).

Groos, K. (1901). *The play of man.* New York: Appleton.

Hall G. S. (1906). *Youth: Its education, regimen, and hygiene.* New York: Appleton.

Hartley, R., & Goldenson, R. (1963). *The complete book of children's play.* New York: Crowell.

Johnson, J. E., Christie, J. F., & Yawkey, T. D. (1999).*Play and early childhood development.* Boston: Allyn & Bacon.

Kavanaugh, R. D. (2001). Understanding the pretense—Theory of mind relationship. *Play and Culture Studies, 3,* 255-260.

Kavanaugh, R. D., & Engel, S. (1998).The development of pretense and narrative in early childhood. In O.N. Saracho and B. Spodek (Eds.),*Multiple perspectives on play in early childhood education.* (pp. 80-99). New York: SUNY Press.

Lazarus, M. (1883). *Die reize des spiels.* Berlin. Fred. Dummlers Verlagsbuch-handlung.

Lillard, A. (1998). Playing with a theory of mind. In O.N. Saracho and B. Spodek (Eds.), (pp. 11-33). *Multiple perspectives on play in early childhood education.* New York: SUNY Press.

Lillard, A. (2001). Pretending, understanding pretense, and understanding minds. *Play and Culture Studies, 3,* 233-254.

Mellou, E. (1994). Play theories: A contemporary view.*Early Child Development and Care, 102,* 91-100.

Mitchell, E. D., & Mason, B. (1948) .*The theory of play* (rev. ed.). New York: A. S. Barnes.

Montessori, M. (1965). *Dr. Montessori's own handbook.* New York: Schocken. (Original published in 1914)

Montessori, M. (1973). *The Montessori method.* Cambridge, MA: Bently.

Murphy, L. (1956). *Methods for the study of personality in young children.* New York: Basic Books.

Nisbet, R. A. (1969). *Social change and history.* Oxford: Oxford University Press.

Opie, I., & Opie, P. (1959). *The lore and language of schoolchildren.* Oxford: Oxford University Press.

Pan, W. H. L. (1994). Children's play in Taiwan. In J. Roopnarine, J. Johnson, & F. Hooper (Eds.), *Children's play in diverse cultures.* (pp. 31-50) Albany: SUNY Press.

Patrick, G. T. W. (1916). *The psychology of relaxation.* Boston: Houghton-Mifflin.

Peller, L. E. (1952). Models of children's play.*Mental Hygiene, 36,* 66-83.

Piaget, J. (1985). Symbolic play. In J. S. Bruner, A. Jolly, K. Sylva (Eds.) *Play: Its role in development and evolution.* Bergenfield NJ: Penguin Books (Originally published in 1951).

Piaget, J. (1962). *Play, dreams and imitation in childhood.* New York: Norton.

Potts, R. (1996). *Humanity's descent: The consequences of ecological instability.* New York: Avon.

Roberts, W. P. (2001). Symbolic play and the evolution of culture: A comparative life history perspective. *Play and Culture Studies, 3,* -108.

Roopnarine, J. L., Lasker, J., Sacks, M., & Stores, M. (1998). The cultural contents of children's play. In O.N. Saracho and B. Spodek (Eds.), *Multiple perspectives on play in early childhood education.* (pp. 194-219). New York: SUNY Press.

Rubin, K.H. (1982). Early play theories revisited: Contributions to contemporary research and theory. In D. J. Pepler & K. H. Rubin (Eds.) *The play of children: Current theory and research, Contributions to human development.* Basel: Karger.

Rogoff, B. (1990). *Apprenticeship in Thinking: Cognitive Development in Social Context.* New York: Oxford University Press.

Saracho, O.N. (1991). The role of play in the early childhood curriculum. In B. Spodek & O. N. Saracho (Eds.). *Yearbook of early childhood education: Issues in early childhood curriculum,* Vol. II (pp. 86-105). New York: Teachers College Press.

Schwartzman, H.B. (1978). *Transformations: The anthropology of play.* New York: Plenum.

Smith, P. K. (1982). Does play matter? Functional and evolutionary aspects of animal and human play. *Behavioral and Brain Science, 5,* 166.

Spodek, B., & Saracho, O. N. (1997). The challenge of educational play. In D. Bergen (Ed.), *Play as a learning medium for learning and development: A handbook of theory and practice* (pp. 11-28). Olney, MD: Association for Childhood Education International.

Stich, S. (1983). *From folk psychology to cognitive science.* Cambridge, MA: MIT Press

Sylva, K., Bruner, J. S., & Genova, P. (1974). The role of play in the problem solving of children. In J. S. Bruner, A. Jolly, & K. Sylva, Eds.), *Play: Its role in development and evolution* (pp. 97-109). Bergenfield, NJ: Penguin.

Takeuchi, M. (1994) Children's play in Japan. In J. Roopnarine, J. Johnson, & F. Hooper (Eds.), *Children's play in diverse cultures.* (pp. 51-72) Albany: SUNY Press.

Takhvar, M. (1988). Play and theories of play: A review of the literature. *Early Child Development and Care, 39,* 221-244.

Vygotsky, L.S. (1962). *Thought and language.* Cambridge, Mass: M.I.T. Press.

Vygotsky, L. S. (1978). *Mind in Society.* Cambridge: Harvard University Press.

Wehman, P., & Abramson, M. (1976). Three theoretical approaches to play. *The American Journal of Occupational Therapy, 30*(9), 551-559.

Wolf, D. & Grollman, S.H. (1982). Ways of playing: Individual differences in imaginative style. In D. J. Pepler & K. H. Rubin (Eds.) *The play of children: Current theory and research, Contributions to human development* (pp. 46-64). Basel: Karger.

CHAPTER 2

SPONTANEOUS PLAY IN THE 21ST CENTURY

Fergus P. Hughes

Children's play is a spontaneous activity whose benefits are well documented in the realm of intellectual development, language and literacy development, and social development. However, all human behavior occurs within a particular sociocultural context, and play is influenced by the characteristics of the environment in which it is found. While it may be spontaneious in that it is generated by the player, play is dependent on the sociocultural context for support. There is reason to believe that the social and cultural conditions that support spontaneous play are less in evidence today than they were in the past, because of the increasing complexity and specialization in children's play materials, increasing organization in children's games, and a growing tendency to characterize rough and tumble play as symptomatic of patholgy.

Play is the most natural of childhood activities and one of the most frequently observed. It is an activity that eludes simple definition, although the criteria used to define play typically include freedom of choice, personal enjoyment, and a focus on the activity as an end in itself rather than on its outcomes (Rubin, Fein, & Vandenberg, 1983). Freedom of choice

Contemporary Perspectives on Play in Early Childhood Education
A Volume in: Contemporary Perspectives in Early Childhood Education, pages 21–39.
ISBN: 1-930608-31-4 (cloth), 1-930608-30-6 (paper)

seems to be an essential component of a definition of play. As Vandenberg (1998) expressed it, "The excitement of play results from the sheer exercise of freedom over necessity" (p. 303).

The major premises of this chapter are that

a. spontaneous child-initiated play facilitates child development;
b. play may be spontaneous in that it is generated by the player, but it occurs within a sociocultural context and is dependent on that context for support, and
c. the social and cultural conditions that support spontaneous play are less in evidence today than they were in the past, for a variety of reasons. These reasons include increasing complexity and specialization in children's play materials, increasing organization in children's games, and a growing tendency to characterize rough and tumble play as symptomatic of pathology rather than as a natural activity of childhood.

Spontaneous Play and Development

Cognitive theorists have long supported the view that spontaneous imaginative play facilitates children's intellectual development. For example, Piaget (1962, 1969) maintained that "games of construction" often arise from symbolic play, and these games "are initially imbued with play symbolism, but tend later to constitute genuine adaptations (mechanical constructions, etc.), or solutions to problems and intelligent creations (1969, p. 59)". Thus he argued that spontaneous play facilitates intellectual development in that it can lead to discoveries about the physical environment. Vygotsky (1986) suggested that pretend play facilitates the mastery of symbolism, the understanding of a relationship between the signifier and the signified, which is one of the cognitive foundations of literacy. Imaginative play frees behavior and thought from the domination of the immediate perceptual field, and represents a middle ground between the literalness of seeing meaning as inherent in objects themselves and a form of thinking that is totally separated from real situations (Kozulin, 1996)

Research on children's intellectual development indicates that a number of cognitive skills, including measurement, equivalency, balance, spatial concepts, conservation, decentration, reversibility, and logical classification are enhanced during play, and particularly during the course of symbolic play (Copple, Cocking, & Matthews, 1984; Elder & Pederson, 1978; Jackowitz & Watson, 1980; Piaget, 1962; Rubin, 1980; Ungerer, Zelazo, Kearsley, & O'Leary, 1981). In addition, symbolic play is thought to afford children the opportunity for creative expression, as well as to actually facilitate creative processes, including divergent thinking (Fein, 1987; Russ, 1993).

Group symbolic play, or sociodramatic play, allows children to create alternative worlds, encouraging them to engage in subjunctive representation of reality. It enhances the child's need to organize a complex environment into meaningful scripts and schemas for possible action in the future, and encourages children to plan, to consider a variety of courses of action, and to communicate their plans and courses of action to other people (Bretherton, 1998; Singer & Singer, 1998). It stimulates the "what if" type of thinking that forms the basis for mature hypothetical reasoning and problem solving. It stimulates children to think creatively, and has been found to predict later creativity (Dansky, 1980). In addition, extensive involvement in sociodramatic play seems to improve children's memory, language development, and cognitive perspective-taking abilities (Burns & Brainerd, 1979; Dansky, 1980; Saltz, Dixon, & Johnson, 1977).

Language and Literacy

There is a growing body of evidence in support of a relationship between various forms of spontaneous play and linguistic development. In fact, all of the four aspects of the human language system (the phonological, the syntactic, the semantic, and the pragmatic) are incorporated into young children's play (Kuczaj, 1985). Garvey (1984) suggested that there are four different types of language play, which roughly correspond to the different aspects of language

1. play with sounds and noises,
2. play with linguistic systems, such as those involving word meanings or grammatical constructions,
3. play with rhymes and words, and
4. play with the conventions of speech.

While the purpose of language play is not fully understood, it is noteworthy that language play involving sounds and sound structures has been observed in lower animal species as well as in human children, and is thought to serve important developmental functions; in human beings such play is thought to facilitate cognitive, social, and linguistic development (Kuczaj, 1998).

As an example of play with sounds, the spontaneous babbling of the infant in the first year could easily fall within the definition of play since it is intrinsically-motivated, freely-chosen, devoid of external goals, and apparently pleasurable for children. Such play can facilitate word usage because parents may unintentionally influence their children to make sounds appropriate to the language that they speak. In that sense, the sound play of the infant may ultimately result in advances in sound production. By the end of the first year, infants produce a variety of playful sounds with their mouths, and sound play occurs among older children as well. Three- and four-year-old children become fascinated with songs, chants, and rhymes, and enjoy producing nonsensical rhyming patterns, and play of this type is related to language development in that the ability to rhyme is highly correlated with early reading achievement in children (Bergen & Mauer, 2000).

Solitary play with the syntactic and semantic elements of language appears in the second year. Children repeat sentences, each time substituting a new word of the same grammatical category: a child might say "Daddy go out", "Mommy go out", "Baby go out" or "Doggie fall down", "Kitty fall down", "Baby fall down" . They construct and deconstruct sentences (e.g., "Give it to me", Give the cup to me"), ask questions and provide their own answers themselves, recite lists of words, numbers, or letters, and engage themselves in conversation.

Solitary experimental play with the rules of word order is thought to form the basis for the development of the grammatical structures of language (Garvey, 1984; Ratner & Bruner, 1978). While the language of social interaction is goal-directed and devoid of the element of playfulness found in the solitary monologue, solitary language play gives children an opportunity to experiment with the elements of speech (Garvey, 1984).

Since language and symbolic play both depend on representational skills, it is not surprising that efforts have been made to relate play to linguistic development, and to literacy. The connection has been clearly established, although the direction of influence is more difficult to ascertain. Experimental research to demonstrate that symbolic play directly influences language comprehension has often taken the form of having one group of children listen to a story and then play out the scenes, while another group either engages in discussion of the story or engages in unrelated activities. Later the children's memory for details of the story is tested. The finding that emerges in studies of this type is that the play group displays the greatest understanding of, and memory for, the story's details (Saltz, Dixon, & Johnson, 1977; Williamson & Silvern, 1990).

The language-symbolic play connection is further supported by the results of correlational studies indicating a relationship between scores on standardized symbolic play inventories and language measures such as the Peabody Picture Vocabulary Test (Laasko, , Poikkeus, Eklund, & Lyytinen, 1999; Lim, 1998; Lyytinen, Laasko, Poikkeus, & Rita, 1999), and between parental reports of symbolic play and literacy tasks such as rhyming and segmenting sentences into word units (Bergen & Mauer, 2000). Finally, there appears to be evidence of a circular relationship between pretend play and linguistic development: Fein, Ardila-Rey, and Groth (2000) reported that the experience of acting out stories as they were read to them resulted in an increased interest in dramatic play in a group of five- and six-year-old children.

Convergent Problem Solving

Single-solution problems require the ability to engage in convergent problem solving (Pepler & Ross, 1981), which is characterized by bringing a variety of isolated pieces of information together to arrive at one correct solution. Illustrative of such problem solving is the task devised by Sylva, Bruner, and Genova (1976), and later replicated by Barnett (1985), who asked preschool children seated at a table to try to obtain an object beyond their reach without standing up or leaving their chairs. Two sticks were provided, neither long enough to reach the desired object, but if the sticks were clamped together, the children could attain the goal. One group played freely with the problem solving materials prior to engaging in the task, a second group watched as the experimenter solved the problem before they were asked to do it, and a third group was given neither the play experience nor the opportunity to observe the problem being solved. The children who either played with the materials in advance or watched an adult solve the problem were the most successful problem-solvers. In addition, the play group appeared to be more highly motivated to solve the problem, and worked at it more persistently than did the observation group, who either solved the problem immediately or simply gave up.

Divergent Thinking

Divergent thinking, the ability to branch out from a starting point and consider a variety of possible solutions, involves fluidity of thinking, broad scanning ability, and free association. It is thought to be a major cognitive process underlying creativity (Guilford, 1968; Russ & Kaugars, 2001). The connection between play and divergent thinking has been established in various lines of research. First, a relationship has been found between divergent problem solving ability and the characteristics of children's play materials (Dansky & Silverman, 1973, 1975; Pepler & Ross, 1981). For example, Pepler and Ross (1981) gave sixty-four preschool children the opportunity to play repeatedly with convergent (e.g., puzzles with one correct solution) or divergent (e.g., blocks, which can be assembled in a variety of ways) materials. When the children were later asked to solve a variety of problems, those who had engaged in divergent object play were more flexible and more original in their problem solving approaches, and quicker than those in the convergent play group to abandon ineffective problem-solving approaches. The researchers concluded that the experience of interacting with toys that suggest a single correct way to be played with may teach children that there are correct answers, and may encourage them to seek them out. Playing with open-ended materials, on the other hand, may suggest that there are numerous approaches that can be taken to any problem.

While object play has clearly been related to divergent problem solving ability in young children, so too has make-believe, or fantasy, play. For example, Dansky (1980) observed ninety-six preschool children in a free-play situation, and categorized them as high or low in their pretend play ability. He then assigned them to one of three conditions:

1. free play,
2. imitative play, and
3. a problem-solving task.

Dansky (1980) found that the children in the free-play situation performed the best on the divergent problem solving task, but only if they were spontaneously high in their level of make-believe play. He concluded that it is not play in itself that predicts problem solving skill, but the extent to which children become involved in make-believe when they are playing.

It has been suggested that the link between fantasy play and divergent thinking can be found in the concept of decentration (Rubin, Fein, & Vandenberg, 1983), which involves the ability to attend simultaneously to many features of the environment and to transform objects and situations while at the same time understanding their original identities and states, to imagine things as they are and as they were at one and the same time. A child engaged in make-believe knows that the object he is sitting in really is a cardboard box, but pretends it is a car; in a sense, it is both a box and a car at once, and perhaps it was a submarine ten minutes earlier. Make-believe play, therefore, provides evidence of a considerable amount of intellectual flexibility in the child, and flexibility is a key ingredient in the creative process.

An alternative explanation of the play-divergent thinking connection was suggested by Russ (1993; 1999; Russ & Kaugars, 2001), who maintained that affect-laden fantasy underlies both symbolic play and creative expression. Thoughts, ideas, or fantasies that contain affective themes such as aggression or anxiety are illustrations of affect-laden fantasy, and such fantasy has been related empirically to creative problem solving (Isen, Daubman, & Nowicki, 1987; Russ & Grossman-McKee, 1990). Symbolic play is characterized by both fantasy and a high degree of affect, and so one might expect to find a relationship between pretend play and creativity. In fact, such a relationship has been found repeatedly in the research literature (Russ & Grossman-McKee, 1990; Russ & Kaugars, 2001; Russ, Robbins, & Christiano, 1999).

As is true of the research on language and literacy, the direction of influence between play and divergent problem solving is neither simple nor direct. Instead, the relationship is both complex and reciprocal: pretend play may enhance divergent problem solving skills, but the acquisition of problem solving skills also enhances the quality of pretend play (Wyver & Spence, 1999).

Play and Socialization

A variety of play forms have been found to facilitate aspects of social development in children. For example, physical play between parent and child is thought to have important socializing functions (Carson, Burks, & Parke, 1993; MacDonald & Parke, 1986), and a relationship has been found between the amount of physical play in the home and children's competence with peers: children rated as popular by their teachers are the most likely to have parents, and particularly fathers, who engage in a good deal of physical play with them (Carson, Burks, & Parke, 1993). The rough and tumble play with peers that occurs throughout childhood but peaks during the elementary school years (Pellegrini & Smith, 1998), is thought to enhance children's abilities to encode and decode social signals, and thus may enhance social cognition (Bjorklund & Brown, 1998).

Involvement in sociodramatic play seems to improve children's ability to cooperate in group settings, to participate in social activities, and to understand human relationships (Smith & Sydall, 1978; Smith, Dalgleish, & Herzmark, 1981). Role-taking skills can be enhanced by gently supervised forms of social fantasy play (Burns & Brainerd, 1979; Golumb & Cornelius, 1977; Saltz, Dixon, & Johnson, 1977). While most of the research in this area points to the necessity of an adult "social director" to stimulate children to play in a way that enriches perspective-taking ability, some psychologists (e.g., Rubin & Maioni, 1975) suggest that role-taking ability may be enhanced by social play that is totally spontaneous and not at all influenced by adults.

The value of spontaneity in child-generated pretense as a facilitator of social development can be seen in an examination of the consequence of using adult-assigned roles in socio-dramatic play as opposed to allowing children to choose roles for themselves. If an adult assigns the roles, the child's freedom to self-regulate is diminished, and the child is less likely to define the activity as play. However, if the adult allows children to choose their own roles, they begin to explore issues of "control and compromise" (Howes, Unger, & Matheson, 1992). They engage in a complicated and delicate process of negotiation while they assign roles to themselves and to their peers. Indeed they often bargain about play roles (E.g., Shelley: "I want to be the airplane pilot. I never get to be the pilot." Scott: "Yes you do. You were the pilot yesterday. Now it's my turn.") and themes (E.g., Jean: "We're a family going to the beach." Joan: "I don't want to go to the beach. That isn't any fun. I want to be a firefighter." Jean: "O.K. You could put out a fire at the beach."). Negotiations of this sort can encourage children to communicate more effectively with peers, and to resolve some of the inevitable conflicts that arise in the interaction of preschoolers (Howes, Unger, & Matheson, 1992).

Spontaneous Play in the Sociocultural Context

Imaginative play cannot and should not be considered without reference to the social context in which it occurs. The freedom to play, and to play as one chooses, can vary from one cultural milieu to another, depending on the amount of play space and free time that is available, and on parental and general societal attitudes about the relative importance of play and work in children's lives (Roopnarine, Lasker, Sacks, & Stores, 1998). It has been suggested (Roopnarine, Shin, Donovan, & Suppal, 2000) that despite an impressive research base detailing the developmental progression of pretend play and its various benefits, there remains a major gap in our understanding of the intersection between pretend play and the sociocultural system in which it occurs.

The necessity of considering the social context of pretend play is underscored by research on the characteristics of representational activity in the one-year-old child. While Piaget (1962) characterized the initial signs of representational ability as solitary in nature, and implied they occur naturally without adult intervention, pretend play is from the outset an intensely social activity between parents and children (Haight & Miller, 1992; Haight, Parke, & Black, 1997). Not only does pretend play usually occur in a social context, but social pretend play in the second year has been found to be more sustained, complex, and diverse than is solitary make-believe (Haight & Miller, 1992). Mothers typically encourage their children to engage in acts of make-believe, particularly when, at the beginning of the second year, the child is less likely to pretend spontaneously (Tamis-LeMonda & Damast, 1993; Tamis-LeMonda & Bornstein, 1991). They demonstrate an activity, such as pretending to talk on a toy telephone, and then offer it to the child with encouragement to do the same thing. As the child matures, mother-generated acts of make-believe decrease and are replaced by spontaneous child-generated pretense; sensitive mothers match their play to the child's level of sophistication and are the most effective at enhancing children's play (Tamis-LeMonda & Bornstein, 1991; Tamis-LeMonda & Damast, 1993).

Research on cultural variations in the group symbolic play of older preschool children reinforces the view that the sociocultural context has a significant impact on play. Imaginative pretend play has been observed most often in cultures that expose children to a greater amount of stimulation and a greater amount of novelty, and/or those in which children have opportunities to make choices about their play activities and companions without adult supervision or interference (Edwards, 2000).

In reaction to the observed cultural differences, some scholars warn of the danger of simply attempting to document whether or not pretend play can be found in a given society, particularly if cross-cultural variations are described as deficiencies. Instead they suggest that we ask how children *use* pretend play differently in the different contexts in which they develop (Roopnarine, Shin, Donovan, & Suppal, 2000). In some cultures play themes resemble the domestic scenes and work roles of adults, and may allow children to practice adult roles; in others the roles and scripts are far removed from reality (Edwards, 2000).

Even within a particular culture, variations in spontaneous imaginative play can be observed, a point that is illustrated by Farver's research on the contrasts between the play of Anglo-American and Korean –American children in Los Angeles nursery schools (Farver & Lee-Shin, 2000; Farver, Kim, & Lee, 1995; Farver, Kim, & Lee-Shin, 2000; Farver & Shin, 1997). Korean pre-school teachers, even if educated in the United States, saw the primary value of early childhood education as teaching academic skills and good work habits. Their classrooms were highly structured and contained few materials that might foster creative play. In fact, play of any sort was a rare occurrence in the Korean-American pre-school. Anglo-American teachers were more likely to encourage independence of thought, they provided a substantial amount of material (e.g., props, miniature life toys) designed to encourage the use of imagination, and spontaneous play was much more in evidence in their classrooms.

The variables that predict the occurrence of spontaneous pretend play seem to transcend culture. When Farver & Lee-Shin (2000) examined the degree to which Korean-immigrant mothers living in the United States had been assimilated into American culture, they found that those mothers who were "separated" or "marginal" in their acculturation styles were less accepting and encouraging of their children's play, and less likely to actually play with their children than were those who were more "integrated" or "assimilated". Similarly, Farver, Kim, & Lee-Shin (2000) reported that children's individual characteristics are better predictors of pretend play than are ethnicity and culture in themselves. Regardless of ethnicity, children's style of interaction with peers, the degree to which they were successful in their interactions, and their scores on a test of creativity were significantly related to their level of make-believe play.

The Future of Spontaneous Play

American children entering the 21st century seem to be less likely to determine when and where they will play because of a number of restrictions in the physical environment, including increasing urbanization, a decreasing sense of community, fear for personal safety, and difficulty in obtaining access to natural play spaces (Dargan & Zeitlin, 2000; Frost & Jacobs, 1995; Frost, Wortham, & Reifel, 2001). Beyond the physical restrictions, there are other indicators of change in sociocultural support for spontaneous play, and these include the increasing prominence of play materials with highly specialized functions, the replacement of invented games by organized sports supervised and directed by adults, and a tendency to view rough-and-tumble play as indicative of pathology.

Specialized Play Materials

As far as can be determined, toys have always been a part of the play experience for children. In wall paintings dating from ancient Egyptian civilization children are depicted as playing with dolls and balls, and jumping rope. The toy manufacturing industry is thought to date back to southern Germany during the Renaissance (1300-1600), when, in addition to homemade toys such as tops and kites that were available during the Middle Ages, there were elaborate wooden dolls, lead soldiers, and little glass animals (Somerville, 1982).

Until the last quarter of the twentieth century, new varieties of toys were slow to emerge, and there was little change from one generation to the next. Recent years, however, have seen the appearance of a variety of new forms of play materials that are highly structured, highly complicated, and technologically advanced. They include television, videos, computer games and programs, CD's and DVD's, and interactive toys that contain computer chips. Such toys appear to encourage activity that might be more accurately referred to as "entertainment" than as spontaneous play, and they often substitute the imagination of their creators for those of the children who interact with them. The nature of spontaneous play may change as a result of the "robot revolution", and the outcomes for children could be negative in terms of restriction of the imagination, a sedentary lifestyle, and decreased interaction with parents and peers (Frost, Wortham, & Reifel, 2001; Oravec, 2001; Saffo & Simon, 1998; Sardar, 1998). Little is known about the long-range outcomes of play with electronic toys since the children who use them have yet to reach adulthood, and since today's adults find themselves providing children with toys that they themselves had never even conceived of when they were young.

An illustration of a toy of recent vintage that could constitute an impediment to spontaneous play in childhood is the "interactive toy". Interactive toys first appeared in the 1960's, when the pull of a string would result in a recorded statement. Today, however, interactive toys are more sophisticated, typically containing microchips and having the capacity to store information and to respond to input from the environment (Oravec, 2001). An example is "Amazing Ally" doll that sings songs, tells jokes, and orders a pizza on her cell phone.

Interactive toys may encourage children to ask the wrong question when playing with them. Instead of asking, "What can I do with this toy?" the child may ask, "What does this toy do?" In addition, these toys have been criticized because they provide inadequate feedback to the child who plays with them. The toy may ask a question, and if the child does not provide a correct response, the toy simply continues to repeat the question, leaving a young child confused. However, one of the most often expressed concerns about interactive toys is that, if the play material defines the parameters of an interaction, children do not have the opportunity to create and define the interaction themselves (Oravec, 2001).

Even traditional toys such as building blocks have changed considerably since they first appeared in terms of complexity and reliance on technology. As an example, the 1958 version of the LEGO block with the patented stud-and-tube coupling system was sold in sets consisted only of standard rectangular bricks and sloping roof tile bricks. By the late 1960's, model sets appeared, complete with building instructions, and there were 57 sets and 25 vehicles available, many of them motorized. Parents today can purchase the "Super Car", introduced in 1994, which contains 13,000 elements.

One wonders if the nature of play with LEGO blocks has changed as the simple "binding brick" gradually evolved into a complex puzzle with 13,000 pieces. There is no correct way to construct with simple blocks, but there is a correct way of assembling a pirate ship or an antique car, and so the complicated block-building materials available today are similar to puzzles and may require a degree of convergent problem solving (Pepler & Ross, 1981), while the simpler open-ended blocks of the past stimulated children to engage in divergent problem solving. Imaginative play may occur with the finished construction in the modern block-building set, since highly structured materials can facilitate sociodramatic play, particularly in a child who is low in fantasy predisposition (Frost, Shin, & Jacobs, 1998; McLoyd, 1983). In fact, young children have been found to play longer with highly realistic toys, although they play more creatively with less realistic ones (McGhee, Ethridge, & Benz, 1984). Regardless of what happens after the building project is completed, however, a lesser degree of imagination, flexibility, and spontaneity is required in the building process itself if the materials are complex and a correct solution is required.

If allowed to do so and provided with interesting materials, children will play freely, spontaneously, and imaginatively. A toy with a specialized function, however, or one so sophisticated that it performs a variety of activities that once were performed only in the mind of the player (e.g., a doll calls out for pizza on her cell phone), then the toy becomes a source of entertainment rather than a plaything. As children come to expect their toys to dazzle and entertain them, they may contribute less of themselves to the play experience. The result is that spontaneous play will be diminished.

An intriguing observation about the changing nature of manufactured toys was made by Roopnarine (Roopnarine, Lasker, Sacks, & Stores, 1998):

as American toys reach a larger market throughout the world, children in other cultures are given play materials that have little cultural significance to them. A Barbie Doll or a G.I. Joe may bear little relationship to the world of a child from a radically different cultural milieu. If children's play reflects the values of their cultures, what significance would such toys have for a child in a small Kenyan or Chinese village? Furthermore, children may feel that these interesting and colorful objects are "better" than the traditional toys that were available to their parents, and by implication may conclude that they are products of a better culture.

Increasingly Organized Games

Piaget (1962) spoke of the difference between games with rules trans-mitted directly from adults or older children and games with rules that emerge spontaneously from the interaction of the children involved. While the former are passed on purely "through the social pressure of children", the latter "are the outcome of socialization...which, though it may involve relationships between younger and older children, is often only a matter of relationships between equals or contemporaries." (p. 143). Self-created and spontaneous games were the most interesting to Piaget and the most meaningful for development because, in the process of creating rather than simply adapting to rules, children develop a more complete under-standing of rules themselves, and particularly for the rules for social engagement.

Rule games invented by children themselves seem to be more valuable in fostering an understanding of the meaning and relevance of rules than are rule games passed down from a higher authority (Castle, 1998; Castle & Wilson, 1993). Invented games encourage children to develop organiza-tional skills, understand the perspectives of others as they attempt to nego-tiate the rules, understand concepts of fairness, and develop a sense of autonomy (Castle, 1998; Castle & Wilson, 1993).

As we enter the 21st century, it seems that commercial games with prede-termined instructions and increasingly organized sports are replacing the invented games of childhood. The culture of sports, with externally imposed rules, referees, uniforms, and an emphasis on outcomes (win-ning) clearly differs from spontaneous, self-regulated play. In fact, sponta-neous play has been described as the "inversion of sport"; unlike organized sport, spontaneous play is intrinsically motivated, flexible, and regulated by the players themselves so that it may change as the interest of the players change from moment to moment (Frost, Wortham, & Reifel, 2001).

Rough-and-Tumble Play as Pathology

Rough-and-tumble play, a form of social engagement consisting of activ-ities such as play fighting, hitting, wrestling, and chasing with the intent of fighting, is believed to constitute approximately 15% of all the vigorous physical play observed in children (Humphreys & Smith, 1984; Smith, 1989). While it is not known why immature organisms engage in such play, Pellegrini and Smith (1998) suggested that its primary function might be to allow children, and particularly boys, to establish their status within a dominance hierarchy. This appears to be the function of rough and tumble in other mammals, such as chimpanzees; it is a relatively safe way to establish one's status within the group without the risk of injury that may occur during genuine aggressive acts (Pacquette, 1994).

There is a correlation between the appearance of this activity and the maturity of the frontal lobes of the brain. The executive functions of the frontal lobes include reflection, imagination, empathy, and play/creativity, and when these develop, they allow for greater behavioral flexibility and foresight, for well-focused goal-directed behavior. As the frontal lobes mature, the frequency of rough-and-tumble play goes down, and damage to the frontal lobes is associated with a higher level of playfulness (Panksepp, Normansell, Coc, & Siviy, 1995). In fact, surgical reduction of the frontal lobes of young rats results in an increased level of playfulness and hyperactivity. However, when these surgically altered rats are given ample opportunity to engage in rough-and-tumble activity, the decline in such play with maturity is even more dramatic than the decline that occurs in the normal rat, leading to the speculation that rough-and-tumble play is not only correlated with frontal lobe development but may actually promote it (Panksepp, Burgdorf, Turner, & Walter, 1997).

Spontaneous rough-and-tumble play may be increasingly seen as a sign of pathology rather than as an ordinary childhood activity, a growing intolerance that corresponds that with one of the more intriguing trends in the diagnosis of childhood psychological problems: the dramatic increase in the diagnosis of attention deficit hyperactivity disorders in the late 20th century (Panksepp, 1998). It has been estimated that in the year 2000 15% of American children (about 8 million) were so diagnosed, up from 1% at the beginning of this century and 5% at the beginning of this decade (Armstrong, 1995). It seems unlikely that there really has been an increased prevalence of genuine neurological disorders in the United States; a more likely interpretation is that we have redefined what we consider to be "normal" childhood behaviors, and spontaneous energetic physical play is sometimes interpreted as a form of pathology (Panksepp, 1998).

There is evidence that genuine attention deficits in children are correlated with reduced frontal lobe size and activity (Barkley, 1997), although brain-imaging data is obviously not a prerequisite for a diagnosis of ADHD. Whether or not a neural disorder is present, however, findings from animal research suggest that rough and tumble play not only reflects frontal lobe development but also promotes it. In other words, active, energetic, spontaneous physical play may facilitate neurological development. If this is the case, the inhibition of play through the use of behavioral restrictions or medication might actually contribute to developmental abnormalities. Indeed, while psychostimulant medications such as Ritalin are quite effective in focusing children's attention, another of their major effects of is to reduce the urge of young organisms to engage in rough and tumble play (Panksepp, Normansell, Cox, Crepeau, & Sacks, 1987).

Since learning requires attention and focus, vigorous physical play may appear to be antithetical to the educational process. Teachers may believe that opportunities for physical play may make children, and particularly those diagnosed with attention disorders, even more difficult to teach. Panksepp (1998) maintained that, as is true of other appetites, the need for rough and tumble is self- regulating process. Once the need is satisfied, the organism will return to a relatively quiet state. In fact, there is evidence to suggest that if children are deprived of physical play, they will play with even greater vigor when given the opportunity to do so (Pellegrini, Huberty, & Jones, 1995; Smith & Hagan, 1980). If there is an appetite for rough and tumble play, and if such play not only reflects but also promotes neurological maturity, it seems that it would be counterproductive and possibly harmful to try to prevent it.

CONCLUSIONS

Several years ago, Brian Sutton-Smith solicited thoughts from a wide variety of scholars on a number of issues related to play. Perhaps the most intriguing question in the survey was, "How do you think children will be playing in the year 2050?" The temptation is to respond that children will always be children and will always find a way to play. Essentially this is the case. When Edwards (2000) re-examined data on play from her *Six Cultures* study done during the 1950's and broadened it with data collected during the 1960's and 1970's, environmental changes over the years resulted in changes in societal reinforcement for play. Improved literacy, increased availability of formal education, a decreasing sense of isolation, and greater exposure to the media and mass communication have all had an influence on play. However, every variety of play could still be found in each of the cultures studied. Edwards (2000) observed that a community may reinforce play to a greater or lesser extent, but it is children themselves who instigate it.

The questions raised in this chapter should not be taken as concerns that spontaneous play will disappear in the 21 [st] century. If the research on play reveals anything, it is that play is a natural and universal activity of childhood. Cross-cultural research reveals, however, that play reflects and is influenced by cultural values, and regional differences in play have been documented repeatedly. If we conceive of cultural variations across time instead of space, there is reason to believe that play will change over time.

If, in fact, spontaneous play arises from an atmosphere of openness and freedom, there is reason for concern that, while play will continue to exist, it will be less spontaneous and less free. The challenge to educators and psychologists is to guarantee that children will continue to have opportunities for spontaneous play.

REFERENCES

Armstrong, T. (1995). *The myth of the ADD child.* New York: Dutton.

Barkley, R.A. (1997). *ADHD and the nature of self-control.* New York: Guilford Press.

Barnett, L.A. (1985). Young children's free play and problem-solving ability. *Leisure Sciences, 7* 25-46.

Bergen, D., & Mauer, D. (2000). Symbolic play, phonological awareness, and literacy skills at three age levels. In K.A. Roskos & J.F. Christie (Eds.), *Play and literacy in early childhood* (pp. 45-62). Mahwah, NJ: Lawrence Erlbaum Associates.

Bjorklund, D.F., & Brown, R.D. (1998). Physical play and cognitive development: Integrating activity, cognition, and education. *Child Development, 69,* 604-606.

Bretherton, I. (1998). Reality and fantasy in make-believe play. In D. Bergen (Ed.), *Play as a medium for learning and development* (pp. 67-69). Olney, MD., Association for Childhood Education International.

Burns, S.M. & Brainerd, C.J. (1979). Effects of constructive and dramatic play on perspective-taking in very young children. *Developmental Psychology, 15,* 512-521.

Carson, J., Burks, V., & Parke, R.D. (1993). Parent-child physical play: determinants and consequences. In K. MacDonald (Ed.), *Parent-child play: Descriptions and implications* (pp. 197-220). Albany: State University of New York Press.

Castle, K. (1998). Children's rule knowledge in invented games. *Journal of Research in Childhood Education, 12,* 197-209.

Castle, K., & Wilson, E. (1993). Creativity through children's invented games. In M. Guddemi and T. Jambor (Eds.), *A right to play: Proceedings of the American Affiliate of the International Association for the Child's Right to Play* (pp. 87-90). Little Rock, AK: Southern Early Childhood Association.

Copple, C.E., Cocking, R.R., & Matthews, W.S. (1984). Objects, symbols, and substitutes: The nature of the cognitive activity during symbolic play. In T.D. Yawkey & A.D. Pellegrini (Eds.), *Child's play: Developmental and applied* (pp. 105-124). Hillsdale, N.J.: Erlbaum.

Dansky, J.L. (1980). Make-believe: A mediator of the relationship between play and associative fluency. *Child Development, 51,* 576-579.

Dansky, J.L. & Silverman, I.W. (1973). Effects of play on associative fluency in preschool-aged children. *Developmental Psychology, 9,* 38-43.

Dansky, J.L. & Silverman, I.W. (1975). Play: A general facilitator of associative fluency. *Developmental Psychology, 11,* 104.

Dargan & Zeitlin (2000). City play. *Educational Leadership, 57,* 73-75.

Elder, J.L. & Pederson, D.R. (1978). Preschool children's use of objects in symbolic play. *Child Development, 49,* 500-504.

Farver, J.A., & Lee-Shin, Y. (2000). Acculturation and Korean-American children's social and play behavior. *Social Development, 9,* 316-336.

Farver, J.A., & Shin, Y.L. (1997). Social pretend play in Korean-and Anglo-American Preschoolers. *Child Development, 68,* 544-556.

Farver, J.A., Kim, Y.K., & Lee, Y. (1995). Cultural differences in Korean- and Anglo-American preschoolers' social interaction and play behaviors. *Child Development, 66,* 1088-1099.

Farver, J.A., Kim, Y.K., & Lee-Shin, Y. (2000). Within cultural differences. Examining individual differences in Korean-American and European-American preschoolers' social pretend play. *Journal of Cross Cultural Psychology, 31,* 583-602.

Fein, G. (1987). Pretend play: creativity and consciousness. In P. Gorlitz & J. Wohlwill (Eds.), *Curiosity, imagination and play* (pp. 281-304). Hillsdale, N.J.: Lawrence Erlbaum Associates, Inc.

Fein, G., G., Ardila-Rey, A.E., & Groth, L.A. (2000). The narrative connection: Stories and literacy. In K.A. Roskos & J.F. Christie (Eds.), *Play and literacy in early childhood* (pp. 27-44). Mahwah, N.J.: Lawrence Erlbaum Associates.

Frost, J.L., Wortham, S., & Reifel, S. (2001). *Play and child development.* Upper Saddle River, N.J.: Prentice-Hall.

Frost, L.L., Shin, D., & Jacobs, P.J. (1998). Physical environments and children's play. In O.N. Saracho & B. Spodek (Eds.), *Multiple perspectives on play in early childhood education* (pp. 255-294). Albany, NY: State University of New York Press.

Garvey, C. (1984). *Children's talk.* Cambridge, MA.: Harvard University Press.

Golumb, C. & Cornelius, C.B. (1977). Symbolic play and its cognitive significance. *Developmental Psychology, 13,* 246-252.

Guilford, J.P. (1968). *Intelligence, creativity, and their educational implications.* San Diego: Knapp.

Haight, W., & Miller, P.J. (1992). The development of everyday pretend play: A longitudinal study of mothers' participation. *Merrill-Palmer Quarterly, 38,* 331-347.

Haight, W.L., Parke, R.D., & Black, J.E. (1997). Mothers' and fathers' beliefs about and spontaneous participation in their toddlers' pretend play. *Merrill-Palmer Quarterly, 43,* 271-290.

Howes, C., Unger, O.A., & Matheson, C.C. (1992). *The collaborative construction of pretend.* Albany, NY: State University of New York Press.

Humphreys, A.P. & Smith, P.K. (1984). Rough-and-tumble in preschool and playground. In P.K. Smith (Ed.), *Play in animals and humans* (pp. 241-270). London: Basil Blackwell.

Isen, A., Daubman, K., & Nowicki, G. (1987). Positive affect facilitates creative problem solving. *Journal of Personality and Social Psychology, 52,* 1122-1131.

Jackowitz, E.R. & Watson, M.W. (1980). The development of object transformations in early pretend play. *Developmental Psychology, 16,* 543-549.

Kozulin, A. (1996). The concept of activity in Soviet psychology: Vygotsky, his disciples, and critics. In H. Daniels (Ed.), *An introduction to Vygotsky* (pp. 99-122). London: Routledge.

Kuczaj, S.A. (1985). Language play. *Early Child Development and Care, 19,* 53-67.

Kuczaj, S.A. (1998). Is an evolutionary theory of language play possible? *Current Psychology of Cognition. 17,* 135-154.

Laasko, M., Poikkeus, A.M., Eklund, K., & Lyytinen, P. (1999). Social interactional behaviors and symbolic play competence as predictors of language development and their associations with maternal attention directing strategies. *Infant Behavior and Development, 22,* 541-556.

Lim, S. (1998). Linking play and language in Singapore preschool settings. *Early Child Development and Care*, **XX**, 21-38.

Lyytinen, P., Laasko, M., Poikkeus, A., & Rita, N. (1999). The development and predictive relations of play and language across the second year. *Scandinavian Journal of Psychology*, *40*, 177-186.

MacDonald, K.B., & Parke, R.D. (1986). Parent-child physical play: The effects of sex and age of children and parents. *Sex Roles*, *15*, 367-378.

McGhee, P.E., Ethridge, L., & Benz, N.L. (1984). Effect of level of toy structure on preschool children's pretend play. *The Journal of Genetic Psychology*, *144*, 209-217.

Oravec, J. (2000-2001). Interactive toys and children's education: Strategies for educators and parents. *Childhood Education*, (Winter), 81-85.

Pacquette, D. (1994). Fighting and play fighting in captive adolescent chimpanzees. *Aggressive Behaviour*, *20*, 49-65.

Panksepp, J. (1998). Attention deficit hyperactivity disorders, psychostimulants, and intolerance of childhood playfulness: A tragedy in the making. *Current Directions in Psychological Science*, *7*, 91-98.

Panksepp, J., Burgdorf, J., Turner, C., & Walter, M. (1997). A new animal model for ADHD: Unilateral frontal lobe damage in neonatal rats. *Society for Neuroscience Abstracts*. *23*, 691.

Panksepp, J., Normansell, L.A., Cox, J.F. & Siviy, S. (1995). Effects of neonatal decortication on the social play of juvenile rats. *Physiology and Behavior*, *56*, 429-443.

Panksepp, J., Normansell, L.A., Cox, J.F., Crepeau, L., & Sacks, D.S. (1987). Psychopharmacology of social play. In J. Mos (Ed.), *Ethnopharmacology of social behavior* (pp. 132-144). Dordrecht, The Netherlands: Duphar.

Pellegrini, A.D., Huberty, P.D., & Jones, I. (1995). The effects of recess timing on children's classroom and playground behavior. *American Educational Research Journal*, *32*, 845-864.

Pellegrini, A.D., & Smith, P.K. (1998). Physical activity play: The nature and function of a neglected aspect of play. *Child Development*, *69*, 577-598.

Pepler, D.J. & Ross, H.S. (1981). The effects of play on convergent and divergent problem-solving. *Child Development*, *52*, 1202-1210.

Piaget, J. & Inhelder, B. (1969). *The psychology of the child*. New York: Basic Books.

Piaget, J. (1962). *Play, dreams, and imitation in childhood*. New York: Norton.

Pulaski, M.A. (1970). Play as a function of toy structure and fantasy predisposition. *Child Development*, *41*, 531-537.

Pulaski, M.A. (1973). Toys and imaginative play. In J.L. Singer (Ed.), *The child's world of make-believe*. New York: Academic Press.

Ratner, N. & Bruner, J. (1978). Games, social exchange, and the acquisition of language. *Journal of Child Language*, *5*, 391-401.

Roopnarine, J.L., Lasker, J., Sacks, M., & Stores, M. (1998) The cultural context of children's play. In O.N. Saracho & B. Spodek (Eds.), *Multiple perspectives on play in early childhood education* (pp. 194-219). Albany, NY: State University of New York Press.

Roopnarine, J.L., Shin, M., Donovan, B., & Suppal, P. (2000). Sociocultural contexts of dramatic play: Implications for early education. In K.A. Roskos & J.F. Christie (Eds.), *Play and literacy in early childhood*, *(pp. 205-230)*. Mahwah, NJ: Lawrence Erlbaum Associates.

Rubin, K.H. & Maioni, T. (1975). Play preference and its relationship to egocentrism, popularity, and classification skills in preschoolers. *Merrill-Palmer Quarterly, 21,* 171-179.

Rubin, K.H. (1980). Fantasy play: Its role in the development of social skills and social cognition. In K.H. Rubin (Ed.), *Children's play.* San Francisco: Jossey-Bass.

Rubin, K.H., Fein, G.C., & Vandenberg, B. (1983). Play. In P.H. Mussen (Ed.), *Handbook of child psychology,* (4th Ed.). New York: Wiley.

Russ, S.W., (1993). *Affect and creativity: The role of affect and play in the creative process.* Hillsdale, NJ: Lawrence Erlbaum Associates.

Russ, S.W. (1999). Play, affect, and creativity: Theory and research. In S. Russ (Ed.), *Affect, creative experience, and psychological adjustment* (pp. 57-75). Philadelphia: Brunner/Mazel.

Russ, S.W., & Grossman-McKee, A. (1990). Affective expression in children's fantasy play, primary process thinking on the Rorschach, and divergent thinking. *Journal of Personality Assessment, 54,* 756-771.

Russ, S.W., & Kaugars, A.S. (2001). Emotion in children's play and creative problem solving. *Creativity Research Journal, 13,* 211-219.

Russ, S.W., Robbins, D., & Christiano, B. (1999). Pretend play: Longitudinal prediction of creativity and affect and fantasy in children. *Creativity Research Journal, 12,* 129-139.

Saffo, P., & Simon, C. (1998). Neo-toys. *Civilization, 5,* 68-69.

Saltz, E., Dixon, D., & Johnson, J. (1977). Training disadvantaged preschoolers on various fantasy activities: Effects on cognitive functioning and impulse control. *Child Development, 48,* 367-380.

Sardar, Z. (1998). Unity against the tyranny of toys! *New Statesman, 127,* 38-39.

Silvern, S.B., Williamson, P.A., & Waters, B. (1982). Play as a mediator of comprehension: An alternative to play training. *Educational Research Quarterly, 7,* 16-21.

Singer, J.L., & Singer, D.G. (1998). Imaginative play and human development: Schemas, scripts, and possibilities. In D. Bergen (Ed.), *Play as a medium for learning and development* (pp. 63-66). Olney, MD., Association for Childhood Education International.

Smith, P.K. (1989). *Rough-and-tumble play and its relationship to serious fighting.* Paper presented at the biennial meeting of the Society for Research in Child Development, Kansas City, April.

Smith, P.K., Dalgleish, M., & Herzmark, G. (1981). A comparison of the effects of fantasy play tutoring and skills tutoring in nursery classes. *International Journal of Behavioral Development, 4,* 421-441.

Smith, P.K., & Hagan, T. (1980). Effects of deprivation on exercise play in nursery school children. *Animal Behaviour, 28,* 922-928.

Smith, P.K. & Sydall, S. (1978). Play and non-play tutoring in preschool children: Is it play or tutoring which matters? *British Journal of Educational Psychology, 48,* 315-325.

Somerville, J. (1982). *The rise and fall of childhood.* Beverly Hills, CA.: Sage.

Sylva, K., Bruner, J.S., & Genova, P. (1976). The role of play in the problem solving of children 3-5 years old. In J.S. Bruner, A. Jolly, & K. Sylva (Eds.), *Play: Its role in development and evolution.* New York: Basic Books.

Tamis-LeMonda, C.S., & Bornstein, M.H. (1991). Individual variation, correspondence, stability, and change in mother and toddler play. *Infant Behavior and Development, 14,* 143-162.

Tamis-LeMonda, C.S., & Damast, A.M. (1993, April). *Individual differences in mothers' play actions and beliefs: Correspondence to toddler-play competence.* Paper presented at the biennial meeting of the Society for Research in Child Development, New Orleans.

Ungerer, J.A., Zelazo, P.R., Kearsley, R.B., & O'Leary, K. (1981). Developmental changes in the representation of objects in symbolic play from 18 to 34 months of age. *Child Development, 52,* 186-195.

Vandenberg, B. (1998). Real and not real: A vital developmental dichotomy. In O.N. Saracho & B. Spodek (Eds.), *Multiple perspectives on play in early childhood education* (pp. 295-305). Albany: State University of New York Press.

Vygotsky, L. (1986). *Thought and language* (Newly revised and edited by A. Kozulin). Cambridge, MA: MIT Press.

Williamson, P. A., & Silvern, S.B. (1990). The effects of play training on the story comprehension of upper primary children. *Journal of Research in Childhood Education. 4,* 130-134.

Wyver, S.R., & Spence, S.H. (1999). Play and divergent problem solving: Evidence supporting a reciprocal relationship. *Early Education and Development, 10,* 419-444.

CHAPTER 3

THEORIES OF PRETENSE, MENTAL REPRESENTATION, AND HUMOR DEVELOPMENT
Answers and Questions

Doris Bergen

During the past 25 years, numerous studies have explored the definitions and characteristics of play in early childhood, the conditions under which it occurs, and its relationships to the development and learning of young children. The type of play that has received the most attention by early childhood researchers has been pretense, which involves the ability to transform the "real" world into the "pretend" world and to act "as if" that world existed. Observational research on social pretense with parents, siblings, and peers, has been especially fruitful in pointing out underlying mental processes that appear to be required for this activity. For example, pretense has been linked to children's development of representational competence (Pederson, Rook-Green, & Elder, 1981), problem solving skills (Smith & Dutton, 1979), and perspective-taking (Rubin & Howe, 1986). More recently, a body of experimental research focused on learning more about young children's mental representation abilities, specifically

Contemporary Perspectives on Play in Early Childhood Education
A Volume in: Contemporary Perspectives in Early Childhood Education, pages 41–51.
Copyright © 2003 by Information Age Publishing, Inc.
All rights of reproduction in any form reserved.
ISBN: 1-930608-31-4 (cloth), 1-930608-30-6 (paper)

their "theory of mind" (TOM) (Leslie, 1987) has provided insights into the development of this process. These studies have typically used language and actions related to pretense to explore whether children understand "false belief." Because results from these studies have raised questions about the role of pretense in the development of such mental processes, there are presently a number of theories being proposed and hypotheses being investigated to attempt to answer these questions. Few studies, whether observational or experimental, have explored potential links between pretense, theory of mind, and young children's humor development, however. This is especially surprising because the characteristics of humor are conceptually very similar to those of pretend play, which has been defined as symbolic, meaningful, pleasurable, active, reality-bending, intrinsically motivated, rule-governed, and episodic (Fromberg, 1992). Most humor also requires an expectation of response from another person, which at least implies that the humor initiator has some type of mental representation of what the humor responder believes. However, few researchers studying social pretense are including reports of the humorous language or behavior children may exhibit in those settings. Experimental theory of mind studies, while including tasks requiring pretense, do not have a humor-oriented bent, nor do observationally-based TOM studies remark on this dimension of observed behavior. It is highly possible, however, that investigation of children's humor development may be relevant in the investigation of young children's mental representational processes.

PRETENSE AND THEORY OF MIND

Building on the theoretical literature that strongly suggests this connection, numerous researchers (e.g., Astington & Jenkins, 1995; Youngblade & Dunn, 1995) have reported that children who engage in pretend role play perform better on perspective taking tasks and are more likely to understand that one can hold false (or inaccurate) beliefs about objects and phenomena. Lillard (1998) has outline five reasons why pretense might enhance children's theory of mind:

1. Pretend play often involves "out-of-playframe" negotiating among different children's wishes, requiring the players to consider others' views;
2. Within the playframe, the ability to think of one situation or object in two ways, real and pretend, at the same time is also an essential ability for understanding what is in other's minds;
3. Pretending involves representations of objects and events, which may lead to flexibility in mental representation;

4. Pretend role play involves social meta-representation i.e., acting out another's thoughts and actions.and

5. Pretense involves dealing with conflicting emotions and being able to portray the emotions appropriate to different situations and actors.

Thus, ability to pretend appears to be connected to children's understanding of mental representation and intentional acts.

Researchers who have studied pretense in natural settings have noted that children younger than age 4 often appear to show understanding of others' thinking and beliefs in their naturally occurring pretend play but whether these behaviors indicate that the children understand the possibility that others can entertain false beliefs is unclear. Experimental research focusing on this question has consistently found that children do not begin to have this understanding until about age 4 to 5, although they can pretend long before that age. Using versions of the "false belief" paradigm, Lillard (1996) and others have explored various possible explanations for this discontinuity between young children's pretense ability and their theory of mind. Lillard has used a protocol that requires children to understand that a particular pretend subject (a troll-like character, Moe) does not know what a certain animal is (e.g., a rabbit), and thus, even if Moe performs hopping motions, he cannot be pretending to be a rabbit. Children are asked whether they understand that Moe doesn't know what a rabbit is, and then they are asked to say whether Moe is pretending to be a rabbit when the experimenter makes Moe do a hopping motion. Most children before age 4 will assert that Moe is pretending to be a rabbit even when they have agreed that Moe doesn't know what a rabbit is, so the researchers have concluded that the children do not have a concept of theory of mind. They have hypothesized that young children may initially see pretend as action rather than as mental representation, and may not even include pretending in their view of what are mental acts. This research indicates children may not fully understand mental representation and intention until elementary age. Because these experimental studies use a limited view of pretense and a few specific types of false belief tasks and they usually do not compare the extensiveness or sophistication of the natural pretense of child subjects to their performance on the experimental set of theory of mind tasks, the studies raise some interesting questions. For example, does the extensiveness of a child's pretend repertoire influence the ability to perform the theory of mind task? Does the experimental context bring forth a different response than would occur in a child-chosen pretend setting? Do relatively minor changes in the experimental vocabulary result in higher performance of children? These questions are being discussed extensively and a number of researchers are attempted to provide answers.

The researchers are using adapted experimental methods or combining experimental and observational methods to try to clarify what aspects of TOM younger children may have. For example, Joseph (1998) conducted a series of experiments that probed 3- and 4-year-olds' understanding of involuntary behaviors and those performed intentionally during pretend. Joseph used questions that differentiated intention-by-pretend versus involuntary acts (e.g., pretending to sneeze; really sneezing) along with false belief tasks. He concluded that 4-year-olds understood intention as a cause of action and that they did represent pretend behaviors mentally, not merely as actions. He asserted that Lillard's questions required more sophisticated reasoning, which resulted in an underestimation of children's TOM. Cassidy (1998), following the view of Bartsch and Wellman (1995) that TOM begins by age 2 with a 'naive' psychology based on desire, conducted a series of studies to investigate whether children's use of desire to solve TOM problems affected their performance. Testing whether young children use the desires of others rather than their beliefs to predict behavior, Cassidy found that more children are able to attribute a false belief to an agent when that belief is about something occurring in pretend play but that a "reality bias" influences their ability to respond correctly in non-play situations. Abu-Akel & Bailey (2001), in a TOM study comparing tasks using indexical language references (e.g., least abstract, such as finger pointing) to symbolic language references (e.g., using labels requiring abstraction), found that a higher percentage of 4 year olds were successful in TOM tasks when indexical references were used. They posit two stages of TOM, the first indexical (ages 4-5) and the latter indexical-symbolic (5-6). In a longitudinal study designed to test the direction of the relationship between children's joint planning and role assignments during social pretense and their TOM, Jenkins and Astington (2000) found that the children's level of TOM predicted the extensiveness of these abilities rather than the pretense abilities predicting the TOM level of the child. Although they point out that the study just begins to explore the directionality of the social pretense/TOM relationship, they suggest that a theory of mind appears to be a gradual acquisition over the age period from 2 to 6.

Studies of younger children do give some indications of the developing ability to understand the thinking of others. For example, in a pretend play situation with parents, Kavanaugh, Eizenman, and Harris (1997) found that children of 2 show independent agency (making dolls do pretend actions) and intersubjectivity (having a shared understanding with the parent in the common activity). When the parent initiated the doll's action, they were able to respond appropriately although often they responded with the appropriate action themselves rather than making the doll perform the action. Sinclair (1996), using naturalistic examples, suggests that very young children's ability to use *practical deception* indicates that they are moving toward a theory of mind, but that their earlier view of false belief is linked to goal-oriented specific social actions rather than to a socially neutral abstract domain. Sinclair points out that children's humor expression at this early age may also be evidence of mental representation development. She states, "the existence of jokes and fantasy, where the invitation is to appreciate the pretence *as a pretence* and find it funny, attests to the capacity to articulate links between the pretence and the real. Even very young children show that they are aware of the pretend nature, inappropriateness or falsity of their pretence; otherwise there is no joke. Jokes work because the truth value or sincerity...proffered by the actor is shared by the audience" (p. 165).

PLAY AND HUMOR DEVELOPMENT

Although pretense/TOM researchers (with the exception of Sinclair) have ignored potential connections between their findings about mental representation and studies of humor development, theorists and researchers focused on humor have long speculated about these connections, and hypotheses regarding the social-emotional and cognitive meanings underlying the emergence of children's humor have been in existence for many years. The first theorist to address the play-humor connection was Freud (1960), who was interested in humor as a method of expressing both meaning and emotion. He characterized three stages of humor development, beginning with a stage called "play" (ages 2-3); followed by "jesting" (ages 4-6), and finally true 'joking,' (about age 7), which provides a socially acceptable way of expressing feelings that can not be otherwise expressed (i.e., hostility, sexuality). Freud characterized the *play* stage as involving repeating sounds, practicing incongruous acts with objects, and "rediscovering the familiar" by using it in incongruous ways. He posited that the *jesting* stage results from children's discovering that adults prefer "reasonableness" rather than "absurdity." Although Freud did not connect his theory of joking to a theory of mind, his observation that very young children intentionally use familiar objects and acts in incongruous ways and deliberately use absurdity to get a reaction from adults suggest that he believed awareness of an audience is present even in these early stages of humor development. According to Wolfenstein (1954), early humor also assists children in mastering their anxieties, because they tend to use "joking pretend" in situations where they have just mastered some concept or experience. This view explains why young children enjoy "wrong name" humor at the time they have begun to establish self-identity. In the clinical treatment of children, the use of humor and play are still recommended as effective methods which free young patients from adherence to rigid defenses (Sanville, 1999).

Following Piaget (1962), McGhee (1979) defined four stages of humor as a cognitive process: "incongruous actions" (ages 1-2), "incongruous language" (beginning about age 2), "conceptual incongruity" (beginning about age 4), and "word play/multiple meanings" (about age 7). The reason cognition (and potentially TOM concepts) is involved in incongruity-based humor is because it is not until children "know" the correct actions, language, concepts, and meanings that they can deliberately play with them to create humor that gets a reaction from an adult or peer. There is evidence that humor based on recognition of incongruous actions appears very early, usually shown by infants' laughter during physical and social 'surprise' play with parents (Pien & Rothbart, 1980; Sroufe & Wunsch, 1972; Stern, 1974). Reacting to incongruity is not the same as reacting to novelty. According to Pien and Rothbart, "an incongruous stimulus is *mis*-expected...while a novel stimulus is *un*expected" (p.3). Panksepp (2000) suggests that infant laughter induced by tickling, peek-a-boo, and other early social routines may be related to the neural development of the brain, and that, although this basic response is evident very early, the *feelings* of joy or humor appear to depend on frontal lobe development during the second half of the first year. It is probably likely that the first *mis*expectations occur at that time, and the first child initiated attempts at humor begin at that time also.

Case studies of infant and toddler humor and play development describe this progression of early humor. In a study of an infant during the first 12 months, the researcher found the infant used pre-verbal symbols, deliberate finger and body movements, and finally symbolic play and humor to engage in interactions with the parent (Hill, 1996). Another study, which followed a toddler (from 15 to 30 months), found that symbolic play and conceptual mastery were precursors of verbal incongruity humor (Johnson & Mervis, 1997). The first verbal humor observed was mislabeling (incongruent labels), followed by puns and production of non-sense words. Adult playfulness cues were not always necessary to produce humor by this age. Aimard (1992) reports that 2-year-olds show "iconoclastic" humor, which seems to be deliberately designed to gain control in social interactions. McGhee (1979) asserts that "in the majority of toddlers" humor is self-generated" (p. 2). Examples of the humor of children in the age range of 2-4 include clowning (making exaggerated movements or vocal sounds designed to make an effect), teasing (using actions or words to provoke another), performing incongruous or fantasy actions in the presence of others, and describing impossible events (Bergen, 1998a). Even these early humor attempts are primarily social acts, which appear to require the child to have some understanding of other people's thinking in order for the humorous act to be effective (i.e., gain a smile or laugh response). Early examples from humor records (Bergen, 2001) are that of Britta (11 months) and Sam (26 months). Britta crawls quickly away from her mother when her mother asks her to come to get dressed. Her mother joins in the play saying, "I'm gonna get you" and Britta shrieks (falsely) and crawls under the table. The routine continues for a few more rounds, then mother catches Britta and both of them laugh. Sam is with a 4-year-old child who asks him what ducks drink. Sam answers "Ducks drink water." The older child responds, "No, ducks drink orange juice." Sam laughs and reiterates "Ducks drink water." This sequence is repeated four times, resulting in escalating laughter. While neither of these example shows child understanding of false belief, they do show that very young children have the ability to deliberately create a teasing effect (Britta) and to enjoy the expression of incongruous (or false) ideas (Sam).

Play, and especially pretend play, may serve as the major context for humor development (Bergen, 1998a; 1998b). Humor expression and pretend play have many similar characteristics, and are often produced concurrently. Pretense and humor both require the ability to be free of reality and to act in an "as if" manner. McGhee (1979, p. 61) states, "humor develops as the child's playfulness extends to recently mastered ideas and images...[and includes]... something that he knows is non-sense, absurd, or impossible." Wolfenstein (1954) theorized that although play and humor may start from the same developmental base, they become separate conceptual entities during the second year of life. At that point pretense becomes two diverging types: "serious" make-believe, in which children attempt to replicate the real world, and "joking" make-believe, in which they deliberately distort the real world through incongruous actions and language (i.e., "nonsense" or "silliness"). In serious pretense children attempt to create a world that differs from the children's actual world only because it is governed by the children. That is, in serious make-believe children try to replicate the real world in ways that make sense to them. In joking pretense, children are not acting as if the pretend world is the real world. Rather, they are deliberately distorting reality through making fictitious deformations of the world in order to make others laugh. Bariaud (1989) states that the incongruities expressed in the actions of joking make-believe are *not incorrect* but of a *pretend nature*, performed in order to "trigger laughter" (p.23). She asserts, "there is a certain "distancing" from the norms of reality, and a combination of being fooled and complicity required from the other" (p. 21). An example from the humor records (Bergen, 2001) is that of Lucy (4-years-old), who in one 10 minute recorded period engaged in clowning (hopping in a "silly" manner and looking to see effect), teasing (poking and hugging another child who was engaged in an activity), verbal/sound play (saying "baby, baby, baby" in an increasing loud voice), and "joking" make-believe (pretending to "comb" the hair of the "baby" (the other child) with a wooden rod and pretending to feed her in an exaggerated manner). Early symbolic play and humor development may have a long-term relationship. In a longitudinal study, pre-school children who spent more than 50% of the observed time period in symbolic play (pretense and literacy related) had higher scores on self ratings of their sense of humor at age 9 and parents of children who spent at least 30% of their preschool observed time in social pretense rated their children higher on both sense of humor and play interests at the later age (Bergen, 2000).

While earlier stages of humor might be explained by reasons other than development of mental representation, by the time children reach the humor stage of conceptual incongruity (McGhee's stage 3 age 4-6), their understanding of false belief is apparently evident (according to TOM researchers). A recent study by Varga (2001), however, calls into question that children need concrete operational thought to express hyperbole in humor. Hyperbole requires the ability to understand figurative language instead of literal meanings. Children do not find outrageous false statements humorous unless they understand that distinction. In this observational study of language during social play, when the preschool children asserted that they had extraordinary abilities (hyperbole), their peers responded by elaborating on the claims, with increasing evidence of laughter as the incongruities were heightened. Other naturalistic studies of children's *humor* expression conducted in social play settings have found that children express a range of humor types, including making outrageous claims and describing impossible events (e.g, Bergen, 1998a; Klein, 1985).

It is surprising, however, that most observational studies of children's *social play* do not indicate whether the play was accompanied by expressions of humor, thus making play appear to be "serious business." That does not appear to be the case. In one review of a set of toddlers' and preschoolers' video records of free play time, 68% of the records had at least one event in which the focal child expressed humor, with the humor instances ranging from one to ten over each child's ten minute videotape record. (Bergen, 2001). Humor occurred during practice play, pretend play, and game play, but not equally in all social contexts. Social pretense had the most instances. The presence of other children elicited more boisterous humor, especially among preschool age children. Major humor types included expressing joy in mastery play, clowning, teasing, and observing/performing incongruous actions and language. There were no significant differences between children with disabilities and typical children or between boys and girls in the number of humor events or in the types of humor expressed, although adults were more involved in humor interactions with younger children and those with disabilities. This study verified the presence of spontaneous expressions of humor during young children's play, but it did not test specific hypotheses about pretense, humor, and TOM connections. There are many questions about this connection that need to be addressed in order to test the theoretical assumptions about their diverging paths of development and their ongoing connections.

THEORY OF MIND AND HUMOR DEVELOPMENT

Evidence from both case studies of individual children and observations of social pretense has provided examples of the intentional nature of children's early humor and the diverging paths taken by serious make-believe and joking make-believe. While it is undoubtedly the case that children's theory of mind is not sufficiently sophisticated to answer false belief task questions until age 4-5, over the period from age 2 to 4 there are sufficient examples of children deliberately distorting factual information and creating incongruous situations for the purpose of making others laugh. If children have no conception of what the other person is thinking, why would they engage in this humor-provoking activity? It may be, as Sinclair says, that practical deception is different from later understanding of false belief because it is a goal-oriented specific social action rather than an understanding of a socially neutral abstract domain. There are presently no studies of social pretense that have separated observational data into categories of serious make-believe and joking make-believe. Perhaps a reason why the predictive nature of social pretense on theory of mind development is unclear is because researchers did not separate their observational data into the categories of joking make-believe and serious make-believe. It may be that the quantity of joking make-believe in a child's repertoire is more predictive of their theory of mind development. The case is made here for considering the role of humor, especially joking make-believe, in influencing theory of mind development.

REFERENCES

Abu-Akel, A., & Bailey, A. L. (2001). Indexical and symbolic referencing: What role do they play in children's success on theory of mind tasks? *Cognition, 80,* 263-281.

Aimard, P. (1992). Genese de phumour. *Devenir, 4*(3), 27-40.

Astington, J. W., & Jenkins, J. M. (1995). Theory of mind development and social understanding. *Cognition and Emotion, 9,* 151-165.

Bariaud, F. (1989). Age differences in children's humor. *Journal of Children in Contemporary Society, 20*(1-2), 15-45.

Bartach, K., & Wellman, H. M. (1995). *Children talk about the mind.* Oxford, England: Oxford University Press.

Bergen, D. (1998a). Development of the sense of humor. In W. Ruch (Ed.), *The sense of humor: Explorations of a personality characteristic.* (pp. 329-358). Berlin: Mouton deGruyter.

Bergen, D. (1998b). Play as a context for humor development. In D. P. Fromberg., & D. Bergen (Eds.) *Play from birth to twelve and beyond: Contexts, perspectives, and meanings.* (pp. 324-327). New York: Garland Press.

Bergen, D. (2000). *Play and development of the sense of humor: A longitudinal study.* Paper presented at the 16th ISSBD Biennial Meeting, Beijing, Peoples Republic of China.

Bergen, D. (2001). Finding the humor in play. In J. Roopnarine (Ed.), *Play and Culture Studies (Vol. 3)*, Stanford, CT: Ablex.

Bergen, D., & Mauer, D. (2000). Symbolic play, phonological awareness, and literacy skills at three age levels. In J. Christie, & K. Roskos (Eds.) *Literacy and play in the early years: Cognitive, ecological, and sociocultural perspectives* (pp. 45-62). New York: Erlbaum.

Cassidy, K. W. (1998). Preschoolers' use of desires to solve theory of mind problems in a pretense context. *Developmental Psychology, 34*(3), 503-511,

Freud, S. (1960). *Jokes and their relation to the unconscious.* New York: Norton.

Fromberg, D. P. (1992). A review of research on play. In C. Seefeldt (Ed.), *The early childhood curriculum: A review of current research* (2nd ed., pp. 42-84). New York: Teachers College Press.

Hill, C. (1996). Ego development, creative humour and play, in a "good enough" mothering experience: An infant observational study. *Australian Journal of Psychotherapy, 15*(1), 82-91.

Jenkins, J. M., & Astington, J. W. (2000). Theory of mind and social behavior: Causal models tested in a longitudinal study. *Merrill-Palmer Quarterly, 46*(2), 203-220.

Johnson, K. E., & Mervis, C. B. (1997). First steps in the emergence of verbal humor: A case study. *Infant Behavior and Development, 20*, 187-196.

Joseph, R. M. (1998). Intention and knowledge in preschoolers? conception of pretend. *Child Development, 69*, 966-980.

Kavanaugh, R. D., Eizenman, D. R., & Harris, P. L. (1997). Young children's understanding of pretense expressions of independent agency. *Developmental Psychology, 33*, 764-770.

Klein, A. (1985). Humor comprehension and humor appreciation of cognitively oriented humor: A study of kindergarten children. *Child Development, 56*, 223-235.

Leslie, A.M. (1987). Pretense and representation: The origins of "theory of mind." *Psychological Review, 94*, 412-426.

Lillard, A. S. (1996). Body or mind: Children's categorizing of pretense. *Child Development, 67*, 1717-1734.

Lillard, A. S. (1998). Playing with the theory of mind. In O. N. Saracho & B. Spodek (Eds.) *Multiple perspectives on play in early childhood education.* (pp. 11-33). Albany, NY: State University of New York Press.

Panksepp, J. (2000). The riddle of laughter: Neural and psychoevolutionary underpinnings of joy. *Current Directions in Psychological Science, 9*(6), 183-186.

Pederson, D. R., Rook-Green, A., & Elder, J. L. (1981). The role of action in the development of pretend play in young children. *Developmental Psychology, 17*, 756-759.

Piaget, J. (1962). *Play, dreams and imitation in childhood.* New York: Norton.

Pien, D., & Rothbart, M. K. (1980). Incongruity humour, play and self-regulation of arousal in young children. In P. McGhee & A. J. Chapman (Eds), *Children's humour* (pp. 1-26). New York: John Wiley.

Rubin, K. H., & Howe, N. (1986). Social play and perspective taking. In G. Fein & M. Rivkin (Eds.). *The young child at play: Reviews of research* (pp. 113-125) Washington, DC: National Association for the Education of Young Children.

Sanville, J. B. (1999). Humor and play. In J. W. Barron (Ed.).*Humor and psyche: Psychoanalytic perspectives* (pp. 31-55). Hillsdale, NJ: Analytic Press.

Sinclair, A. (1996). Young children's practical deceptions and their understanding of false belief. *New Ideas in Psychology, 14*(2), 152-173.

Smith, P. K., & Dutton, S. (1979). Play and training in direct and innovative problem solving. *Child Development, 50*, 830-836.

Sroufe, L. A., & Wunsch, J. P. (1972). The development of laughter in the first year of life. *Child Development, 43*, 1326-1344.

Stern, D. N. (1974). Mother and infant at play: The dyadic interaction involving facial, vocal, and gaze behaviors. In M. M. Lewis & I. Rosenblum (Eds.) *The effect of the infant on its caregiver* (pp.187-213). New York: John Wiley.

Varga, D. (2001). Hyperbole and humor in children's language play.*Journal of Research in Childhood Education, 14*(2).142-146.

Wolfenstein, M. (1954). *Children's humor: A psychological analysis.* Glencoe, IL: Free Press

Youngblade, L. M., & Dunn, J. (1995). Individual differences in young children's pretend play with mother and sibling: Links to relationships and understanding of other people's feelings and beliefs.*Child Development, 66*, 1472-1492.

CHAPTER 4

PLAY IN SCHOOL—THE TEACHER'S ROLE
Reforms and Recent Research

Ole Fredrik Lillemyr

In some Western countries play is now becoming an integral part of the school's curriculum. The main reason for this is that early childhood education now is seen to encompass both the preschool years and the early years of primary school, from the age of 0 up to 9 or 10 years. In Norway and other Scandinavian countries two educational traditions are being integrated in the curriculum according to new reforms, the tradition of preschool education and the tradition of primary school education. On this background a change in the teacher's role in relation to children's play is necessary, although it represents a challenge. This call for a change in the teacher's role can be seen as a tendency in other countries as well, however, not to the same extent as in the Nordic countries.

In this chapter it is maintained that the inclusion of play in the first years of school implies development towards a new and broader concept of school

Contemporary Perspectives on Play in Early Childhood Education
A Volume in: Contemporary Perspectives in Early Childhood Education, pages 53–73.
Copyright © 2003 by Information Age Publishing, Inc.
All rights of reproduction in any form reserved.
ISBN: 1-930608-31-4 (cloth), 1-930608-30-6 (paper)

learning. First of all this means seeing learning as processes providing increased capacity to comprehend, experience, feel, reflect and act. A new and broader concept of school learning has to include both the acquisition of knowledge and skills, as well as the applications of knowledge, as it is seen in experimentation and creativity. Furthermore, learning affects the whole personality of the child, as the personality also affects learning.

Research on children's play, learning, and sense of competence in the classroom, and research focusing the teacher's role in relation to children's play in particular, is presented here based on European studies, in addition to studies from United States, New Zealand, and Australia. Clearly, teachers look at play both as an inspiration and a challenge. In terms of the teacher's role in play, the concept of "scaffolding" has been used as an effective way of helping children enhance and extend their knowledge. Further, teachers seem to support and emphasize choice for the children. However, the activities in class were often determined by the teacher. Nonetheless, adult interventions are needed in order for children to explore available choices during play sessions. This indicates that adult involvement in play and children's development of independence need not to be mutually exclusive. Today it is meaningful to look at two conceptions of play; learning through play and the value of play as such.

In particular, research studies presented in this chapter, disclose that the extent to which play really is an integral part of the curriculum varies strongly from one country to another. However, even in countries like Norway, where play has a rather strong position in the curriculum guidelines, the students does not seem to expect much free learning to take place in school, e.g. learning where students can choose among alternatives and make decisions about what and how in the activities. Nevertheless, a strong emphasis on play actually implies varied forms of learning as far as student autonomy is concerned. In the change of the teacher's role certain elements from research have to be highlighted. Some of these are presented and discussed in this chapter, first of all from the perspective of transition between day care and school. These elements will definitely contribute to a change in the teacher's role in children's play in the future.

Only recently has play really become an integral part of the school's curriculum in some Western countries. The main reason for this is that early childhood education now not only encompasses the pre-school years, but has also spread to the early school years. It has been argued that in years to come, early childhood education will integrate with the primary school tradition to evolve into new early school pedagogy, with play as a vital element. However, one of the most challenging dilemmas connected with play in day care institutions and primary schools is how *the teacher role* should be carried out and developed in relation to children's play (Bennett, Wood & Rogers 1997; Dockett & Fleer 1999; Lillemyr, 1999a).

INTRODUCTION

Children's play was introduced to the field of early childhood education as one of the main areas many years ago, based on the theories and perspectives of kindergarten of Friedrich Froebel (1782-1852). George H. Mead (1863-1931) discussed the relation of play and education, in terms of the first years of school, more than a hundred years ago (Mead, 1896).

For many years, the field of early childhood education and care was defined as the pre-school period. This is still the case today; for example in New Zealand, where the field "refers to the non-compulsory provision of education and care for young children and infants before they begin school" (Ministry of Education, 1995; May, 1996). However, early childhood education is now often considered to include the first three years of the primary school as well (Klugman, 1990; Wasserman, 1990; Wood & Attfield, 1996; Lillemyr, Fagerli & Søbstad, 2001). The extent to which this is realized in recent reforms, however, differs from one country to another (see Broström, 1999a; Dockett & Fleer, 1999; Lillemyr, 1999a).

In early childhood education today, it is meaningful to look at two conceptions; "learning through play" and "playful learning". Some want to see these leading to what has been called meaning making; e.g. to actively seek for the underlying meaning of knowledge and learning (Dahlberg, Moss & Pence, 1999; Samuelsson & Sheridan, 1999; Broström & Vejleskov, 1999). In curriculum development, some prefer to refer to the conception of *varied forms of play and learning*, reflecting the extent to which children are allowed to make decisions about their activities, being either play or learning (Lillemyr et al., 1998). Characteristically, play has been related to different areas of school learning, like language literacy (Vedeler, 1997; Einarsdottir, 2000), creativity (Vandenberg, 1990), humor (Søbstad, 1999), and art and aesthetics (Eisner, 1990; Lindqvist, 1995). Some even highlights the value of play for its own sake (Olofsson, 1992).

A core issue in the discussion of the function and legitimacy of play in school is whether free play is at all possible or useful in a school setting. As a matter of fact, what has been called the play/work divide reflects the dilemmas connected with the role of the teacher in play, which according to some researchers (Bennett, Wood & Rogers, 1997), is directly linked to the constructivist principles of Piaget and Vygotsky. Both theoretical approaches aim at a level of independent learning, although through slightly different premises (Piaget, 1972; Vygotsky, 1978). Yet does this level of independent learning really happen in a free play setting in the school? Meadows & Cashdan (1988) found that children involved in free play were content and busy, but three things were rare:

1. sustained conversation or play with an adult,
2. high complexity of play activities, and

3. lively, purposeful involvement leading to creative, exciting discovery.

Based on these findings, they recommend that the traditional free play curriculum should be reconsidered since the optimal conditions for learning are not always present in free play activities. These researchers recommend a social-constructivist model based on "tutorial dialogue". This is a suggestion closely related to other propositions for what is called "scaffolding" or arguments for "frame play" (see Broström, 1998; Dockett & Fleer, 1999). In both cases, the purpose is to bring together the intentions of both children and teachers in a reciprocal relationship. Several studies have documented that children's activity spans during the play session increase when an adult is present and when children are offered choices or alternative activities (Sestini, 1987; Hutt et al., 1989; Bennett, Wood & Rogers, 1997; Lillemyr et al., 1998). These studies indicate that in order to implement and retain changes in the teacher role, the teachers' expressed need for practical and theoretical support must be met. This is momentous, since the teachers' "theories of play" will probably function as a frame of reference to ascertain a close relationship between theory and practice, as a foundation for the development of the teacher role. This is particularly important at a time when educational reforms demand major changes in the teacher role.

SCHOOL REFORMS

In Norway, 'Reform 97' for the 10-year compulsory education (primary and lower secondary school) with students aged 6 to 15, was launched in June 1997. The implementation period lasted from June 1997 to June 2000. Following 'Reform 97' new curriculum guidelines were implemented (Curriculum Guidelines of 1997). The changes in "Reform 97" included lowering the school starting age to 6, outlining certain main principles of teaching, and dividing the compulsory education into three stages: the primary school/initial stage (grades 1-4), middle school/intermediate stage (grades 5-7), and lower secondary stage (grades 8-10). Quite a few elements were emphasized to enhance the motivation of students. Greater emphasis is given in the guidelines to making students become involved and take responsibility for activities and learning, in order to be able to cope with the demands of independence and creativity in later life.

A central element designed to catch students' interest and motivation was the inclusion of play in the curriculum. This was done to an extent that is probably unique in Western countries today. One reason for the inclusion of play is to ensure students' involvement, and to enhance their motivation, thereby promoting their personal investment in learning. This can be seen as a motivational approach to education, focusing upon intrinsic motivation and self worth. This coincides with the recommendations made by researchers in the field of motivation with regard to school reforms (Maehr, 1984; Covington, 1992; 1998; Deci & Ryan, 1994; Skaalvik, 1997). As I have argued elsewhere, by sustaining the value of motivation, "Reform 97" in Norway also implies a movement towards a new and broader perspective on school learning (Lillemyr, 2001).

INTERNATIONAL TENDENCIES

Norway is an example of a country where a recent school reform has heavily emphasized children's play. However, this emphasis can also be found in several other countries, although perhaps not to the same extent as in Norway. In many countries, questions related to the teacher's role in relation to play, particularly in the primary school, have been under debate (Bennett, Wood & Attfield, 1997; Dockett & Fleer, 1999). In recent years early childhood educators and school educators alike have increasingly come to see that play is most certainly not "only play". Play actually affects development, stimulates and influences learning, and *is* sometimes the learning process itself, whether in a day care institution or in a school (Smilansky & Shefatya, 1990; Hellendoorn, van der Kooij & Sutton-Smith, 1994; Pellegrini & Smith, 1998; Dockett & Fleer, 1999). However, controversy and criticism are often (justifiably) directed towards how play in school and in other settings functions in practice (Sutton-Smith, 1997; Steinsholt, 1998; Trawick-Smith, 1998).

In the last decade or so, school reforms have often integrated perspectives from early childhood education. In some countries, however, the learning perspective, in a somewhat narrow sense, is the primary focus. This is the reason behind British politicians' fear that formal teaching starts too early in the UK, when compared to other countries (The Times, 1998).

A national curriculum for day care institutions has now evolved in some countries, such as Norway (Framework Plan, 1996) and New Zealand (May, 1996). A "school-orientation" has also influenced the curriculum programs for nurseries and day care institutions. An increasing interest in literacy, learning and evaluation appears to be the result (cf. Curtis, 1998). This tendency is also present in other countries, but to a lesser degree (Broström, 1999b; Einarsdottir, 2000; Framework Plan, 1996).

The Integration of Teacher Education Traditions: A Third, Shared Tradition?

In most countries early childhood educators (preschool teachers) undergo a different form of training than primary school teachers. This is still the case in many countries, even if the two traditions have come closer together in recent years, particularly since the appointment of both pre-school teachers and primary school teachers is now common at primary level in some countries. Cooperation between both kinds of teachers is strongly encouraged in order to create a new kind of pedagogy, founded on the best elements from each tradition.

In the early childhood tradition, the areas of *play* and *learning* are typi-cally quite differently defined and understood compared to the way in which they are understood in the primary school tradition. In the latter tra-dition, learning is often related to problem-solving and progression, and to systematic training of formal knowledge. In early childhood education, developmental objectives have been the main focus, as learning has often been related to fundamental physical and social skills and to the develop-ment of a sense of competence and self-worth. In day care programs, free play and learning through play are important, in contrast to the primary school where play was often the activity reserved for recess time or in play-related activities in music or other aesthetic subjects. Traditionally, several dissimilarities could be found between the two traditions. Still, the under-standing and practice of play and learning are perhaps the two most important issues when comparing the traditions.

The integration of these two traditions has been seen as a third, shared tradition, constituting a platform for a new pedagogy for early school edu-cation in the years to come (Broström, 1999b; Lillemyr, 1999a). The important issue here is how the integration of the two traditions should be handled. How is it possible to include the best from both traditions in developing a third tradition? In Great Britain a lack of visibility of play is documented in the curriculum guidelines, but nonetheless many teachers are highly aware of the importance of play (Wood & Attfield, 1996; Ben-nett, Wood & Rogers, 1997). In conclusion, the integration between the two traditions implies certain changes in the teacher's role in relation to children's play.

PLAY AND LEARNING IN DAY CARE AND SCHOOL

In the last few decades several perspectives from theory and research on play have been put forward. Levy (1978) discussed three dimensions as fundamental to our understanding of children's play: intrinsic motivation, suspension of reality, and internal locus of control. Pellegrini (1991) defines play along three dimensions: play as disposition, play as context, and play as observable behavior. Definitions are typically multidimensional since no single definition is satisfactory or sufficient (Dockett & Fleer, 1999). For this reason it has become more common to delineate dimen-sions for our understanding of the phenomenon of play or as a set of atti-tudes towards play, as seen in the expression of "homo ludens" (Huizinga,

1955; Berg, 1992; Fromberg, 1992; Pellegrini & Smith, 1998). Some even go so far as to maintain that play typically withdraw from our attempts at a definition. Still, understanding play according to dimensions seems to be meaningful (Lillemyr, 1999a; 1999b). Others conceive of play as an important element in the quality of life as such, or as the highest form of human expression, as did Friedrich Schiller (see Levy, 1997; Kibsgaard, 1999).

Against this background I would like to present a holistic perspective on play, drawing on different theories, and with four main dimensions (Levy, 1978; Lillemyr, 2001):

- intrinsic motivation
- children's suspension of reality
- internal base of control
- play as social interactions, or communication at different levels

I find these four dimensions useful in understanding play. Nonetheless, play typically escapes definition. Several scholars in the field draw attention to the strength of play as such, and see play as a societal and cultural phenomenon. It is important to assert that two perspectives of play should be recognized in relation to education:

- the unique value of play for its own sake
- learning through play

In the context of education, it is hard to understand play without referring to learning. In this chapter, *learning* is understood in a broad sense, corresponding with perspectives and discussions that have recently been presented (Bjørgen, 1997; Schoenfeld, 1999). In this sense, learning can be related to five main points (Lillemyr, 1999a; 2001):

- Learning is internal processes caused by training/experiences, providing increased capacity to comprehend, experience, feel, reflect and act.
- Learning includes the acquisition of knowledge and skills, as well as application, as in experimentation and creativity.
- Learning comprises individual processes, but is influenced by social competence, feelings of relatedness, and socio-cultural aspects.
- Learning affects personality, and vice-versa. Learning affects the whole child.
- Learning changes the child's competence, and hence its sense of competence.

Based upon these components, it can be argued for a new and broader concept of learning in day care institutions and schools alike. Accordingly, it will be necessary to get rid of the old-fashioned concept of school learning.

Recent Research on the Teacher's Role in Children's Play

As shown above, recent theory and research on children's play has been critical of applying one single definition of play as a point of departure. Still, a perspective of some kind is needed as the background or foundation for research efforts. Often, different forms of play occur during the period of childhood from which distinct antecedents, contexts and functions for the child or group can be derived (Pellegrini, 1995; Fromberg & Bergen, 1998; Pellegrini & Smith, 1998). In most cases different kinds of play form the starting point for research approaches aiming at enhancing our knowledge and insights into the world of play. In relation to play in school, the function of play itself, and not least the teacher's role in relation to play, have been pursued in research. This approach has been necessary, as some recent school reforms heavily emphasize teaching through play.

In recent research, there has been a tendency to emphasize the objective of social competence in day care institutions as well as in schools (Backe-Hansen & Ogden, 1998; Ladd, Birch & Buhs, 1999). For this reason, including play in the educational program seems necessary to ensure both a harmonic school start and a socio-cultural perspective on schooling (Broström, 1999a; Samuelsson & Sheridan, 1999; Lillemyr, 1999a). In New Zealand it was clearly documented in a study among 5-year-old school starters (Patrick & Townsend, 1995) that their *sense of social competence* is clearly affected their perception of academic competence. Yet play and social competence often are ignored in teaching at the expense of teacher-directed activities (Wood & Attfield, 1996).

In a British research study (Bennett, Wood & Rogers, 1997) the background assumption was that the teacher's cognitive and pedagogical behaviors are guided by a personally-held system of *beliefs, values and principles*. Teachers' "theories" were considered to be imbedded in their practice and made explicit through their teaching orientation. The study covered 9 reception teachers, each with highly different amounts of teaching experience. The researchers included five key areas:

- the area of play and learning
- control, ownership and the role of the teacher
- play in the curriculum
- assessing and interpreting children's learning through play
- constraints

They found that teachers' assumptions about how children learn were in some cases, strongly challenged. Some key points could be pointed out, in particular the *discontinuities* existing between teachers' theories, intentions and practice:

- Teachers emphasized social skills in their theories, but there were few examples showing cooperative play unless an adult was present
- Role-play continued to preoccupy teachers, providing them with challenging issues
- Teachers emphasized the importance of *choice*, but in reality most activities were determined by the teachers themselves
- The practice of "rotating" play and more formal activities interfered with teachers being involved in play for sustained periods

It was concluded as follows:

In their theories, most teachers adhered strongly to the view that play and learning are interrelated through a variety of processes. These included promoting children's interests, choice and ownership, developing autonomy and control and fostering intrinsic motivation, engagement and concentration. .... In general, play was far more structured in practice than teachers' theoretical accounts indicated. (p. 75)

More than half the teachers said that play activities were largely determined by the teachers themselves with relatively little choice allowed for the children. In the reasons given for these contradictions of theory and practice, a key issue was their assumptions about the teacher role in relation to a broad knowledge base, comprising ideology, values, child development, pedagogy, curriculum content, and classroom processes. Nonetheless, the teachers' theories indicated a strong commitment to play as an integral part of the curriculum, since play was seen as contributing to "quality learning", providing the ideal conditions in which to learn.

One of the registered constraints was the pressure of the National Curriculum on the assessment of children's learning through play. A major outcome of the process of teacher reflections was the elaboration of a set of dilemmas about practice regarding choice and ownership, independence, discovery learning, the teacher's role, teachers' and children's intentions, and assessment. The researchers concluded that this would definitely have specific implications for educational practice. Furthermore, these research results seem to document what others in Britain have also asserted (see Wood & Attfield, 1996), namely that there is a gap between the rhetoric about play in school and the reality, representing a main weakness, not least because the National Curriculum deals with play in a rather unsatisfactory way. However, it has been found to be necessary to include play beyond the level of 4-5-year-olds in the school. This means that teachers must then reconsider their role, with the intention of improving the quality of play.

In the United States as well, early childhood education in some instances comprises both the day care institution level and the early school level (Klugman, 1990; Ceglowsky, 1997). A study in the United States and Israel examined kindergarten teachers' attitudes toward the use of play in teaching. A clear tendency that teachers considered play important was revealed, although play was not an element of awareness in their classroom practice (Smilansky, 1990).

An American study on play (Cooney, 1995) indicated that children perceive play in a broader sense of the word than teachers do. It was concluded that the school culture needs to be permeated by the attitude that play is an integral part of the teaching program, in order for children to achieve an adequate level of readiness for learning in the first year of school. Cooney argues that the organization of the school day has to take into consideration the fact that children at this age are first and foremost *learning through play*.

In another American study, focus was placed on the conception of investment in learning, through what is seen as the purpose of schooling and the purpose of learning in school, in order to obtain a fundamental change in the school culture (Maehr & Midgley, 1996; 1999). Meetings and discussions were held with teachers and leaders of elementary and middle schools to change their work from a performance-oriented to a task-oriented learning strategy, based on a goal theory perspective (Pintrich & Schunk, 1996; Maehr & Midgley, 1999). The perspective of children's play was not included in this research on motivation and learning, but it could have been, as play must be considered a typical task-oriented activity (cf. Levy, 1978). Over a period of three years, most of the teachers had changed their attitudes towards task-oriented motivation and "investment in learning", a fact that fundamentally influenced their perception of the teacher's role in relation to learning in school. Interestingly, the achievement records of the school increased, even if performance-orientation and competition among students were given less emphasis.

Longitudinal studies over four years carried out in Austria (Hartmann & Rollett, 1994) reported interesting results. Studies on integrating a play intervention program in the Viennese elementary school curriculum documented that children in the intervention classes were more content with school than children in the control classes. Teachers in play-enriched classes reported children to be more companionable and candid and straightforward, and less aggressive, with fewer behavioral disorders. In general, children from "play classes" showed more positive attitudes towards learning and stronger intrinsic motivation, than the control groups. These effects were obtained without any forfeit of scholastic achievement. For this reason, the concept of "learning through play" was introduced as a recommended form of learning in the Austrian elementary school curriculum in 1987.

A recent study of teachers in the first and second year of school in Australia reveals a strong interest in the teacher's role in play in accordance with recommendations in the curriculum documents (Jones, Dockett, Westcott & Perry, 2000). The attitudes and approaches towards play were examined among six Kindergarten and Year One teachers. All teachers utilized play within their classroom, but they still had diverse understandings of the potential role of play in the early school curriculum. The results showed that the teachers were committed to the value of play for children, preferred to work as a team with play, and were able to support and encourage each other when colleagues and parents questioned the value of play in school. Teachers interviewed twice in each of four school terms about the play program, their expectations and their role, revealed that they:

- regarded their prime role in play as a respondent to, rather than an initiator of play,
- emphasized that play was based upon children's choice, to help them develop independence,
- were focused on their role in managing play,
- emphasized the importance of team work among the school staff in promoting a play approach,
- applied play as a means of 'revisiting' concepts or topics previously introduced in class, rather than for exploring new and different areas,
- regarded play as primarily providing opportunities for children to develop language, and social and motor skills.

In connection with the focus on children's choice in play, it was found that they needed a range of *adult interventions* in order to explore the available choices. In other words, adult involvement in play and the development of children's independence need not be mutually exclusive. Issues regarding the learning potential of play were also raised. For example, does play provide a chance for refining understanding or for generating new understandings? These researchers found both forms of learning existent in play. It was concluded that despite considering their play program as successful, these teachers saw themselves as observers rather than participants in play (Dockett, 2000; Jones, Dockett, Westcott & Perry, 2000). In terms of the teacher role in play, the concept of 'scaffolding' has been used, as an effective way of helping children enhance and extend their knowledge, understanding and skills (Dockett & Fleer, 1999). Scaffolding is utilized not only as a means to enhance learning, but to mediate to the child something about his or her competencies and interests, that is, his/her worth as a human being. Thus, effective scaffolding ensured children's activity as well as the teacher's extent of involvement. Even so, it was considered that there was a delicate balance between supporting children's play and overtaking it (Dockett & Fleer, 1999), as many researchers have pointed out, in particular with regard to play in school (Sutton-Smith, 1994; Steinsholt, 1998).

As mentioned, the emphasis on play in Norwegian schools, according to Reform 97 and the Curriculum Guidelines of 1997, is relatively strong.

This fact, which is a unique characteristic in an international perspective, should provide a well-suited point of departure for the integration of the early childhood education tradition and the school education tradition. However, research seems to indicate that such integration has not yet occurred. On the contrary, Norwegian studies directed towards children's play and the teacher role just before and during the first couple of years after Reform 97 was implemented, seem to reveal differing tendencies, which will be discussed below.

A Norwegian interview study of 6-year-olds and the same children when they were 8 years old, just before Reform 97 was implemented, took a holistic perspective to learning as a starting point (Eide & Winger, 1996). Although the 8-year-olds clearly had less freedom in their learning activities in school, compared to the freedom they had had as 6-year-olds in the last year of day care, the children themselves did not see this as a major problem. In both cases the children expressed a clear perception of the difference between play and learning. The researchers suggested in their conclusion that varied methods of how children can be active and concurrent in decisions may be necessary to obtain a holistic approach on play and learning. They argue that much depends on the teacher's attitude to the value of play in school. Other (Bae 1994) interviews with children have documented the value of teachers promoting positive interpersonal relations in the classroom, based on a supportive teacher attitude, particularly in the transition years between day care and school.

A set of research studies carried out in the central area of Norway (Lillemyr et al. 1998), called "The transition preschool-school project" (translation), started out by recognizing that students' competence and self worth at the school start, and focusing students' interests in play and learning. Self-determination theory and goal theory were combined to form the guiding theory (Deci & Ryan, 1991; Maehr & Midgley, 1996), supplemented by main principles from the (national) curriculum guidelines. Four theoretical ideas were especially stressed in development projects carried out in the schools:

1. promoting students' positive self-perception,
2. supporting autonomy,
3. structuring expectations and objectives, and
4. involvement in students' self worth and relationship to others.

The studies were carried out in the period 1995 to 1998. It was found that students' interest in play, in particular play where students can make choices, represents a considerable potential in school learning. Further, it was found that interchanging play and learning activities had positive effects, as documented through observations and interviews. Surprisingly, students' interest in free learning, defined as learning where students can to a great extent decide the nature and form of the activity, dropped dramatically from 5 to 9 years of age. The interpretation given for this was that students do not expect free learning to take place in school, even if this is a clearly expressed objective in the Curriculum Guidelines of 1997 (Lillemyr, 2001). If this is a general tendency, it will represent a challenge, as well as affecting the teacher role considerably. In these studies early childhood educators and primary school teachers worked together, either in the same class or across classes. It was learned that the early childhood educator valued children's need for play significantly more strongly than the primary school teacher. Furthermore, early childhood educators had greater trust in the independence of children starting school, with regard to school activities. It was found that female teachers emphasized the need for enhancing students' self- perceptions in the first years of school to a greater extent than did male teachers (Lillemyr et al. 1998).

Another Norwegian study (Germeten, 1999) studied attitudes among first and eighth grade teachers towards Reform 97. Through interviews it was noted that through collaboration between the early childhood educator and the primary school teacher, a well-balanced combination of play and free activities, theme working and formal activities of literacy and mathematics was obtained. In general, the teachers in this study expressed different attitudes to Reform 97 and to the curriculum guidelines. However, all first grade teachers considered the integration of the two educational traditions, and emphasis on such aspects as play, social competence, and relatedness, to be successful. A surprisingly large convergence was found between early childhood educators' and primary school teachers' perspectives on play. Both groups of teachers included *learning through play* as well as the *value of play* itself in their conception of play in school. The main result indicates that teachers seem to find a mismatch with regard to the relationship between play and free activities at primary level, and the emphasis on evaluation of achievements at lower secondary level (op. cit.). This may represent a challenge for the school and the teacher role in the future.

Studies in Norway have also disclosed a tendency for teachers to be more supportive of play in school, rather than interactive. That is, they support play opportunities for the students, but hesitate to interact with students' play, although more of an interactive tendency was found among teachers in the first year than in the second year of school. Obviously, teachers see play in school both as an inspiration and a challenge (Tangen, 1998; Aspaas, 1999; Hanssen, 1999). There may be hesitation amongst some teachers to involve too much in role-play themselves, even if this is recommended in the literature when done with caution (Smilansky, 1990; Hellendoorn, van der Kooij & Sutton-Smith, 1994; Dockett & Fleer, 1999). However, a lack of play competence among teachers was also detected. Some studies claim to have found indications of a change taking place, concerning the teacher's role in relation to play in school (Hanssen, 1999). There have also been studies in this country which indicate that teachers see play in school as being primarily related to objectives of *social learning* and *self esteem*, and less related to academic subjects like language and mathematics (Zachrisen, 2000). This could be caused by the fact that teachers have often drawn a clear distinction between their role in play as opposed to their role in learning, as Vejleskov has pointed out. It is said that the teacher's role in play has often been conceived as passive, while the role in learning is regarded as more active and more strongly connected with teaching (Vejleskov, 2000).

A few studies have also been carried out in other Scandinavian countries. However, the degree of integration of play in the school curriculum and the meaning of integration of educational traditions will vary across the countries. Accordingly, this will also mean differences in influences on the teacher role. Some of the studies have focused on the relation between children's play and early literacy (Vedeler, 1997; Einarsdottir, 2000). In a comparative study, the Danish researcher Broström (1992; 1998) examined everyday life in Danish and American kindergarten classes. In the American class he found teaching the three R's to be predominant, whereas play was the norm in the Danish class. The American teacher-controlled 'academic' practice and the children's background contributed to the development of motivation for learning. On the other hand, the American children were egocentric and had some difficulty participating in group activities. The "child-controlled" practice in the Danish kindergarten developed social competence but neglected the development of motivation for learning. He concluded that a combination of the two traditions was preferable. Later, Broström (1999c) elaborated his perspective of the concept of educational play, taking the greater emphasis on literacy in the Danish kindergarten classes into account. Broström is concerned about this tendency, as its consequence will be a decreased emphasis on the typical Danish child-oriented tradition. Nevertheless, he also argues in favor of the growing interest in coordinating kindergarten and the early years of school. Educational play, as Broström presents it, can be an opening for play in school, while at the same time introducing reading and writing activities in kindergarten. He suspects that one of the challenges is that primary school teachers and kindergarten teachers have different understandings and definitions of play and learning. In this concern he still thinks "frame play" (Broström, 1996)—a play activity in which the children and the teacher plan and play together—represents an exciting opportunity in school. He thinks it is important to formulate and express an approach to learning in accordance with young children's needs, taking play into account.

In Sweden, Samuelsson et al. have carried out research on how children learn, and understand learning in preschools, as opposed to schools, during recent decades. These researchers regard children's play as an important path to learning in the last year of day care and the first years of school (Pramling, Klerfelt & Graneld, 1995). What they call 'ethnographic education', with play and a broad perspective on learning, is found to enhance students' abilities for reflection and creativity. They found acquired knowledge to be individual, but still dependant on social interactions. They argue that communicative interaction and freedom of choice is, like in play, fundamental to learning for children. In particular, learning how to learn and social cognition are of great importance (Pramling, 1990; 1992). Play and learning are considered as different ways for the child to react to the outside world, with both phenomena being closely connected with communication. For teachers it is momentous to understand how children learn, in order to be able to empower the child as a learner. As a result, it appears necessary, not least because of recent reforms in day care and schools, to move toward a new and broader concept of learning (Pramling, 1996; Doverborg & Pramling, 1996).

CONCLUSIONS

In many countries there is now a tendency towards strong emphasis on play in the first years of school. This suggests a change in the teacher's role concerning the stimulation of children's play and investment in learning. The integration of the play element, both as learning through play and for the value of play as such, will pave the way for a new and broader understanding of school learning. To capture this broader concept of learning, varied forms of play and learning, as interchangeable activities, are needed. To be successful in this endeavor a thorough collaboration between day care institutions and schools is required, as well as further research. In particular, research on the teacher's role in play seems necessary, since research in different countries reveals uncertainty among teachers, especially primary school teachers. Nevertheless, reforms for the early years of school are increasingly often emphasizing the importance of play as an integral part of the school's curriculum.

Is it possible to outline some elements of the teacher's role based on recent research and developments? Even if the teacher role does change and develop in accordance with changes in society and school policies, some elements can be suggested. The teacher will have to take specific responsibility for:

- developing competence in guiding, supporting, and involving himself/herself in children's play,
- discussing the value of play in the school curriculum with colleagues,
- managing the interchange of play and learning activities, providing children with opportunities for choice and learning through play,
- organizing learning in a holistic sense of the word, related to the child as a whole,

- developing competence in relating play, creativity, humor and aesthetics in children's activities,
- promoting positive interpersonal relations in the classroom, based on a "supportive teacher attitude",
- emphasizing students' competencies in the different areas, in order to support their sense of competence (self-esteem),
- supporting students' independence, and moving towards increased responsibility for activities and learning,
- making clear structures, such as to the teacher and student expectations and school objectives,
- showing engagement with students and their self worth.

It is anticipated that these components will influence a change in the teacher's role in the future, in addition to societal demands and reform perspectives and curriculum principles. It is sometimes hard to say from research alone whether play is in fact enhancing learning, though several studies indicate an increase in motivation, which should be considered important enough in itself. The famous researcher on play, Sutton-Smith (1994: 15) once said: "In general, it seems that the use of play in the classroom greatly contributes to children's motivation for classroom studies and is quite justified for that reason." The recent research on intrinsic motivation thus seems to be of great relevance (Deci & Ryan, 1991; 1994; Maehr & Midgley, 1996; 1999).

Certainly, in many countries the ongoing integration of the early childhood education tradition and the primary school tradition will influence the teacher's role, both in general and in relation to play in particular. However, the overall aim will be to achieve a high quality environment for children's development, learning and well-being, which is of particular importance in the transition between day care and school.

REFERENCES

Aspaas, I. (1999). *Lek eller alvor? En studie av læreres oppfatning av lek i første klasse.* ("Play or Serious?" A study of teachers' attitudes towards play in first grade) Graduate dissertation Oslo College: Oslo Norway.

Backe-Hansen, E. & Ogden, T. (Eds.) (1998). *10-åringer i Norden. Kompetanse, risiko og oppvekstmiljø.* (Ten-year-olds in the Nordic countries. Competence, risk and the educational environment) Copenhagen: *Nordic Council of Ministries,* 1998, no. 3.

Bae,B. (1994). "Hei Løve! Er du farlig eller grei?" Om lekende samspill. ("Hello, Lion! Are you dangerous or OK?" About play interactions) *Norsk Pedagogisk Tidsskrift* (*Norwegian Journal of Education*), *1994*(5).

Bennett, N., Wood, L., & Rogers, S. (1997). *Teaching through play: Teachers' thinking and classroom practice.* Buckingham, UK: Open University Press.

Berg, L.-E. (1992). *Den lekande människan. En socialpsykologisk analys av lekandets dynamik.*(The Playing Man. A social-psychological analysis of the playing dynamic) Lund: Studentlitteratur.

Bjørgen, I. (1997). Ansvar for egen læring. (Responsibility for one's own learning. In a Norwegian anthology *Learning in play and social interaction*) Report from a national conference in Trondheim, Norway. Trondheim: *The Queen Maud's College Publications, 1997*(1).

Broström, S. (1992). Quick Response: An Ethnographic Analysis of a Drama-Game in a Danish Preschool. *The Quarterly Newsletter of the Laboratory of Comparative Human Cognition, 14*(1), 317-325.

Broström, S. (1997). Frame play with 6 year old children. *European Early Childhood Education Research Journal, 3*(2), 89-102.

Broström, S. (1998). Kindergarten in Denmark and the USA. *Scandinavian Journal of Educational Research, 42*(2), 109-122.

Broström, S. (1999a). *En god skolestart—fælles ansvar og fælles udvikling.* (A good school start—Common responsibility for common development) Copenhagen: Systime.

Broström, S. (1999b). Changes in Early Childhood Education in Denmark: The appearance of literacy in early childhood education. In Brougère & Sylvie,R. (Eds.) *Culture, Childhood and Preschool Education.* Paris: Université Paris-Nord & INRP. UNESCO.

Broström, S. (1999c). Educational Play. Paper presented at the 21. International Council for Children's Play World Play Conference in Oslo, September 15–17, 1999.

Broström, S., & Vejleskov, H. (1999). *Lærerig leg og legende læring.* (Learning through play and playful learning) Copenhagen: The Danish University of Education Press.

Ceglowsky, D. (1997). Understanding and Building upon Children's Perceptions of Play Activities in Early Childhood Programs. *Early Childhood Education Journal, 25*(2), 107-112.

Cooney, M. H. (1995). Socialization and play as indicators of readiness to learn: A school culture perspective on goal one. Paper presented at annual meeting of American Educational Research Association, April 1995, San Francisco, California.

Covington, M. V. (1992). *Making the Grade: A self-worth perspective on motivation and school reform.* Cambridge, UK/NY: Cambridge University Press.

Covington, M. V. (1998). *The will to learn. A guide for motivating young people.* Cambridge, UK/NY: Cambridge University Press.

Curriculum Guidelines (1997). (In Norwegian: Læreplanverket for den 10-årige grunnskolen) See the following brochures in English: *Core curriculum,* for primary, secondary and adult education 1993, Oslo: Ministry of Education, Research and Church Affairs; and *Reform 97: The compulsory school reform.* Oslo: Ministry of Education, Research and Church Affairs.

Curtis, A. (1998). *A curriculum for the pre-school child* Sec. Ed. London/NY: Routledge & Kegan Paul.

Dahlberg, G., Moss, P., & Pence, A. (1999). *Beyond Quality in Early Childhood Education and Care. Postmodern Perspectives.* London/Philadelphia: Falmer Press.

Deci, E. L. & Ryan, R. M. (1991). A motivational approach to self: integration in personality. In Dienstbier, I. R. (Ed.) *Nebraska Symposium on Motivation: Perspec-*

tives on Motivation. 38, pp. 237-288. Lincoln, Nebraska: University of Nebraska Press.

Deci, E. L. & Ryan, R. M. (1994). Promoting Self-determined Education. *Scandinavian Journal of Educational Research, 38*(1).

Dockett, S. (2000). The state of play in Australia. Paper presented at The International Association for the Study of Play, Baltimore Maryland, 2000.

Dockett, S., & Fleer, M. (1999). *Play and pedagogy in early childhood: Bending the rules.* Marrickville, NSW: Harcourt Brace & Company.

Doverborg, E., & Pramling, I. (1996). *Mangfoldets pedagogiske muligheter.* (The educational opportunities of diversity) Oslo: Pedagogisk Forum.

Eide, B., & Winger, N. (1996). *Kompetente barn og kvalifiserte pedagoger i den nye småskolen.*(Competent Children and Qualified Teachers in the New Primary School) Oslo: Cappelen Academic Publications

Einarsdóttir, J. (2000). Incorporating literacy resources in the play curriculum of two Icelandic preschools. In Roskos, K. A. & Christie, J. F. (2000) *Play and literacy in early childhood.* London: Lawrence Erlbaum.

Eisner, E. W. (1990). The Role of Art and Play in Children's Cognitive Development. In Klugman, E. & Smilansky, S. (Eds.) *Children's Play and Learning: Perspectives and Policy Implications.* New York/London: Teachers' College Press.

Framework Plan for Day Care Institutions: A brief presentation (1996). English ed. Oslo: The Ministry of Children and Family Affairs.

Fromberg, D. P. (1992). A review of research on play. In Seefeldt, C. (Ed.) *The early childhood curriculum: A review of current research.* 2nd ed. (pp. 42-84). New York: Teachers College Press.

Fromberg, D. P., & Bergen, D. (Eds.) (1998). *Play from birth to twelve and beyond: Contexts, perspectives, and meanings.* New York/London: Garland.

Germeten, S. (1999). Evaluering av Reform 97 "På vei mot ny grunnskole i Oslo". (The Evaluation of Reform 97: "Heading towards a new obligatory education in Oslo") Report I: Results from a questionnaire fall 1998. Oslo: Oslo College Publications.

Hanssen, T. (1999). "Me ska' vel leka i dag o'?" Lekens vilkår i 1. klasse i grunnskolen. ("We're gonna' play to day too, aren't we?" Play Conditions in the First Grade of School) Graduate dissertation Queen Maud's College/Norwegian University of Science and Technology Trondheim Norway.

Hartmann, W. & Rollett, B. (1994). Play: Positive intervention in the elementary school curriculum. In Hellendoorn, J., van der Kooij, R. & Sutton-Smith, B. (Eds.) *Play and intervention* Albany, New York: State University of New York Press.

Hellendoorn, J., van der Kooij, R., & Sutton-Smith, B. (1994). *Play and Intervention.* Albany, New York: State University of New York Press.

Huizinga, J. (1955). *Homo Ludens: A study of the play element in culture.* London/Boston: Beacon Press.

Hutt, S. J., Tyler, C., Hutt, C. & Cristopherson, H. (1989). *Play, Exploration and learning.* London: Routledge.

Jones, K., Dockett, S., Westcott, K. & Perry, B. (2000). Play in kindergarten. Paper presented at the annual Australian Research in Early Childhood Education Conference, Canberra January 2000.

Kibsgaard, S. (1999). Lek som livskvalitet. (Play as the quality of life) In Kibsgaard, S. & Wostryck, A. (Eds.) *Mens leken er god.* ("While the play is good") Oslo: Tano Aschehoug.

Klugman, E. (1990). Early Childhood Moves into the Public Schools: Mix or Meld. In Klugman, E. & Smilansky, S. (Eds.) *Children's play and learning: Perspectives and policy implications* (pp. 188-210). New York/London: Teacher's College, Columbia University.

Ladd, G. W.; Birch, S. H. & Buhs, E. (1999). Children's social and scholastic lives in kindergarten: Related spheres of influence? *Child Development, 70,* 1373-1400.

Levy, J. (1978). *Play behavior.* New York: Wiley.

Levy, J. (1997). Play: The highest form of human expression. In Carpenter, C. (Ed.) *Childhood in Canada: Cultural images and contemporary issues.* Waterloo: Wilfried Laurier University Press.

Lillemyr, O.F. (1999a). *Lek—opplevelse—læring, i barnehage og skole.* (Play—Experience—learning, in preschool and school.) Oslo: Tano Aschehoug.

Lillemyr, O.F. (1999b). Hvorfor er barns lek så viktig ved overgangen barnehage—skole? (Why is children's play so important in the preschool-school transition?) In Kibsgaard,S. & Wostryck,A. (Eds.) *Mens leken er god.* (While the play is good.) Oslo: Tano Aschehoug.

Lillemyr, O.F. (2001). Play and Learning in School: A Motivational Approach. In McInerney, D. & VanEtten, S. (Eds.) *Research on sociocultural influences on motivation and learning* Greenwich, Connecticut: Information Age Publishing.

Lillemyr, O.F., Bergstrøm, S., Eggen, A., Skevik, S., Støp, K., & Voll, A. L. S. (1998). Overgangen barnehage—småskole. Et forsknings-og utviklingsprosjekt i Nord-Trøndelag. (The Preschool—School Transition. A research and development project in North Trøndelag) Report Ministry of Education, Research and Church Affairs. Steinkjer: North Trøndelag Research Institute.

Lillemyr, O. F., Fagerli, O., & Søbstad, F. (in press). A Global Perspective on Early Childhood Care and Education: Need of a new Model. Paris: Monograph published by UNESCO.

Lindqvist, G. (1995). *The aesthetics of play: A didactic study of play and culture in preschools.* Uppsala, Sweden: Uppsala Studies in Education, no.62.

Maehr, M. L. (1984). Meaning and motivation: Toward a theory of personal investment. In Ames, R. E. & Ames, C. (Eds.) *Research on motivation in education volume 1: Student motivation* (pp. 115-144). New York: Academic Press.

Maehr, M. L., & Midgley, C. (1996). *Transforming school cultures.* Westview Press. In the Series Csikszentmihalyi, M., (Ed.) *Lives in context,* Boulder/Oxford: Westview.

Maehr, M. L., & Midgley, C. (1999). Creating optimum environments for students of diverse sociocultural backgrounds. In Block, J., Everson, S. T., & Guskey, T. R. (Eds.) *Comprehensive school reform: A program perspective.* Dubuque, IA: Kendall/Hunt.

May, H. (1996). The politics and processes of the implementation of TE WHAARIKI, The New Zealand national early childhood curriculum 1993-6 The Weaving Webs Conference, University of Melbourne, 11-13 July.

Mead, G. H. (1896). The relation of play to education, *University of Chicago Record, 1,* 140-145.

Meadows, S., & Cashdan, A. (1988). *Helping children learn: Contributions to a cognitive curriculum* London: David Fulton.

Ministry of Education (1995). Better beginnings: Early childhood education in New Zealand. Wellington, New Zealand: Ministry of Education/Learning Media Limited.

Olofsson, B. K. (1992). *I lekens värld*. (In the world of play) Stockholm: Almqvist & Wiksell.

Patrick, H., & Townsend, M. A. R. (1995). The influence of perceived social competence on school beginners' emergent academic intrinsic motivation. Paper presented at the annual meeting of American Educational Research Association, April 1995, San Francisco, CA.

Pellegrini, A. D., Ed.(1995). *The future of play theory: A multidisciplinary inquiry into the contributions of Brian Sutton-Smith*. Albany, New York: State University of New York Press.

Pellegrini, A. (1991). *Applied child study: A developmental approach*. Hillsdale, NJ: Lawrence Erlbaum.

Pellegrini. A., & Smith, P. K. (1998). The development of play during childhood: Forms and possible functions, *Child Psychology and Psychiatry Review, 3*(2).

Piaget, J. (1972). *Play, dreams and imitation in childhood* London: Routledge & Kegan Paul.

Pintrich, P. & Schunk, D. (1996). *Motivation in education: Theory, research and applications*. Columbus, OH: Merill/Prentice Hall.

Pramling, I. (1990). *Learning to learn*. N.Y: Springer Verlag.

Pramling, I. (1992). To be 6 years old in Sweden in the 1990's, *Early Years, 12*(2).

Pramling, I. (1996). Understanding and empowering the child as a learner. In Olsen, D., & Torrance, N. (Eds.) *Handbook of Education and Human Development: New Models of Learning, Teaching and Schooling* (pp. 565-592). Oxford: Basil Blackwell.

Pramling, I., Klerfeldt, A., & Graneld, P. W. (1995). Barns möte med skolans värld. (Children's meeting with the school world) Goetenburgh: *Goetenburgh Studies in Educational Sciences, 1995*(9).

Samuelsson, I. P. & Sheridan, S. (1999). *Lärandets grogrund* (The growing ground of learning) Lund, Sweden: Studentlitteratur.

Schoenfeld, A. H. (1999). Looking Toward the 21st century: Challenges of educational theory and practice. *Educational Researcher, 28*(7), 4-14.

Sestini, E. (1987). The quality of learning experiences for four year olds in nursery and infant classes. In NFER/SCDC, *Four year olds in school policy and practice*. Slough: NFER/SCDC.

Skaalvik, E. M. (1997). Issues in research on self-concept. In Maehr, M. L. & Pintrich, P. R. (Eds.) *Advances in motivation and achievement*, vol. 10, Greenwich, CT/London, United Kingdom: JAI Press.

Smilansky, S. (1990). Sociodramatic play: Its relevance to behavior and achievement in school. In Klugman, E., & Smilansky, S. (Eds.) *Children's play and learning: Perspectives and policy implications* (pp. 18-42). New York/London: Teachers' College Press.

Smilansky, S., & Shefatya, L. (1990). *Facilitating play: A medium for promoting cognitive, socio-emotional and academic development in young children*. Silver Spring, MD: Psychosocial & Educational Publications.

Steinsholt, K. (1998). *Lett som en lek!* (Easy As play) Trondheim, Norway: Tapir.

Sutton-Smith, B. (1994). Paradigms of intervention. In Hellendoorn, J., van der Kooij, R., & Sutton-Smith, B. *Play and intervention*. Albany, NY: State University of New York Press.

Sutton-Smith, B. (1997). *The ambiguity of play* Cambridge, MA/London, UK: Harvard University Press.

Søbstad, F. (1999). Humor i lekfamilien. (Humor in the play family) In Kibsgaard, S., & Wostryck, A. (Eds.) *Mens leken er god. (While the play is good)*. Oslo: Tano Aschehoug.

Tangen, D. (1998). Jeg lærer meg å leke med kunnskapen på en måte. Lek i småskolen—et studium av barns lek i to småskoleklasser. (I am learning to play with knowledge in a way. Play in primary school—a study of children's play in first and second grade classrooms) Graduate dissertation 1998 Oslo College, Oslo, Norway.

The Times, (1998). Early learning may put boys off school, (March 24).

Trawick-Smith, J. (1998). School-based play and social interactions: Opportunities and limitations. In Fromberg, D. P. & Bergen, D. (Eds.) *Play from Birth to Twelve and Beyond: Contexts, Perspectives, and Meanings* (pp. 241-247). New York/London: Garland.

Vandenberg, B. (1990). Play, problem-solving, and creativity. In Rubin, K. H. (Ed.) *Children's play* London/San Francisco/Washington: Jossey–Bass.

Vedeler, L. (1997). Dramatic play: a format for "literate" language? *British Journal of Educational Psychology, 67,* 153-167

Vejleskov, H. (2000). Undervisning, indlæring og leg i skolestarten. (Teaching, learning and play at the start of school) In Heilä-Ylikallio (Ed.) *Aspekter på skolestarten i Norden.* (Aspects on school start in the Nordic countries) Lund: Studentlitteratur.

Vygotsky, L. S. (1978). *Mind in society: The development of higher psychological processes.* Cambridge, MA: Harvard University Press.

Wasserman, S. (1990). *Serious players in the primary classroom: Empowering children through active learning experience.* New York/London: Teachers' College Press.

Wood, E. & Attfield, J. (1996). *Play, learning and the early childhood curriculum.* London: Paul Chapman.

Zachrisen, B. (2000). *Når leken blir skolemoden. (When play is becoming ready for school)* Hamar, Norway: College of Hedmark Publications.

CHAPTER 5

YOUNG CHILDREN'S PLAY AND COGNITIVE STYLE

Olivia N. Saracho

For more than a decade, studies on young children's play and cognitive style have emerged. Most research acknowledge that young children use both their cognitive and play behaviors to arrange their physical world and to attempt to understand the others' distinct social points of view. Children's cognitive styles are observed when they accumulate and organize information. The ways in which children process information and react to different circumstances characterizes their cognitive style, which has components of perceptual styles, personality, intelligence, and social behavior. These individualistic tendencies, grounded on cognitive style theory, affect children's play. This chapter presents an overview of cognitive style, play, and studies that explore the relationship between the two.

COGNITIVE STYLE

Cognitive style has its theoretical foundation in Piaget's (1962) developmental framework that describes the individuals' method of processing,

Contemporary Perspectives on Play in Early Childhood Education
A Volume in: Contemporary Perspectives in Early Childhood Education, pages 75–96.
Copyright © 2003 by Information Age Publishing, Inc.
All rights of reproduction in any form reserved.
ISBN: 1-930608-31-4 (cloth), 1-930608-30-6 (paper)

interpreting, and responding to information within their environment. Armstrong and Priola (2001) see cognitive style as reflecting the way that different individuals conduct these processes differently, supposedly idio-syncratically, although Riding and Rayner (1998) believe that it may be the barring interface that accounts for human behavior. Cognitive styles are far-reaching stylistic characteristics in the way that individuals process exist-ing information and the new knowledge that becomes available, and then assimilate that knowledge within their cognitive systems. Individuals' cogni-tive style indicates how they comprehend, preserve, and apply information. It usually denotes the individuals' distinct procedures to understand, remember, and think and as "an individual's characteristic and consistent approach to organising and processing information and experience?" (Tennant, 1988, p. 3). Young children's learning relies on the method they use to handle and process incoming information. Their method of decid-ing, deciphering, assembling, conserving, recapturing, interpreting, and creating information are intermeshed with their cognitive style.

One dimension of cognitive style is field dependence independence (FDI; Kogan, 1987; Witkin & Goodenough, 1981). FDI is ingrained in the individual's method of performing, describing how field dependent (FD) and field independent (FI) individuals behave under different circum-

TABLE 1
Comparison Between Field Dependent and Field-Independent
Individuals

Field Dependent Individuals	*Field Independent Individuals*
1. rely on the surrounding perceptual field;	1. perceive objects as separate from the field;
2. experience their environment in a rela-tively global fashion by conforming to the effects of the prevailing field or con-text;	2. can abstract an item from the surround-ing field and solve problems that are presented and reorganized in different contexts;
3. are dependent on authority;	3. experience an independence from authority which leads them to depend on their own standards and values;
4. search for facial cues in those around them as a source of information;	4. are oriented towards active striving;
5. are strongly interested in people;	5. appear to be cold and distant;
6. get closer to the person with whom they are interacting;	6. are socially detached but have analytic skills;
7. have a sensitivity to others which helps them to acquire social skills;	7. are insensitive to others, lacking social skills;
8. prefer occupations which require involvement with others.	8. prefer occupations that allow them to work by themselves (p. 154).

stances. Since FD and FI individuals have different cognitive and personal characteristics, they vary in the way they process information. Saracho and Spodek (1981) present a comparison of cognitive style characteristics for FD and FI individuals (See Table 1).

These characteristics are extensive and constant; they influence numerous domains including the individuals' socialization. For example, FD individuals are more sensitive to the emotions of others, which provides them with better social skills (Witkin, Dyk, Faterson, Goodenough, Karp, 1974/1962; Witkin, Lewis, Hertzman, Machover, Meisner, & Wapner, 1972/1954); whereas FI individuals are insensitive to others, antisocial (Saracho & Spodek, 1981, 1986), able to cognitively structure skills (Renninger & Sigel, 1987), but possess analytic abilities (Ohnmacht, 1968). Research suggests that the individuals' social orientation is grounded on their cognitive style and their play.

PLAY

Play helps young children understand the world and includes several factors such as the cognitive, creative, language, social, and physical constructs of play (Saracho, 1986a). It has an extensive social application. Researchers identify important factors in preschool children's play including

1. imitative experiences,
2. communication of ideas,
3. concrete objects, and
4. parallel/associative levels of socialization in young children's social play (Saracho, 2001).

These factors demonstrate the importance of discussing ideas, engaging in sociodramatic play, and using actions in their play activities and confirm the patterns in children's play in their cognitive, social, and emotional development (Saracho & Spodek, 1998). When children play, they confront social circumstances and learn to collaborate, help, share, and resolve social difficulties (Saracho, 1986a). In such social behaviors, children think, contemplate their peers' points of view, assess conventions, generate social abilities, and learn harmony concepts. Becoming aware and recognizing their peers' feelings assists children to adopt perspective-taking skills (Rubin & Coplan, 1998). The children's formation of their perspective-taking skills helps them to interpret their peers' impressions of them and compensate for them (Small, 1990).

Social pretend play encourages children to imagine the world from someone else's point of view. When children assume a role, they need to appreciate briefly someone's perspective. Role play allows young children to explore unfamiliar roles and to understand their peers' thoughts and feelings. From this perspective, role playing involves more than a progression of concise and playful interactions between two voluntary collaborators. Actually it is this essence that generates full-grown concepts (Kavanaugh & Engel, 1998). Appropriate social behaviors help children develop self-confidence when they succeed in dealing with their peers' desires and accordingly address predicaments with assurance and are independent of the solicitation and direction from others. Children reflect their cognitive systems in their social performance, which Rubin (1980) refers to as social-cognition. Investigations into social-cognition concentrate on the implications of cognitive systems on social behaviors. Shantz (1983) concludes that in social-cognition children's perspective taking skills transform their concepts of self and others. The merit of the cognitive and social dispositions of young children's play has been documented (see Saracho, 1995a, 1995b, 1994, 1992b). Using a scalable step developmental sequence of cognitive levels, Corrigan (1987) uses play to determine the children's cognitive level in two distinctive settings and two actor-role undertakings.

PLAY AND COGNITIVE STYLE

Studies that examine the association between the social realm and FDI have mostly been conducted with adults and school-age children. They suggest that FD individuals possess a sensitive radar system aligned to social elements in the social environment and are more socially directed than are FI individuals (Saracho, 1985). Armstrong and Priola (2001) show that FD individuals initiate more social-emotional-oriented behaviors. In contrast, FI individuals prefer a more structured, less ambiguous, and more technique oriented environment (Armstrong, 2000).

Research with adults demonstrates that FD individuals are more stimulated by and are more attentive to social prompting (Fitzgibbons & Goldberger, 1971; Eagle, Goldberger, & Breitman, 1969; Fitzgibbons, Goldberger, & Eagle, 1965). They concentrate on the faces of others as their basic source of knowledge in connection with their peers' feelings and thoughts (e.g., Konstadt & Foreman, 1965; Ruble & Nakamura, 1972). The more FDs are more emotionally expressive, submissive, relatively friendly (Witkin et al, 1972/1954, 1974/1962, 1981); interpersonal, popular, warm toward others (Pascual-Leone, 1989), and more nurturing (Armstrong, 1999). FD individuals focus more on verbal communications that contain social substance than do FI individuals (e.g., Eagle, Fitzgibbons, &

Goldberger, 1966; Fitzgibbons & Goldberger, 1971). In contrast, FI individuals recall and choose non-social stimuli (Goldberger & Bendich, 1972) and have more psychosocial acts during interpersonal relationships (Armstrong, 2000; Armstrong & Priola, 2001).

These results are supported by research that examines the relationship between social behavior and FDI with school-age children. Such studies suggest that FD children look at the examiner's face for information more than do FI children (Ruble & Nakamura, 1972; Konstadt & Forman, 1965). In addition, they are more interpersonally dependent (Beller, 1958), sensitive to the adults' negative feedback (Konstadt & Forman, 1965), and rely more on social cues to resolve difficulties (Ruble & Nakamura, 1972) than do FI children. In exploring the effectiveness of task and social behaviors of nine- to twelve-year-olds, Nakamura and Finck (1980) show that FI children are low-social but task-effective; while FD children are more socially oriented. Undoubtedly, field dependence affects social sensitivity; however, research results are ambivalent concerning the elementary school age FD children's social competence or effectiveness (Kogan, 1987), which may challenge those findings with preschool children. Kogan and Block (1991) declare that FI individuals are verbally fluent, attentive, competent, employ and react to reason, and are reflective. In addition, they use high performance standards, are diligent, plan and think ahead, and become absorbed in tasks. Kogan and Block (1991) describe FI children as creative, curious and exploring, and embracing atypical thought processes; but they assume FD children pursue others to certify their self worth, display a drive to please, manipulate individuals by flattering themselves, and are distrustful of others. They are also envious and resentful of others, are effortlessly antagonized, and request the guidance of adults (Kogan & Block, 1991). FD individuals manage their social world with a feeling of avid vulnerability. These characteristics are compatible with Witkin and his associates' (1972/1954, 1974/1962, 1981) characterizations of FD and FI children. The FD individuals' exclusive consciousness and their adjustment to the social environments assist them to enjoy a repertoire of highly developed social skills.

The results of most of the studies with preschool children are analogous to those found with adults and school-age children. For example, a longitudinal study by Halverson and Waldrop (1976) examines young children's social orientation and FDI. Its findings indicate that young children's social behavior corresponds to their cognitive style. A primary focus in Halverson's and Waldrop's (1976) study is their belief that children's high levels of activity and impulsiveness affects their development of cognitive and social behaviors. In their research, Halverson and Waldrop (1976) categorize social behaviors as high active, vigorous, and impulsive and show a correlation with FDI. FI children tend to be highly active during play, but FD children tend to be less active during play. Kagan (1971) supports these results in his assumption that a child's play tempo, as reflected in differences in play levels, has an impact on young children's social and cognitive performance. Consequently, children draw upon their cognitive style to understand the socialization process during their play experiences. Similar social elements of FDI are found in the preschool studies. The relationship between social behaviors and FDI with preschool children focus on their play, because it provides a natural environment (e.g., Beller, 1958; Coates, 1972; Coates, Lord, & Jakabovics, 1975; Halverson & Waldrop, 1976; Steele, 1981). These studies are discussed in detail in the following section.

The greater social interest of FDI is confirmed in the studies of play preferences among preschool children. Coates, Lord, and Jakabovics (1975) and Steele (1981) show that preschool FD children engage in social play more than do their FI peers. FD preschool children are more socially oriented in their play; inasmuch as FI children engage in solitary play. Such findings suggest a relationship between play and cognitive style. In analyzing the relationship between young children's play and their cognitive style, Steele (1981) classifies the play behaviors of five- and six-year-old children into pretend play events, talkativeness, playfulness, sense of humor, and aggression acts. Her findings indicate significant relationships between two play behaviors (pretend play and playfulness) and cognitive style. She concludes that FD children are more aggressive than FI children. Coates et al. (1975) and Steele (1981) show that in natural settings preschool FD children spend more of their available free time in social play than do their FI playmates. FD preschool children prefer socially oriented play; whereas FI preschool children choose solitary play. Several studies that examine the relationship of FDI to young children's play support the greater social interest of FDI, that is, that FD children possess better greater social skills and sensitivity about their playmates' feelings. Such social skills are boosted during the children's social play.

The relationship between children's play and cognitive style is further supported in Coates' (1972) two play studies where children have the opportunity to select from three play alternatives: block building, playing house, or other play activities (e.g., painting, making collages, working with puzzles). Her first study supports the relationship between the play preferences and cognitive styles. FD girls engage in social play, but FI girls prefer non social play activities . Coates' (1972) study indicates a relationship between four- and five-year-old children's play and cognitive styles. Evidently, most FD girls favor a social activity (such as playing house) where they collaborate with several children; inasmuch as most FI girls favor non-social activities where they play independent of their peers, although they occasionally interact with their peers. Saracho (1995a) also shows that FI children participate more in social play than do FD children who are considered to possess more FD characteristics. Such outcomes suggest that play behaviors can be defined in a two-dimensional mode as contemplating both a field independence cognitive style and social orientation. These results are also confirmed by Coates and her associates (1975) who investigate the children's play preferences and FDI in a natural setting. They show that FD four- and five-year-olds prefer social activities; while FI children engage in non social activities. Both FD girls and boys are more socially oriented in their play; whereas the FI ones prefer solitary play. Thus, social play corresponds to a FD cognitive style whereas solitary play corresponds to a FI cognitive style in spite of the presence of others. Children who prefer social instead of solitary play are somewhat more FD. In comparison, children who favor solitary play (e.g., working alone on projects) are somewhat more FI.

Play and cognitive style have been additionally examined in a series of studies conducted by Saracho (1987, 1989b, 1989c, 1990, 1991a, 1991b, 1992a, 1992b, 1994, 1995a, 1995b, 1995c, 1996a, 1996b, 1997, 1998, 1999) and Saracho and Spodek (1998) with three- to five-year-old children. Saracho (1996b) demonstrates that FD and FI individuals play differently. That is, FD children play more than do FI ones. In this study, it is apparent that FD and FI children display all the behaviors under investigation, although FD children have higher scores in most of the play behaviors. In addition, cognitive style influences the children's play behaviors including the following:

1. *Frequency of play.* FD children usually exhibit more play behaviors in all of the play areas than FI children.
2. *Communication of ideas.* FD children more than FI children were observed to engage in communicating ideas.
3. *Socialization levels.* FD children exhibited higher levels of socialization. That is, they engage in cooperative play, whereas FI children engage in solitary play.

In another study, Saracho (1996a) uses different measures and procedures to assess the relationship between cognitive style and play. Since research confirms that FD children are more socially oriented, she anticipated that FD children would undertake more social play activities and display more social play behaviors. As a result, most FI children show higher scores in their play behaviors. That is, Saracho (1996a) does show that FD and FI children play differently. However, in this study FI children engage more in play than do FD ones. Thus, the prominent social interest of FD adults and children is partially supported in Saracho's (1996a) study. FI children absorb themselves more in play activities than do FD children. Three of her studies (Saracho, 1987, 1992b, 1995b) support these results. FI children play more than FD ones. Also FD and FI children (Saracho, 1987, 1992b) have contradictory play behaviors (e.g., ability and creativity to communicate ideas, social levels of participation, capacity to lead in their play). FI children display more play behaviors and play more often than do FD children. Both FD and FI frequently engage in cooperative play, but rarely have the ability and creativity to communicate ideas (Saracho, 1987). Armstrong and Priola (2001), like Saracho (1996a), show an amazing outcome where FD adults indicate more task-oriented behaviors. They attribute this result to the adult's work environment as being structured and organized. The play environment in Saracho's (1996a) study may have been too structured and systematic that FI children felt at ease which prompt them to engage more in their play.

Research that investigate the preschool children's cognitive style and their play preferences demonstrate that

1. FD children participate more than FI children in physical, manipulative, block, and dramatic play (Saracho, 1991a, 1991b, 1995a),
2. FI children favor physical and block play more frequently than do FD children (Saracho, 1990, 1991a, 1991b, 1994),
3. FI children prefer manipulative play (Saracho, 1991a, 1991b, 1994), and
4. FI children have more ability and creativity to communicate ideas, social levels of participation, and capacity to lead in their play than do FD children (Saracho, 1992b).

Saracho (1995a) also shows cognitive style differences according to developmental levels in age and gender.

DEVELOPMENTAL LEVELS DIFFERENCES

Cognitive style influences the developmental levels of children's play behaviors. Many studies indicate a cognitive style-play developmental trend according to age. Research demonstrate ambivalent outcomes with age differences in the relationship between cognitive style and play. Many investigations display age differences, although others do not. Saracho (1994) examines young children's cognitive style and their play preferences but did not find any age differences in the children's play. Other studies with young children support these results with children ages three to four (Renninger & Sigel, 1987; Steele, 1981), three to five (Saracho, 1989c, 1990, 1991a, 1991b, 1992b, 1994), three to five years, 10 months (Coates, 1972), and four to five (Coates, 1972; Coates et al., 1975). Steele (1981) only shows age differences with older children (ages five and six), while Saracho (1987, 1989b) indicates age differences with young children. Although Steele (1981) reports no age differences for three- and four-year-old children with pretend play and playfulness, she shows age differences for five- and six-year-old children.

Saracho (1987) indicates similar findings. Older (five-year-olds) FD and FI children play, communicate and create ideas, participate in cooperative play, and lead in play more than three- and four-year-old children. However, five-year-old FI children demonstrate more of all the play behaviors than the younger and FD children. Saracho (1996a) supports these results. Apparently, there are developmental indicators of cognitive style and play. Usually older children exhibit more field independence and play behaviors; whereas younger FD children exhibit less field independence and play behaviors. She reveals that five-year-old FI children exhibit more field independence and play behaviors; whereas three-year-old FD children exhibit less field independence and play behaviors. Her study demonstrates that five-year-old FI children achieve higher play scores for all behaviors; whereas three-year-old FD children achieve lower play scores.

Obviously, older FI children display more play behaviors, while the younger FD children demonstrate less play behaviors. This suggests that older children attain higher scores on both cognitive style and play behaviors; whereas younger children achieve lower scores on both. In addition, three- to five-year old FD and FI children differ in their social levels of participation. Although FI children engage more in play than do FD ones, older children tend to engage more in a higher socialization level of play. Apparently, three-year-old children engage more in a lower socialization level of play. Also FD and FI children's have different developmental levels in their leadership abilities. Five-year-old FI children have more leadership abilities whereas three-year-old FD and four-year-old FD and FI children have the least leadership abilities. In another study, Saracho (1996b) uses a larger sample, different assessments, and dissimilar procedures. She shows that four-and five-year-old FD children usually have the most play behaviors except for their leadership abilities where three-year-old FI children have the highest scores in dramatic play. In contrast, three- and four-year-old FI children have the least play behaviors except for frequency of play where five-year-old FI children have the lowest scores in all forms of play. Specifically, developmental differences in the children's play behaviors include the following:

1. *Frequency of play.* Four-year-old FD children engage the *most* in physical, block, manipulative, and dramatic play; whereas four-year-old FI children engage the *least* in manipulative play and five-year-old FI children engage the *least* in physical, block, and dramatic play.

2. *Communication of ideas.* Five-year-old FD children communicate the *most* ideas in physical, block, manipulative, and dramatic play; whereas three-year-old FI children communicate the *least* ideas in all of these areas.

3. *Socialization levels.* Four-year-old FD children have the *highest* socialization level in physical and dramatic play and five-year-old FD children have the *highest* socialization level in block, manipulative, and dramatic play. In contrast, four-year-old FI children have the *lowest* socialization level in physical play and three-year-old FI children have the *lowest* socialization level in block, manipulative, and dramatic play.

4. *Leadership abilities.* Three-year-old FI children display *most* leadership abilities in dramatic play and five-year-old FD children display *most* leadership abilities in physical, block, and manipulative play; whereas four-year-old FI display the *least* leadership abilities in physical, block, manipulative, and dramatic play.

The children's developmental levels also influences the FD and FI children's forms of play. Saracho (1996a) demonstrates that usually four-year-old FD children engage more in physical play, five-year-old FD children engage more in block play, and five-year-old FD children have higher socialization levels of play. In contrast, five-year-old FD children engage the least in physical, manipulative, and dramatic play; three-year-old FD and FI children engage the least in block play and have a lower socialization level in manipulative play; four-year-old FD children have the least leadership abilities in physical, block, and manipulative play; and five-year-old FD children have the least leadership abilities in dramatic play (Saracho, 1996a). These results are also confirmed by Coates and her associates (1975) who investigate the children's play preferences and FDI in a natural setting. They show that four- and five-year-olds prefer activities that consist of (1) social interaction (e.g., playing in the doll corner, playing formal games, playing with others in the block corner), and (2) nonsocial interaction (e.g., constructing with blocks, working on tasks at a table, making paintings and collages, working with puzzles, string beads, weaving pot holders). A later study by Saracho (1995a) reveals that FD four-year-olds engage more in physical, block, and dramatic play; whereas FI five-year-olds engage more in manipulative play. In contrast, FI three-year-olds engage less in physical and dramatic play and FI four-year-olds engage less in block and manipulative play (Saracho, 1995a). FI children participate more in social play than do FD children who are considered to possess more FD characteristics. Such outcomes implies that the play behaviors can be defined in a two-dimensional mode as contemplating both field independence cognitive style and social orientation.

Each age group also differs in their social factors. Saracho (1989b) shows two dependent dimensions of play behaviors for each age group of FD and FI children. Three-year-old FD children engage in social play and utilize play equipment; four-year-old FD children designate social roles and play with others, communicate social ideas, and duplicate motor activities; while five-year-old FD children play with objects in social roles to conceive ideas and enact social roles in movement. In contrast, three-year-old FI children assume leadership in social roles, construct ideas, and establish and direct their play with others; four-year-old FI children define social roles; and five-year-old FI children interact with others; employ their body, their motor skills and objects with others during physical play, and manipulate objects in social roles. The results from the cited studies suggest a cognitive style-play developmental trend in young children (Saracho, 1996a).

GENDER DIFFERENCES

Investigations reveal gender differences in the relationship between young children's cognitive style and their play. Coates (1972) identifies a number of gender differences in her study. Most FD girls play house, although some engage in other activities. In contrast, FI girls prefer non social activities. Evidently,

1. FD girls play with others in a social activity, like playing house and
2. FI girls play independently in nonsocial activities, although occasionally they intermingle with other children.

Numerous investigations have similar findings. Coates et al. (1975) reveal that FD girls play in the doll corner, but FI girls play with blocks. In respect to boys, FI boys engage in table tasks; but FD boys play socially in the doll and block centers. Saracho (1987, 1990, 1994) demonstrates that boys play more than girls. Saracho (1990) confirms that

1. FD and FI boys play more than girls and
2. play preferences vary between boys and girls. Boys prefer physical, block, dramatic, and manipulative play; but girls prefer dramatic, physical, manipulative, and block play.

In a later study, Saracho (1994) finds that

1. boys play more than girls in physical, manipulative, block, and dramatic play;
2. boys play more in physical play and less in manipulative play; and
3. girls play more in dramatic play and less in block play.
   Cognitive style and gender also affect the children's play choices.

Coates et al. (1975) show that

1. FD girls prefer to play in the doll corner, whereas FI girls prefer to play with blocks and
2. FI boys prefer to play at table tasks, inasmuch as FD boys prefer social play (e.g., doll corner, block corner).

Thus, social play corresponds to a FD cognitive style whereas solitary play corresponds to a FI cognitive style in spite of the presence of others. Children who prefer social instead of solitary play are somewhat more FD. In comparison, children who favor solitary play (e.g., working alone on projects) are somewhat more FI. Saracho (1995a, 1996b) also shows cognitive style and gender differences. In her earlier study, Saracho (1995a) indicates that FD girls engage more in physical, manipulative, and dramatic play, inasmuch as FD boys engage more in block play. In contrast, FI girls engage less in physical and block play and FI boys engage less in manipulative and dramatic play. Gender differences demonstrate that (1) girls are more socially oriented than boys and (2) girls spend more time in the block corner. Both FD girls and boys are more socially oriented in their play; whereas the FI ones prefer solitary play. The gender differences in Saracho's (1996b) later study indicate that FD girls display more play behaviors than FD boys in manipulative and dramatic play, while FI girls display the least play behaviors in physical and block play. Since this study did not examine the reasons for greater social interest in females than in males, it is assumed that the teachers in the study socialize the children into commonly accepted sex roles of their culture. The teachers' communications of their sex-role stereotypes may have influenced the children's play behaviors. Thus, girls engage more in social activities, while boys engage more in nonsocial activities. Although the teachers' behaviors may have increased the gender differences, it is doubtful that their influence affects the findings in the study (Saracho, 1995a). Coates (1972) shows that 3-0 to 5-10 year-old girls are moderately more FI than boys of the same age. Her study indicates a relationship between four- and five-year-old children's play and cognitive styles. It seems that (1) most FD girls prefer a social activity (such as playing house) where they must cooperate with numerous children and (2) most FI girls prefer nonsocial activities where they engage in solitary play, although they occasionally interact with their peers.

Social orientation factors in children's play and cognitive style also vary according to gender. FD girls identify social roles with others, initiate play activities, and play with objects in social roles; but FI girls conceive ideas, specify social roles that interact with others, and utilize their body and objects to move with others. In comparison, FD boys play with equipment, play in several activities, presume social roles, communicate social ideas, imitate motor activities, and conceive ideas with objects; while FI boys direct and initiate their play with others, apply motor skills, and presume social roles with objects (Saracho, 1989b).

SOCIAL ORIENTATION FACTORS

Social factors are incorporated into children's cognitive style and can be observed within a play setting. Saracho (1989c) investigates those factors underlying the play of 300 FD and FI preschool children. She uses the *Preschool Embedded Figures Test* to determine the children's cognitive style. Her results indicate two dimensions of play behaviors for each group of children: (1) social relations and (2) concrete objects for FD children and (1) role-playing ideas and (2) block building activities for FI children. In a recent study, Saracho (1998) uses the *Articulation of the Body-Concept (ABC) Scale* to assess the preschool children's cognitive style. She shows that FD children exhibit more play behaviors and play more in the different play constructs than do FI children. Although both FD and FI children highly favor dramatic play, they prefer

1. dramatic,
2. physical,
3. block, and
4. manipulative play;

whereas FI children prefer

1. dramatic,
2. block,
3. manipulative, and
4. physical play (hierarchal preference).

In addition, FD children participate in associative play where children interact more with each other; whereas FI children participate in parallel play where children play next to each other but do not interact. The dominant incongruity between the FD and FI children is that FI children are assuming more leadership roles. For example, FD children

1. participate, and engage in play;
2. participate broadly in play activities;
3. participate in associative and imitative play; and
4. engage in several forms of play;

whereas FI children

1. engage in imitative and independent activities;
2. improvise, imitate, and communicate in play activities;
3. engage in physical and cognitive play; and
4. initiate and communicate ideas during manipulative and dramatic play.

Saracho (1999) observes, records, and analyzes the children's play behaviors of 2400 three-, four-and five-year-old children attending an early childhood program. She uses the *Goodenough-Harris Drawing Test* to determine the children's cognitive style. Factors underlying the play of preschool children based on their cognitive style are identified for each group of children. The factors indicate that FD children participate more in social play activities, whereas FI children engage more in nonsocial play activities.

Saracho (1989c) identifies (1) social relations and (2) concrete objects in the play of FD children and (1) role-playing ideas and (2) block building activities in the play of FI children. Saracho (1989b) observes FD children in more play activities with others and with concrete objects, although FI children reorganize the play environment. Evidently, FD children engage in more social activities and forms of play than do FI children. FD children, more than FI children, show more play behaviors, participate more in all the play areas, select social play areas, and engage more in associative play. For example, FD children select from play equipment to play with others, which is one of the FD characteristics. FD individuals are attentive toward others (Saracho & Spodek, 1981, 1986), interpersonal, popular, warm toward others (Pascual-Leone, 1989), and nurturing (Armstrong, 1999). They convey more psychosocial performances during interpersonal relationships (Armstrong, 2000; Armstrong & Priola, 2001) and generally learn definite and logical knowledge. In contrast, FI children generate innovative concepts and initiate their own play activities.

Even when FI children assume social roles, they create the different roles or delineate the roles, which are FI characteristics. Saracho and Spodek (1981, 1986) define FI individuals as being (1) able to resolve problems that emerge and have disorganized contexts and (2) detached from authority. Nonetheless, some FI children display numerous FD characteristics (e.g., assuming social roles, speaking with others in manipulative play). Although assuming social roles and speaking with others are FD characteristics, two debatable inferences may have been ignored: (1) manipulative and physical play may actually be FI ilks of play that includes many FI activities and (2) children's play behaviors and cognitive style may be more astonishing than researchers and educators have originally agreed upon. Saracho (1992a) pinpoints those factors underlying the play of 1276 FD and FI three-, four-, and five-year-old children whose cognitive style is assessed using the *Articulation of the Body Concept (ABC) Scale.* She shows two dimensions of play behaviors for each group of children: (1) communicating ideas through the use of dramatic, manipulative, and physical activities, and (2) communicating ideas in physical and block activities for FD children; and (1) communicating ideas in all forms of play, and (2) engaging in block and physical play for FI children.

Using a sizable sample, Saracho (1992b) specifies play factors of FD and FI preschool children. Her factors show that both FD and FI children communicate ideas in physical, manipulative, block, and dramatic play; and that FI children play more often in the block and physical ilks of play. These outcomes are comparable to the ones in earlier studies that examine the children's FDI and play preferences in a natural setting. The basic purpose of these activities are for children to engage in (1) social interaction (e.g., playing in the doll corner, playing formal games, playing with others in the block corner) and (2) nonsocial interaction (e.g., constructing with blocks, working on tasks at the table, making paintings and collages, working with puzzles, string beads, weaving pot holders). Four-and five-year-old FD children prefer socially oriented activities, but FI ones favor solitary activities (Coates et al., 1975). Saracho (1987) concludes that children's cognitive style guides their play. FI children play more than FD children, but both FD and FI children exhibit play behaviors that define their cognitive style. Young children who play in a group convey their private symbolism into communicable configurations within play events. Their development in language and cognitive skills encourages them to engage in solitary play (Saracho, 1986a). Rubin, Watson, and Jambor (1978) affirm that some children purposely select solitary play. Children who participate in parallel play appreciate the partnership of their peers; while those children who consider their peers' view point select associative and cooperative play (Rubin, 1976, Saracho, 1985). These studies (e.g., Saracho, 1983, 1985, Saracho & Spodek, 1981, 1986) confirm the relationship between cognitive style and play.

SOCIAL COMPETENCE

Social competence is important in helping understand group processes. Cognitive style characteristics can influence the way play groups function. Apparently, discrepancies and congruencies in cognitive style seem to have an impact on the behavioral characteristics of the group members. and Priola (2001) assume that cognitive style characteristics may convey defining sets of categories to describe units of interactions that are simply task or nontask in nature. For example, Armstrong and Priola (2001) show that teams select FD individuals rather than FI analytic individuals as their team leaders. They assume that individuals may perceive the more FD team members as displaying relatively more task and social-emotional oriented behaviors.

Children's social competence in play conveys their cognitive style. Saracho (1991a, 1991b) shows a relationship between the children's FDI and their social competence. She demonstrates FI children are more efficient in adopting a social role and resolving a social problem. In a sociometric study, Saracho (1991b) identifies various social correlates of FD and FI kindergarten children. She shows that teachers view (1) FI children as more socially effective and (2) FD dyads of children (where one child is accepted and the other is rejected) to be more socially effective. Those FD and FI children who are rejected by other children engage more in social play.

A different study (Saracho, 1991a) supports that teachers view FI children to be more socially effective. Previous studies (e.g., Saracho, 1980; Saracho & Dayton; 1980; Saracho and Spodek, 1981) support these results. They determine the teachers' perceptions of their FD and FI children on academic achievement. Teachers underestimate FD children but overestimate FI children. The findings on social competence and academic achievement imply that teachers judge FD and FI children similarly across the board. Although FD children in these classrooms may be more socially effective, the teachers' perceptions may be similar with both academic or social competence.

Teachers view FI children more competent disregarding the task they are evaluating, although FI children may be more socially effective. The children's sociometric selections support the teachers' perceptions of their classroom children. It seems as if young children are applying the teachers' criteria in assessing their peers. FI children are more popular, engage more in social play, and instigate their own play activities more regularly than their FD peers (Saracho, 1991a). Apparently, FI children seem to be more popular. Both FD and FI children prefer FI children to be their playmates. Both the children's and teachers' evaluations are similar (e.g., FI children are more socially effective), even though FI children are described as socially detached, cold and aloof; while FD children are considered to be sensitive to others and describe social skills (Saracho & Spodek, 1981, 1986). FI children are selected as preferred playmates, while FD children mutually reject each other as playmates. This study is conducted in public school settings that concentrate on academic achievement. FD and FI children may perceive the requirements for success in these settings and use the FI characteristics as criteria in their sociometric evaluations. This perception may have an impact in their choice of FI playmates. It seems that FI children are more accepted than FD children (Saracho, 1991a).

Gullo (1988) shows similar outcomes with a separate dimension of cognitive style, reflectivity-impulsivity. He reports that reflective children, who are analogous to FI children, are considered to be more socially competent. FD individuals are assumed to be interpersonally oriented, but Kogan and Block's (1991) study challenges the evidence that social orientation provides effective interpersonal skills. Black (1992) indicates that children's communication in social pretend play is a feeling of social status. FI children may be considered to have a higher social status because of their analytic skills that FD and FI children may notice the FI children's verbal expressions of their thoughts. In assuming social roles, FI children arbitrate the composition of a dialogue, appoint roles, and define pretense in episodes of social play (Saracho, 1997).

The FDI theory shows similar outcomes. For example, Saracho and Spodek (1981, 1986) demonstrate that FI individuals are able to resolve problems they confront in different types of settings. FDI is a bipolar dimension that has an analytic domain on one extreme and the global domain on the other extreme. These domains describe the way individuals resolve problems or view undertakings. Additionally, FDI characterizes the individuals' analytic competence and their capacity to refine knowledge. Solving problems compels individuals to apply their analytic reasoning;

therefore, FI individuals can assess and resolve problems with ease. Cognitive stylistic incongruities depend on the individuals' atypical characteristics (Saracho, 1987). Although a few number of studies exist, these support a relationship between young children's play behaviors and their cognitive style, suggesting important ramifications for research and education.

RESEARCH IMPLICATIONS

Researchers must persevere in testing the relationship between young children's play behaviors and their cognitive style to authenticate the reliability of this branch of research. Investigations, like the ones cited above, can be completely or partially replicated by broadening the domain of subjects (e.g., children from diverse socioeconomic classes, ethnic circles, age clusters), early childhood contexts (e.g., Head Start, child care, public school, nursery school), and methods of assessing play and cognitive style. Contrasting assessments can be applied in determining the children's cognitive style and correlated with one another. In spite of their fragmentary relationship, the studies demonstrate high reliability and validity estimates with their measures and procedures. Perhaps more than one assessment of cognitive style and play must be employed when investigating the relationship between the children's play and cognitive style.

Investigations can embody numerous constructs of play (e.g., manipulative, block, physical, dramatic) and play behaviors (e.g., communication of ideas, levels of social behavior, and leadership roles). The children's presence in these play constructs can be analyzed in countless methods (e.g., mean time invested in each play construct). Teachers can apply a cognitive style classroom instrument in relation to the children's play behaviors, preferences, and constructs. Saracho's (1984a) observation scale assesses the children's play behaviors (e.g., communication of ideas, levels of social behavior, and leadership roles) and play constructs, which can be related to FDI cognitive style. For example, communication of ideas, solitary play, and leadership roles indicate field independence. Children's persistence in these behavior patterns within each play construct and across the distinct play constructs can be examined, although researchers should eschew generalizing exclusive impressions of the children's behavior. Their deductive explanations for their play behaviors and choices of the distinctive play constructs may effortlessly be ignored. Children can be interviewed, further observations can be indexed, and other ilks of data may be aggregated to analyze the children's ripostes to contrasting instances during their play. The relationship between young children's play and cognitive style clearly suggests a longitudinal study before making generalizations concerning this relationship.

EDUCATIONAL IMPLICATIONS

Teachers can determine children's needs and abilities by assessing their cognitive style and play behaviors. Teachers can embark this procedure by analyzing the children's play and cognitive style. First, they can appraise the children's cognitive style at the beginning of the academic year. Teachers can then examine their understanding by evaluating children and making inferences in a variety of play contexts and comparing these play contexts and analyses with other observations from several adults (Saracho, 1998; Saracho & Spodek, 1981). They can assess the children's play by using Saracho's (1984a) *Play Rating Scale* and assess cognitive style using several classroom instruments like

1.   the field sensitive instruments (e.g., Ramírez and Castañeda, 1974)
2.   the *Learning Style Inventory* (Dunn, Dunn, & Price, 1978) and/or
3.   standardized measures such as the *Rod-and-Frame test, tilting room-tilting chair test, Articulation of the Body-Concept (ABC) Scale,* and the different forms of the *Embedded Figures Test,* (Saracho, 1983, 1984b, 1985, 1986b, 1989a).

These assessments and a play scale can assist teachers to design the children's play experiences. Play experiences based on the children's cognitive styles can be initially presented to the children until they are comfortable and confident in the classroom (Saracho & Spodek, 1981). Teachers then can provide social play experiences (e.g., dramatic play) for FD children, and nonsocial activities (e.g., manipulative play, block play) for FI children (Saracho, 1998).

Once children experience security, teachers can slightly introduce play experiences that challenge the children's foremost cognitive style, where some level of "cognitive-style dissonance" emerges (Saracho, 1998; Saracho & Spodek, 1981). For instance, FI children can slowly play in social activities (e.g., working within a group on a social experience like dramatic play) where they apply their social sensitivity, a FD attribute. In comparison, FD children slowly begin playing in nonsocial activities where they apply their analytic skills like working independently to solve a problem in block or manipulative play (Saracho, 1998).

Early childhood education programs need to bear in mind the children's play and their cognitive style. Teachers can adapt the curriculum and their instructional strategies to each child's cognitive style, but this procedure confines the children's possibility to do what emerges "naturally." A more acceptable procedure may be to assist children to become cognitive flexible (Saracho & Spodek, 1986), to expand their repertoire beyond their foremost cognitive style (Saracho & Spodek, 1981).

The measurement of play and cognitive style can assist teachers to provide compatible early childhood education programs that acknowledge young children's needs and can guarantee that divergent information-processing capabilities that are innate among individual children and the children's play behaviors are addressed. Children's play behaviors and cognitive styles should be acknowledged in their educational programs for meaningful learning. Therefore, teachers must learn and understand the young children's FDI characteristics and the relationship between play behaviors and cognitive style. This information can assist teachers to adapt developmentally appropriate ilks of teaching and educational programs for young children.

REFERENCES

Armstrong, S. J. (2000). The influence of individual cognitive style on performance in management education. *Educational Psychology, 20,* 323-340.

Armstrong, S. J. (1999). Cognitive style and dyadic interaction: A study of supervisors and subordinates engaged in working relationships. Unpublished doctoral thesis. University of Leeds, UK.

Armstrong, S. J., & Priola, V. (2001). Individual differences in cognitive style and their effects on task and social orientations of self-managed work teams. *Small Group Research, 32,* 283-312.

Beller, E. K. (1958). A study of dependence and perceptual orientation. *American Psychologist, 13,* 347.

Black, B. (1992). Negotiating social pretend play: Communication differences related to social status and sex. *Merrill-Palmer Quarterly, 38,* 212-232.

Coates, S. (1972). *Preschool Embedded Figures Test.* Palo Alto, CA: Consulting Psychologists Press.

Coates, S., Lord, M., and Jakabovics, E. (1975). Field dependence independence, social-nonsocial play, and sex differences. *Perceptual and Motor Skills, 40,* 195-202.

Corrigan, R. (1987). A developmental sequence of actor-object pretend play in young children. *Merrill-Palmer Quarterly, 33,* 87-106.

Dunn, R., Dunn, K., & Price, G. E. (1978). *Learning Style Inventory.* Lawrence, KS: Price Systems.

Eagle, M., Fitzgibbons, D., & Goldberger, L. (1966). Field dependence and memory for relevant and irrelevant incidental stimuli. *Perceptual and Motor Skills, 23,* 1035-1038.

Eagle, M., Goldberger, L., & Breitman, M. (1969). Field dependence and memory for social vs. neutral and relevant vs. irrelevant incidental stimuli. *Perceptual and Motor Skills, 29,* 903-910.

Fitzgibbons, D., & Goldberger, L. (1971). Task and social orientation: A study of field dependence arousal and memory for incidental stimuli. *Perceptual and Motor Skills, 32,* 167-174.

Fitzgibbons, D., Goldberger, L., & Eagle, M. (1965). Field dependence and memory for incidental stimuli. *Perceptual and Motor Skills, 21,* 743-749.

Goldberger, L., & Bendich, S. (1972). Field-dependence and social responsiveness as determinants of spontaneously produced words. *Perceptual and Motor Skills, 34,* 883-886.

Gullo, D. F. (1988). An investigation of cognitive tempo and its effects on evaluating kindergarten children's academic and social competencies. *Early Child Development and Care, 34,* 201-215.

Halverson, C. F., & Waldrop, M.F. (1976). Relations between preschool activity and aspects of intellectual and social behavior at age 71/2. *Developmental Psychology, 12,* 107-112.

Kagan, J. (1971). *Change and continuity in infancy.* New York: Wiley.

Kavanaugh, R. D., & Engel, S. (1998). The Development of Pretense and Narrative in Early Childhood. In O.N. Saracho & B. Spodek (Eds.), *Multiple Perspectives on Play in Early Childhood Education* (pp. 80-9). New York: State University of New York Press.

Kogan, N. (1987). Some behavioral implications of cognitive styles in early childhood, *Early Child Development and Care, 29,* 595-598.

Kogan, N., & Block, J. (1991). Field dependence-independence from early childhood through adolescence: Personality and socialization aspects. In S. Wapner, & J. Demick (Eds.) *Field dependence-independence cognitive style across the life span* (pp. 177-207). Hillsdale, NJ: Erlbaum.

Konstadt, N., & Forman, E. (1965). Field dependence and external directedness. *Journal of Personality and Social Psychology, 1,* 490-493.

Nakamura, C. Y., & Finck, D. N. (1980). Relative effectiveness of socially oriented and task oriented children and predictability of their behaviors. *Monographs of the Society for Research in Child Development, 45* (3-4, Serial No. 185).

Ohnmacht, F. W. (1968). Factorial invariance of the teacher characteristics schedule and measures of two cognitive styles. *Journal of Psychology, 69,* 193-199.

Pascual-Leone, J. (1989). An organismic process model of Witkin's field dependence-independence. In T. Globerson & T. Zelniker (Eds.), *Cognitive style and cognitive development—Human development* (3rd ed., pp. 36-70). Norwood, NJ: Ablex.

Piaget, J. (1962). *Play, dreams, and imitation in childhood.* New York: International Press.

Ramírez, M., & Castañeda, A. (1974). *Cultural democracy, bicognitive development, and education.* New York: Academic Press.

Renninger, K. A., & Sigel, I. E. (1987). The development of cognitive organisation in young children: An exploratory study. *Early Child Development and Care, 29,* 133-161.

Riding, R., & Rayner, S. (1998). *Cognitive styles and learning strategies.* London: David Fulton.

Rubin, K. H. (1980). Fantasy play: Its role in the development of social skills and social cognition. *New Directions for Child Development, 9,* 69-84.

Rubin, K. H. (1976). Relation between social participation and role-taking skill in preschool children. *Psychological Reports, 39,* 823-826.

Rubin, K. H., & Coplan, R. J.1(998). Social and non-social play in childhood: An individual differences perspective. In O.N. Saracho & B. Spodek (Eds.), *Multi-*

ple Perspectives on Play in Early Childhood Education. (pp. 144-170). New York: State University of New York Press.

Rubin, K. H., Watson, K. S., & Jambor, T. w. (1978). Free play behaviors in preschool and kindergarten children. *Child Development, 49*, 534-536.

Ruble, K. N. & Nakamura, C. Y. (1972). Task orientations versus social orientation in young children and their attention to relevant social cues.*Child Development, 43*, 471-480.

Saracho, O. N. (2001). Factors in three- to five-year-old children's play,*Play and Culture Studies, 3*, 401-416.

Saracho, O. N. (1999). A factor analysis of preschool children's play strategies and cognitive style. *Educational Psychology, 19*, 165-180.

Saracho, O. N. (1998). Socialization factors in the cognitive style and play of young children. *International Journal of Educational Research, 29*, 263-276.

Saracho, O. N. (1997). Some implications of cognitive style on young children's play. *Early Child Development and Care, 131, 131*, 19-30.

Saracho, O. N. (1996a). Preschool children's cognitive style and their play behaviors. *Child Study Journal, 26*, 125-148.

Saracho, O. N. (1996b). The relationship between the cognitive style and play behaviors of 3 to 5-year-old children. *Personality and Individual Differences, 21*(6), 863-876.

Saracho, O. N. (1995a). Preschool children's cognitive style and their selection of academic areas in their play.*Early Child Development and Care, 112*, 27-42.

Saracho, O. N. (1995b). Relationship between the cognitive styles and play behaviors of preschool children.*Educational Psychology, 15*, 405-415.

Saracho, O. N. (1995c). Relationship between young children's cognitive style and their play. *Early Child Development and Care, 113*, 77-84.

Saracho, O. N. (1994). Relationship of preschool children's cognitive style to their play preferences. *Early Child Development and Care, 97*, 21-33.

Saracho, O. N. (1992a). Factors reflecting cognitive style in young children's play. *Learning and Individual Differences, 4*, 43-58.

Saracho, O. N. (1992b). The Relationship between preschool children's cognitive style and play: Implications for creativity. *The Creativity Research Journal, 5*, 35-47.

Saracho, O. N. (1991a). Cognitive style and social behavior in young Mexican American Children. *International Journal of Early Childhood, 23*(2), 21-38.

Saracho, O. N. (1991b). Social correlates of cognitive style in young children.*Early Child Development and Care, 76*, 117-134.

Saracho, O. N. (1990). Preschool children's cognitive style and their social orientation. *Perceptual and Motor Skills, 70*, 915-921.

Saracho, O. N. (1989a). Cognitive style and the evaluation of young children's educational programs. *Early Child Development and Care, 51*, 13-28.

Saracho, O. N. (1989b). Cognitive style in the play of young children.*Early Child Development and Care, 51*, 65-76.

Saracho, O. N. (1989c). The Factorial structure of three- to five-year-old children's social behavior: Cognitive style and play.*Journal of Research and Development in Education, 22*(4), 21-28.

Saracho, O.N. (1987). Cognitive style characteristics as related to young children's play behaviors. *Early Child Development and Care, 28*, 163-179.

Saracho, O. N. (1986a). Play and young children's learning. In B. Spodek (Ed.), *Today's kindergarten: Exploring the knowledge base, expanding the curriculum*, (pp. 91-109). New York: Teachers College Press.

Saracho, O.N. (1986b). Validation of two cognitive measures to assess field-dependence/independence. *Perceptual and Motor Skills, 63*, 255-263.

Saracho, O.N. (1985). Young children's play behaviors and cognitive styles. *Early Child Development and Care, 21*, 1-18.

Saracho, O.N. (1984a). Construction and validation of the *Play Rating scale. Early Child Development and Care, 17*, 199-230.

Saracho, O.N. (1984b). The Goodenough-Harris Drawing Test as a measure of field-dependence-independence. *Perceptual and Motor Skills, 59*, 887-892.

Saracho, O.N. (1983). Assessing cognitive style in young children. *Studies in Educational Evaluation, 8*, 229-236.

Saracho, O.N. (1980). The relationship between the teachers' cognitive style and their perceptions of their students' academic achievement. *Educational Research Quarterly, 5*(3), 40-49.

Saracho, O.N., & Dayton, C.M. (1980). Relationship of teachers' cognitive styles to pupils' academic achievement gains. *Journal of Educational Psychology, 72*, 544-549.

Saracho, O.N., & Spodek, B. (1981). The teachers' cognitive styles and their educational implications. *Educational Forum, 45*, 153-159.

Saracho, O.N., & Spodek, B. (1986). Cognitive style and children's learning: Individual variations in cognitive processes. In L.G. Katz (Ed.) *Current topics in early childhood education*, Vol. VI, (pp. 179-194). Norwood, NJ: Ablex.

Saracho, O. N., & Spodek, B. (1998). Preschool children's cognitive play: A factor analysis. *International Journal of Early Childhood Education, 3*, 67-76.

Shantz, C. (1983). Social cognition. In P. Mussen (Ed.), *Handbook of child psychology. Vol. 3. Cognitive Development*. New York: Wiley.

Small, M. (1990). *Cognitive development*. New York: Harcourt, Brace Jovanovich.

Steele, C. (1981). Play variables as related to cognitive constructs in three- to six-year-olds. *Journal of Research and Development in Education, 14*(3), 58-72.

Tennant, M. (1988). *Psychology and adult learning*. London: Routledge.

Witkin, H. A., Dyk, R. B., Faterson, H. F., Goodenough, D. R., & Karp, S. A. (1974). *Psychological differentiation: Studies of development*. Potomac, MD: Erlbaum. (Originally published, NY: Wiley, 1962)

Witkin, H. A., & Goodenough, D. R. (1981). Cognitive styles: Essence and origins. New York: International Universities Press.

Witkin, H. A., Lewis, H. B., Hertzman, M., Machover, K.,Meissner, P. B., & Wapner, S. (1972). *Personality through perception*. Westport, CT: Greenwood Press. (Originally published, NY: Harper & Row, 1954)

CHAPTER 6

ON THE RELATION BETWEEN PLAY AND SYMBOLIC THOUGHT
The Case of Mathematics Manipulatives

David H. Uttal

Most developmental psychologists and early childhood educators agree that young children learn best through play and exploration. As the chapters in this volume suggest, play and learning are intertwined for young children. Indeed, a focus on natural, play-based activities lies at the core of developmentally appropriate curricula. Organizations such as the National Association for the Education of Young Children (NAEYC) and the National Council for Teachers of Mathematics (NCTYM) stress that children's natural play should be the focus of preschool, kindergarten education, and (to a lesser extent) early elementary education (Uttal, Scudder, & DeLoache, 1997).

As used here, the term "play" does not mean only free play that lacks direction or purpose. Instead, I also use the term play to refer to structured

Contemporary Perspectives on Play in Early Childhood Education
A Volume in: Contemporary Perspectives in Early Childhood Education, pages 97–114.
Copyright © 2003 by Information Age Publishing, Inc.
All rights of reproduction in any form reserved.
ISBN: 1-930608-31-4 (cloth), 1-930608-30-6 (paper)

activities in which teachers (or parents) guide children's activities. Teachers often plan activities and choose particular playthings with the goal of facilitating children's development or learning.

This chapter focuses on a quintessential example of this type of structured play, the use of mathematics *manipulatives*. Manipulatives are concrete objects (rods, blocks, etc.) that are designed to facilitate children's mathematical development. They are used extensively in early education. Their use is encouraged for children of all ability levels, including not only typical preschoolers but also gifted children and those with developmental disabilities (Ball, 1992; Uttal, Scudder, & DeLoache, 1997).

Manipulatives are constructed to allow children to learn naturally through play and exploration. There are formal manipulative systems, such as Dienes Blocks and Cuisenaire Rods, which are designed specifically to teach mathematics. However, teachers also use many informal types of manipulatives, which can include household objects (paper clips, coins, etc.) and pieces of candy or cereal. In addition, manipulatives have moved into the digital age. There are now several digital libraries of manipulatives, and computer scientists have created systems that combine the features of traditional hand-held manipulatives with advanced electronic technologies (Resnick et al., 1996, 1998). These "digital manipulatives" indicate electronically when children have combined the manipulatives in the correct or expected way. For example, manipulatives representing the tens units in an addition problem may turn red and those representing the ones units may turn blue when the child places the objects in a particular order.

Obviously there are real and important differences in the types of manipulatives that young children are asked to use. It seems likely that different forms of manipulatives affect children's mathematical thinking in different ways (Chao, Stigler, & Woodward, 2000). However, our focus here is on a characteristic that most manipulative systems share; each is intended to represent mathematical information in a form that is tractable and does not require the use of written representations. It is this substitution for written representations, and the consequences of this substitution, that is the focus of this chapter. Accordingly, I have treated the term manipulatives in a general way, using it to refer to any physical system of objects that is (a) intended to help young children learn mathematical concepts, and (b) does not require that children use or comprehend written representations of the same concepts.

The fundamental assumption that motivates the enthusiasm regarding manipulatives is that young children understand mathematical concepts and relations in fundamentally different ways than older children's and adults' do. Young children's conception of mathematics is more concrete and tied to manipulations and transformations that can be performed manually. The theoretical basis for this belief is derived from the writings of Bruner (1966), Piaget (1964), and others. Each of these scholars stressed, in different ways, the importance of concreteness and concrete objects on the development of children's concepts.

These theoretical backgrounds have been extended substantially in early childhood education, perhaps beyond the original intent of the theorists. Educators and developmental theorists alike have assumed that "concrete is inherently good; abstract is inherently not appropriate—at least at the beginning, at least for young learners." (Ball, 1992, p. 16) Manipulatives are thought to be particularly appropriate for young children because they encourage learning through natural exploration and play. On this view, manipulatives allow children to learn through play or at least in a playful manner (Ball, 1995; Uttal, Scudder, & DeLoache, 1997).

Despite the enthusiasm for the use of manipulatives, some researchers and teachers have raised questions about their efficacy. Both meta-analyses and intensive, longitudinal studies of children's mathematical development have not demonstrated that using manipulatives conveys a clear and consistent advantage in young children's learning of mathematics (Chao, Stigler, & Woodward, 2000; Hiebert, 1996; Sowell, 1989; Uttal, Scudder & DeLoache, 1987). In this chapter, I focus on one important difficulty that children seem to have that arises from the use of manipulative. Specifically, young children often fail to make a connection between concepts that they learn from manipulatives and written representations of the same or similar concepts. For example, a child might learn about the base-ten system through the use of Dienes Blocks, but the same child might gain no advantage in mastering the written representation of the base-ten system. Similarly, children might learn basic principles of addition from manipulatives but then fail to see a connection to the + sign (Bialystok, 1992; Resnick & Omanson, 1988; Fuson & Briars, 1991).

The difficulty that children sometimes have in connecting manipulatives with written, symbolic representations of the same problem is a fundamentally important one. At its core, mathematics is a formal symbol system, and learning written representations allows children to work on complex problems quickly and efficiently. Single symbols (the + sign, a function sign, etc.) can stand for a series of complex operations. Learning these symbols allows children to reason about relations independent of any physical instantiation of the concepts. For example, we can say, "What's 2 + 3?" without thinking "2 of what?" or "3 of what?" A goal of mathematics education therefore should be the acquisition of a rich understanding of written symbols systems and of the ability to manipulate these symbols both on paper and mentally.

The symbolic demands of mathematics lead to an interesting paradox in regard to early education. On the one hand, children must acquire a symbol system that is distinctly not concrete; even simple mathematical symbols (such as + or -) bear no clear relation to their referents. Yet on the other hand, it is assumed that the best way to teach young children to understand mathematics concepts is through the use of concrete materials such as manipulatives. This paradox highlights the challenges and importance of helping children to establish linkages between manipulative-based solutions or representations and the corresponding written representations (Resnick & Omanson, 1988; Hiebert, 1986; Uttal, in press; Uttal, Liu, & DeLoache, 1999; Uttal, Scudder, & DeLoache, 1997).

The focus of this chapter is on both the opportunities and the difficulties that manipulative use engenders. I address the specific question of why children seem to have so much difficulty relating physical (concrete or manipulative) representations to written representations. I begin by documenting the problem, based on a review of several studies of classroom-based manipulative use. Next, I situate the problem of understanding the relation between manipulative-based representations and written representations within cognitive research on children's understanding of symbolic and representational relations. This literature review provides insights into the special challenges that children face when they are asked to relate one system of representation (e.g., manipulatives), to another (e.g., written representations). Finally, I conclude with specific recommendations regarding how teachers can best help children to understand and use manipulatives.

Two limitations of scope should be noted at the outset. First, the goal is not to provide a comprehensive review of research on the use of manipulatives. Instead, this chapter attempts to establish connections between research on manipulative use and other bodies of work in cognitive development. These linkages help to shed light on why young children may have difficulty relating manipulatives to written representations. Second, this chapter is intended to be neither an endorsement of manipulatives nor a critique of manipulatives per se. Manipulatives can be extremely effective, but like any instructional technique, they also have limitations and disadvantages. There are specific reasons why young children may have trouble linking manipulative mathematic solutions with written representations of the same problem. This information may prove very useful to teachers, curriculum designers, and parents who are interested in using manipulatives in an effective manner.

CHILDREN'S DIFFICULTIES IN RELATING MANIPULATIVES TO WRITTEN REPRESENTATIONS

The difficulty that children have in relating manipulatives to written representations is evident in many different contexts. The problem has been documented across a wide age range; it shows up in children as young as 4, but even high school students may have difficulty relating physical geometry constructions to written representations of the same problem (Von Glaserfeld, 1996). In this section I briefly review studies that have demonstrated that children seem not to relate manipulatives-based representations to written representations of the same, or similar problems.

Resnick and Omanson (1988) conducted a particularly rich and detailed study of the acquisition of mathematical concepts from manipulatives and children's transfer (or lack of transfer) to written representations. Their study included a wide array of methods, ranging from intensive interviews of individual children to reaction time measures of children's processing of numerical information. Many of these measures were collected longitudinally, from the beginning to the end of the second grade. For these reasons, Resnick and Omanson's study provides a unique window onto children's manipulative-based learning and their (lack of) transfer of this knowledge to written skills.

The research documented that manipulative use can facilitate children's acquisition and fluid use of mathematics concepts. For example, children who regularly used Dienes Blocks acquired flexibility in subtraction skills such as borrowing. Many children who began the year with little or no knowledge of subtraction were able to perform well with the Dienes Blocks by the end of the year. In particular, many children's understanding of the borrowing procedures in subtraction, as evidenced by their Dienes Blocks constructions, increased substantially throughout the year.

However, there was very little correspondence between children's performance with the Dienes Blocks and their use of written representations of the same concepts. Indeed, the child who performed the best with the Dienes Blocks performed the *worst* when the testing involved written representations of what were essentially the same problems. And the opposite was also true: children who performed well with the written representations often had the most trouble using the Dienes Blocks.

Based on their results, Resnick and Omanson attempted to improve children's understanding by providing direct instruction about the relation between manipulative-based and written representations of subtraction facts. This was not an easy task; it took extensive, repeated instruction to help children grasp the relation between the two forms of representation. Many children did eventually appreciate the relation, but some persisted in treating the two systems as independent. Put simply, seeing the relation between the two systems of representation was a formidable challenge for these second graders; some never succeeded, and those that did succeed needed repeated, direct instruction about the relation between the two forms of representation.

Hughes (1986) documented a similar problem in elementary school children's use of concrete objects. He studied directly the relation between children's comprehension of manipulatives and their understanding of written representations of the same problems. In one task, children were asked to represent with manipulatives simple written addition problems, such as 1 + 7. The children were given written problems and asked to show how the same problem could be represented with the manipulatives.

In general, children did not perform well; they had difficulty using the manipulatives to express written representations of the problems. The most striking examples illustrate children's difficulties in relating the two systems of representations. For example, some children simply *copied* the written problems with the manipulatives. They literally used the manipulatives to replicate the written problem. For example, the children would lay out the bricks to write "1 + 7 = ?" They saw the manipulatives as simply another way to write the problem; they used the bricks as if they were writing elements. The children either stuck with the manipulatives representation or with the written representation; they seemed to have difficulty construing the possibility of two *alternate* forms of representation. Hence they could not go back and forth between two forms of representation.

Children in this example had already acquired some understanding of written representations, and the problems that they faced were in some ways different from those illustrated in the Resnick and Omanson study. In Hughes' research, children had difficulty using manipulatives to represent written problems. In contrast, in Resnick and Omanson's study, children had difficulty moving from manipulatives to written representations. However, there is an important similarity between the two studies that will be explored further below: In both situations, the children had difficult dealing simultaneously with two, alternate forms of representation. They often could succeed with manipulatives or with written representations, but they failed to connect the two (See also Hiebert, 1989; Hiebert & Carpenter, 1992; Lesh, 1999).

THE DEVELOPMENT OF CHILDREN'S CONCEPTIONS OF SYMBOLS AND REPRESENTATIONS

The examples discussed in the previous section illustrate that children have trouble linking representations based on manipulatives with written, symbolic representations. In this section, I demonstrate that research on the development of children's understanding of symbolic representations is highly relevant to understanding the difficulty that children have in linking manipulatives to written representations. I review the results and implications of two lines of research on specific aspects of cognitive development in preschoolers and young elementary school children. The first concerns how children establish an initial insight into the relation between a symbol and its intended referent. The second concerns the development of the ability to reason systematically about relations between two alternate representations or construals of the same fact or concept. Taken together, these two programs of research highlight the likely sources of the difficulty that very young children experience in using manipulatives. In addition, reviewing these lines of research leads directly to specific solutions regarding how best to help children make connections between alternate forms of representations of mathematics concepts.

It should be noted that the relation of these research programs to manipulative use might not be immediately obvious. Neither research program has dealt specifically with manipulative use. Moreover, neither research program has focused on the development of children's mathematical concepts, and each program involves relatively short testing sessions. Nevertheless, these basic research programs shed light on the fundamental challenges of using symbols and of relating one form of representation to another. The research highlights critical aspects of children's thinking that ultimately are very relevant to the challenges that children face in using manipulatives.

Symbolic Development

Children's comprehension of symbols is obviously related to their understanding of mathematics. This is especially true given that much of the value of mathematics is gained from learning to manipulate a symbol system. Many of the challenges that children encounter in learning to understand symbolic relations are similar to those that they encounter in relating manipulatives to written representations.

Recent work in cognitive development has investigated the development of what is perhaps the core aspect of symbol use: understanding that one thing stands for another. A particularly relevant set of tasks involves the child's use of a novel symbol, a simple model, to find a hidden object (DeLoache, 1987; 1991; 2000; DeLoache, Miller & Rosengren, 1997; Uttal, Schreiber, & DeLoache, 1995). The child is asked to perform a familiar task, looking for a hidden object, in an unfamiliar way. The task is interesting and motivating to young children, who very much want to find the hidden object. These characteristics of the task allow researchers to gain a window onto the process by which children come to understand the basic relation between a symbol and its referent.

The task begins with an extensive orientation, during which the experimenter points out the correspondence between the model and the room. First, the experimenter points out the correspondence at a general level, referring to the model as "Little Snoopy's Room" and the room as "Big Snoopy's Room". Then, the experimenter points out correspondences between individual pieces of furniture in the model and in the room. For example, the experimenter demonstrates the relation between "Big Snoopy's Sofa" and "Little Snoopy's Sofa." Next, the experimenter hides the miniature toy, Little Snoopy, in the model and asks the child to find Big Snoopy in the room. The experimenter reminds the child that Big Snoopy is hiding the same place in his room that Little Snoopy is hiding in his room. The child is allowed to search until he or she finds the toy, but searches are scored as correct only if the child's first search is at the correct location.

This task has been conducted with children approximately ages 2 to 4. 2-½-year-olds typically fail, performing at chance levels. However, children only 6 months older perform dramatically better; 3.0-olds average approximately 75 % correct searches.

What accounts for the 2.5-year-olds' poor performance and for the dramatic improvement in 3.0-year-olds' performance? The younger children's failure is *not* due to memory. The task includes a memory check; after searching in the room, the child is asked to return to the model and find the miniature toy. If the child succeeds in this second retrieval (*Retrieval 2*), then memory for the location of the miniature toy cannot be the cause of the difficult finding the larger toy in the room. Almost all children succeed on Retrieval 2, regardless of their performance on Retrieval 1. Thus the children did know where the toy was hidden in the model but they could not use this knowledge to find the larger toy in the room that the model represented.

If memory is not the problem, then why do very young children have so much difficulty using the model as a symbol for the room? The answer lies in children's appreciation of symbolic relations. A specific challenge concerns an appreciation of what DeLoache and colleagues have termed *dual representation*. There are two ways to think of the model. The first is as an interesting object in its own right; the model contains, for example, several miniature pieces of furniture, a toy dog, etc. The second is as a representation of the room; the model is intended to stand for the room. To find the toy, the child must focus on one of these construals and not on the other. The children must think about the model as a symbolic representation rather than as an interesting object in its own right.

To an adult, these two interpretations of the model may seem almost inseparable; it is difficult to think of the model in isolation—to ignore that it is a representation of the room. In the mind of an adult, the purpose of the model *is* to represent the room. This interpretation of the purpose of the model would be difficult for an adult to put out of mind, particularly after the extensive orientation in which the experimenter pointed out the correspondence between the model and the room.

However, young children probably do not share with adults an understanding of the relation between the model and the room. Several lines of research suggest that the challenge for young children is to think of the model as a representation of the room, rather than as simply an interesting thing in it's own right. For example, manipulations that *increase* the salience of the model as a representation in its own right *decrease* the likelihood of children using the model as a symbol. This claim is based on research in which children were encouraged to play with the model before they were asked to use it as a symbol (DeLoache, 2000). When the child arrived at the laboratory, the model was sitting in the middle of the room. Several toys, including the miniature dog, were placed in and around the model. The children were allowed to play with the model freely for 10 minutes. Thereafter, the experimental procedures were identical to the prior studies. Children in this group averaged only 41% correct searches, compared to more than 75% in the typical task in which children do not play with the model before they are asked to use it as a symbol.

Interestingly, the opposite is also true. Manipulations that *decrease* the salience of the intended symbol as an object in its own right *increase* children's success in establishing the symbolic correspondence. In this research, DeLoache and colleagues (2000) placed the model behind a pane of glass. Children could see the model but they could not touch it or otherwise interact with it. The experimenter pointed to the object that corresponded to the hiding location in the room. Two-and-a-half-year-olds, who typically fail the standard model task, performed much better when the model was placed behind glass. Placing the model out of reach made it impossible for the children to treat the object as a plaything and to focus on its properties as an object per se. Consequently, they were more able to focus on the model's relation to the room and hence they succeeded in the search task.

A fascinating line of research provides very strong evidence that the unique problem for young children involves using the model as a symbol. In this research (DeLoache, Miller, & Rosengren, 1997), 2.5-year-olds were made to believe the model *was* a shrunken version of the room rather than a symbolic representation of the room. The children were told that the experimenter had invented a shrinking machine that could shrink the room, the furniture, and the toys. The "room" in this study was actually a large tent-like structure composed of fabric suspended from PVC pipe. This "portable room" allowed the experimenter to easily disassemble the room and to replace it with a much smaller version during the shrinking procedure. Likewise, the small room (the model) could easily be replaced with the full size version during a "blowing up" trial.

The experiment began with a demonstration trial. The experimenter showed the child a full-size troll doll and said that a shrinking machine would now shrink the troll. The experimenter and the child left the room, but the child could hear strange sounds coming from the room; the child believed that these sounds were the shrinking machine in action. While the child and experimenter were out of the room, an assistant replaced the full-size troll with a miniature version. The experimenter and child then returned to the room. The experimenter pointed out the "success" of the shrinking machine.

Next, the experimenter introduced the test trials. She told the child that the troll would be hidden in the room and that the machine would then shrink (or blow up) the room, the troll, and the furniture. The experimenter hid the toy while the child watched. The experimenter and child then left the room, and the experimenter "activated" the shrinking machine. Upon return, the child found that the room and its contents had been shrunken (or blown up). (In reality, a group of assistants had replaced the full size room with the miniature model). This basic procedure was repeated several times. On each trial, the experimenter either "blew up" the model to form the room or "shrunk" the room to form the model. The child saw where the toy was hidden before the size change was simulated. Then, he or she had to find the toy in the shrunken (or blown up) version of the space.

The 2.5-year-old children performed well in the "shrunken room" task, even though they almost always failed the standard model task. This finding is particularly interesting when one considers that the two tasks are essentially the same: In both cases, the child must use the model (or small room) to find a toy that is hidden in the larger room. There is, however, one important change in terms of what the child thinks about the two spaces. In the standard task, the child needs to think of a symbolic, representational relation. In contrast, in the shrunken-room task, the child needs only to think about one room. This room is altered in size, but in the mind of the child it *is* the same room he or she saw before. In sum, the shrunken room task eliminates the need to think about symbolic relations, and consequently very young children succeed. These results provide very strong evidence that the challenge for young children is to think of the model as representing the room. Once this challenge is removed, children who normally fail do very well.

Seeing One Thing in Two Different Ways

A second, related line of research also sheds light on children's difficulty in understanding the relation between manipulatives and written mathematical symbols. This research program focuses on children's appreciation that a single stimulus or object can be interpreted in more than one way. Young children only gradually develop an ability to see one thing in two different ways. This ability may be critical to reasoning simultaneously about the relation between manipulatives and other forms of mathematics representation, particularly written symbols.

A classic demonstration of developmental differences in children's appreciation of multiple perspectives on the same stimulus concerns children's perception and understanding of ambiguous figures. These figures are well known in psychology. They include, for example, a figure that can be seen either as wrinkled old lady or a beautiful young lady. Similarly, another figure can be perceived either as a man or a mouse. A third ambiguous figure can be perceived either as a rabbit or a duck. Most adults have noticed that these figures can be perceived in both ways. For example, adults acknowledge that the figures could be interpreted either as an old or young women, either as a rabbit or a duck, etc. This does not mean that they can see both interpretations of the figure simultaneously. Instead, adults often report that the figure seems to switch back and forth from one construal to another.

Interestingly, children less than five or six do not seem to see or think about ambiguous figures in the same way as adults. Young children do not reverse ambiguous figures, even when prompted to do so. In one study, Gopnick and Rosati (2001) asked 3-, 4-, and 5-year-olds to look at an ambiguous figure and to describe what the figure looked like. The children were prompted to think of alternate interpretations of the figure. The researchers even went so far as to suggest the specific alternate interpretation of the figure. For example, if the child said that the figure looked like a bunny, the experimenter would ask if it could also be seen as a duck. The children were also asked to look at the figure for an additional minute to see if an alternate interpretation came to mind.

Most of the 3- and 4-year-olds interpreted the figures in only one way; even after prompting, they persisted with their original interpretation of the figures. Five-year-olds, however, often reported that the figures could be construed in more than one way; many spontaneously pointed out that the figure could be, for example, either a duck or a bunny. These children acknowledged the inherent ambiguity of the figures and said that other children might also see the figure in more than one way (See also Rock, Gopnick, and Hall, 1994).

Other lines of work point to the generality of these findings; young children's difficulty in appreciating multiple perspectives or interpretations is not limited solely to ambiguous figures. For example, Taylor, Cartwright, & Bowden (1991) investigated 4- and 6-year-olds understanding of ambiguity in drawings. Specifically, they showed children portions of drawings and asked them to identify the represented object. Because the researchers initially showed the child only a small portion of the drawing, the interpretation was often ambiguous. For example, the researcher would show the child a triangle, which was part of a large drawing of a witch; the triangle represented the witch's hat. Then the experimenter would expose the entire figure and ask the child what he or she saw. Almost all children said, "A witch". Next, the experimenter described a hypothetical task in which another child was asked to look at the triangle portion of the figure, with the remainder covered up. The 4-year-olds said that the new child would see a witch, even though only a triangle was visible. The children failed to appreciate that the figure could be seen in two different ways, and that which version one saw depended upon how much information was exposed. Once the children had seen the disambiguating information (e.g., the entire witch), they seemed unable to think simultaneously about the other interpretation (the triangle that formed the witch's hat (See also Chandler & Sokol, 1999; Sodian, 1990; Taylor, 1988).

These results have been interpreted as suggesting that children develop the ability to interpret the same stimulus in two different ways around age 5 or 6. Before this age, children do not seem to reverse ambiguous figures or to appreciate the ambiguity that is inherent in many representations. Once they see something one way, they find it almost impossible to see the same thing in another way. As discussed below, this finding may have important implications for understanding the challenges that children face when working simultaneously with manipulatives and written, symbolic representations.

RELATION OF RESEARCH ON SYMBOLS USE AND REPRESENTATION TO MANIPULATIVES

There are at least three important similarities in the *process* of understanding symbolic relations and problems that children encounter in understanding relations between manipulatives to written representations (Uttal, DeLoache, & Scudder, 1997). First, the research reviewed in the prior section illustrates that achieving insight into a symbolic relation is not an easy or automatic process for young children. Children's understanding of symbolic relations is easily affected by many factors, and children quickly lose sight of the intended relation between a symbol and what it represents. Likewise, there is no guarantee that children will grasp the relation between a mathematics problem that uses manipulative and a similar problem that is expressed in writing. To a teacher, the correspondence between the two may seem obvious and even trivial, but to young children, the correspondence may remain opaque. Adults are experienced in using multiple symbol systems, but each new symbolic insight may be a challenge for young children.

Second, both research programs provide insight into why children may have trouble reasoning simultaneously about two different forms of representation, even if children understand written representations of mathematics problems. The research demonstrates that children tend to conceive of a stimulus or a concept in a single way, and that they do not spontaneously (and sometimes even with prompting) consider alternate construals of the same stimulus. Thus, when they are asked initially to reason about the relation between manipulatives and written representations, they may have substantial difficulty thinking about the two representational forms at the same time. Viewed from this perspective, Hughes' (1986) results also make sense; children sometimes copied the written representation with the manipulatives because they had difficulty thinking simultaneously about the two forms of mathematic representations at once. Just as children in Gopnick and Rosati's experiment failed to see that an ambiguous figure could be either a duck or a rabbit, children may fail to see in their kindergarten classroom that a manipulative-based problem could also be interpreted in terms of a written representation. Tasks that require children less than 7 to think about the same stimulus or concept in two different ways may be inherently difficult.

Third, the research on symbolic development has a very strong implication regarding the central themes in this volume: Play may not be the best way to learn about symbolic relations. Recall that playing with the scale model actually decreased children's use of the model as a symbol. This example clearly illustrates that play may not be helpful when the educational task involves learning symbolic relations. Playing with an object that is intended to represent something else may increase children's attention to the properties of the object per se. Consequently, children may find it more difficult to focus on the object as a symbol. The same may well hold true for using manipulatives; playing with concrete objects may increase children's interest in mathematics but it may also make it more difficult for children to understand how the manipulatives relate to written representations. Therefore it is perhaps not surprising that the children in Resnick and Omanson's study who were most successful with the manipulatives were the least successful in using written representations.

IMPLICATIONS FOR INSTRUCTION WITH MANIPULATIVES

The previous discussion has several implications for understanding how to help young children to use manipulatives. In this final section, I consider implications for instruction involving manipulatives.

Manipulatives Cannot Be an End in Themselves

Perhaps the most general contribution of this chapter is to demonstrate that manipulatives cannot be used in isolation. Simply playing with a manipulative is unlikely to help children learn information that will facilitate their understanding of written representations. Indeed, it may sometimes be counterproductive.

However, this admonition does *not* mean that children do not learn from using manipulatives. Manipulatives can facilitate specific types of mathematical reasoning (Chao, Stigler, & Woodward, 2000; Resnick & Omanson, 1988). The problem is that this knowledge if often disconnected from other (written) representations. Manipulatives therefore can be only one part of an integrated system of instruction (Hiebert et al., 1997). The problem from the point of view of this chapter is not that manipulatives do not work; the problem is that they sometimes have been assumed to work in an almost magical fashion (Ball, 1992). Like all instructional techniques, manipulatives have their advantages and disadvantages.

Manipulatives Do Not Obviate Teachers.

The examples throughout this paper make one point especially clear: Whether manipulatives will help, hurt, or make no difference in children's acquisition of mathematics concepts depends greatly upon the role of the teacher in the process. Students must be guided to help make a discovery with the manipulative. Without such guidance, manipulatives may do as much harm as good.

More specifically, teachers play a critical role both in helping children understand how the manipulative system represents number *and* in linking those representations to written representations. The challenge for the teacher will be to figure out when, and how, to introduce and reinforce correspondences between the manipulative representation of a mathematics problem and it's corresponding written representation. Traditionally, it has often been assumed that manipulative use should precede the introduction of symbolic representations (Uttal, Scudder, & DeLoache, 1997). Proponents of this view suggest that children should first grasp the initial concepts through manipulatives, and that written representations should be introduced only after the child has fully grasped the concept that the manipulatives can represent. It may be useful, however, to consider introducing written representations at the same time as manipulatives-based representations, so that children do not segregate the two types of solutions. This suggestion would be most appropriate for children of ages 6 or older, who are more likely to appreciate that the same problem can be represented in more than one way.

Effective Manipulative Use Takes Time

Several lines of research have shown that for manipulatives to be effective, they must be used repeatedly for the same concept (Chao, Stigler, & Woodward, 2000; Fernandez, Clea; Yoshida, Makoto; Stigler, J.W, 1992; Hiebert & Carpenter, 1992; Hiebert & Wearne, 1993, 1996; Hiebert et al., 1997). Part of the reason is practice; children need time to learn how the manipulatives work, how different numbers and operations are represented, etc. However, research on symbolic development also points to another reason: over time children lose interest in the manipulatives as objects in themselves. Consequently, it may be easier for the children to think about how the manipulatives relate to written representations. In other words, when manipulatives are first introduced, they are interesting as objects in themselves, and hence the potential relation to written representations may be difficult for children to perceive. However, with extensive practice, the manipulatives become a normal part of the classroom activities, and hence the students may now be able to focus on what the manipulatives are intended to represent in writing.

Attractive or Interesting Manipulatives May Not Always be Best

A related suggestion concerns the validity of a common assumption regarding the value of interesting or attractive manipulatives. It is often assumed that manipulatives should be interesting and attractive to be effective. However, the review of research on symbolic development strongly suggests that attractive manipulatives may sometimes be counterproductive; they may cause children to focus on the superficial properties of the manipulatives as objects rather than on their relation to written representations (See also Gentner & Ratterman, 1991).

In this regard, it is interesting to note that not all teachers emphasize diversity in choosing manipulatives. For example, Japanese teachers tend to stick with a limited set of manipulatives and use these consistently throughout the early elementary school years. Stevenson and Stigler (1992), who have conducted extensive research on cross-cultural differences in mathematics achievement, have observed the following:

> Japanese teachers... use the items in the math set repeatedly throughout the elementary school years... American teachers seek variety. They may use Popsicle sticks in one lesson, and marbles, Cheerios, M&M's, checkers, poker chips, or plastic animals in another. The American view is that using a variety of representational materials may confuse children, and thereby make it more difficult for them to use the objects for the representation and solution of mathematics problems (pp. 186-187).

SUMMARY AND CONCLUSIONS

There is no doubt that play is critical to child development. But when learning involves an appreciation of symbolic relations, play may be a dual-edged sword. On the one hand, playing with an object may increase children's interest in and attention to the object. But on the other hand, playing with an object may cause children to have difficulty focusing on what the object is intended to represent. Put another way, the development of an understanding of symbolic relations requires that children *distance* themselves (Sigel, 1993) from the properties of the symbols as objects. Play may at times make distancing more difficult. In this chapter, I have applied this analysis to the use of manipulatives in early mathematics instruction. My goal in this chapter has been to bring a new perspective to understanding both the advantages and disadvantages of using manipulatives to help children gain insight into mathematics concepts.

The general enthusiasm that many teachers have for manipulative use is well motivated. No one would want to return to the days in which the teaching of mathematics involved the repeated memorization of facts that were meaningless to young children. Manipulatives are developmentally appropriate in the sense that they are designed to match young children's level of understanding, which often focuses on concrete properties of objects and relations. But acquiring a mathematics concept from manipulatives does not guarantee that children will understand how or why the same concept can be expressed in writing. While it is certainly true that young children learn best through play, it is also equally true that teachers must place this play into an educational context. There is nothing magical about manipulatives; like any form of instruction, they have both strengths and weaknesses. Teachers have the critically important task of taking advantage of what manipulatives can offer while helping to prevent the problems that they can engender.

Acknowledgments: Portions of this chapter were supported by NSF Grant NSF 0087516 and NIH R29HD34929 awarded to Northwestern University. I thank Judy DeLoache for her continuing support and discussion of these topics.

REFERENCES

Ball, D. (1992). Magical hopes: Manipulatives and the reform of math education. *American Educator, 16,* 14-18.

Bialystok, E. (1992). Symbolic representation of letters and numbers. *Cognitive Development, 7,* 301-316.

Bruner, J. S. (1966). *Toward a theory of instruction.* Cambridge, MA: Bilknap.

Chandler, M. J., & Sokol, B. W. (1999). Representation once removed: Children's developing conceptions of representational life. In I. Sigel (Ed.) *Development of mental representation* (pp. 201-230). Mahwah, NJ: Erlbaum.

Chao, S. J.; Stigler, J., Woodward, J. A. (2000). The effects of physical materials on kindergartners' learning of number concepts. *Cognition & Instruction, 18,* 285-316.

DeLoache, J. S. (1987). Rapid change in the symbolic functioning of very young children. *Science, 238,* 1556-1557.

DeLoache, J. S. (1991). Symbolic functioning in very young children: Understanding of pictures and models. *Child Development, 62,* 736-752.

DeLoache, J. S. (2000). Dual representation and young children's use of scale models. *Child Development, 71,* 329-338.

DeLoache, J. S., Miller, K. F., & Rosengren, K. S. (1997). The credible shrinking room: Very young children's performance with symbolic and non-symbolic relations. *Psychological Science, 8,* 308-313.

Fernandez, C., Yoshida, M., Stigler, J. W. (1992). Learning mathematics from classroom instruction: On relating lessons to pupils' interpretations. *Journal of the Learning Sciences, 2,* 333-365.

Genter, D., & Ratterman, M. (1991). Language and the career of similarity. In S. A. Gelman & J. P. Byrnes (Ed.), *Perspectives on language and thought: Interrelations in development* (pp. 225-277). New York: Cambridge University Press.

Gopnick, A., & Rosati, A. (2001). Duck or rabbit: Reversing ambiguous figures and understanding ambiguous representations. *Developmental Science, 4,* 175-183.

Hiebert, J. (1989). The struggle to link written symbols with understandings: An update. *Arithmetic Teacher, 36,* 38-44.

Hiebert, J., & Carpenter, T. P. (1992). Learning and teaching with understanding. In D. A. Grouws (Ed), *Handbook of research on mathematics teaching and learning,* (pp. 65-97). New York: Macmillan.

Hiebert, J., Carpenter, T. P., Fennema, E., Fuson, K.C., Wearne, D., Murray, H., Human, P., & Olivier, A. (1997). *Making sense: Teaching and learning mathematics with understanding.* Portsmouth, NH: Heinemann.

Hiebert, J., & Wearne, D. (1993). Instructional tasks, classroom discourse, and students' learning in second-grade arithmetic. *American Educational Research Journal, 30,* 393-425.

Hiebert, J., & Wearne, D. (1996). Instruction, understanding, and skill in multidigit addition and subtraction. *Cognition and Instruction, 14,* 251-283.

Hughes, M. (1986). *Children and number: Difficulties in learning mathematics.* Oxford, England: Basil Blackwell.

Lesh, R. (1999). The development of representational abilities in middle school mathematics. In I. Sigel (Ed.), *Development of Mental Representation* (pp. 323-349). Mahwah, NJ: Erlbaum.

Piaget, J. (1964). *The child's conception of the world.* London: Routeledge & K. Paul.

Resnick, L. B., & Omanson, S. F. (1987). Learning to understand arithmetic. In R. Glaser (Ed.), *Advances in instructional psychology.* (Vol. 3, pp. 41-96). Hillsdale, NJ: Erlbuam.

Resnick, M., Martin, F., Sargent, R., and Silverman, B. (1996). Programmable Bricks: Toys to Think With. *IBM Systems Journal, 35,* 443-452, 1996.

Resnick, M., Martin, F., Berg, R., Borovoy, R., Colella, V., Kramer, K., and Silverman, B. (1998) Digital Manipulatives, *Proceedings of CHI '98,* Los Angeles.

Rock, I., Gopnick, A., & Hall, S. (1994). Do young children reverse ambiguous figures? *Perception, 23,* 635-644.

Ruzic, R. & O'Connell, K. *Manipulatives.* National Center on Accessing the General Curriculum. Retrieved December 5, 2001. Available at http://www.cast.org/ncac/Manipulatives1666.cfm

Sigel, I. E. (1993). The centrality of a distancing model for the development of representational competence. In R. R. Cocking & K. A. Renninger (Eds.), *The development and meaning of psychological distance* (pp. 141-158). Hillsdale, NJ: Erlbaum.

Sodian, B. (1990). Understanding verbal communication: Children's ability to deliberately manipulate ambiguity in referential messages. *Cognitive Development, 5*, 209-222.

Sowell, E. J. (1989). Effects of manipulative materials in mathematics instruction. *Journal for Research in Mathematics Education, 20*, 498-505.

Stevenson, H. W., & Stigler, J. W. (1992). *The learning gap: Why our schools are failing and what we can learn from Japanese and Chinese education.* New York: Summit Books.

Taylor, M. (1988). Conceptual perspective-taking: children's ability to distinguish what they know from what they see. *Child Development, 59*, 703-718.

Taylor, M., Cartwright, B.S., & Bowden, T. (1991). Perspective-taking and theory of mind: do children predict interpretive diversity as a function of differences in observer's knowledge? *Child Development, 62*, 1334-1351.

Uttal, D. H. (in press). Dual Representation and Children's Understanding of Educational Symbols. *Journal of Applied Developmental Psychology.*

Uttal, D. H., Schreiber, J. C., & DeLoache, J. S. (1995). Waiting to use a symbol: The effects of delay on children's use of models. *Child Development, 66*, 1875-1889.

Uttal. D. H., Liu, L. L., & DeLoache, J. S. (1999). Taking a hard look at concreteness: Do concrete objects help young children learn symbolic relations? In L. Balter & C. S. Tamis-LeMonda (Eds.), *Child Psychology: A Handbook of Contemporary Issues* (pp. 177-192). Philadelphia: Psychology Press.

Uttal, D. H., Scudder, K. V., & DeLoache, J. S. (1997). Manipulatives as symbols: A new perspective on the use of concrete objects to teach mathematics. *Journal of Applied Developmental Psychology, 18*, 37-54.

Von Glaserfeld, E. (1996). Aspects of radical constructivism and its educational recommendations. In L. P. Steffe, P. Nesher, P. Cobb, G. A. Goldin, & B. Greer (Eds.), *Theories of mathematical learning* (pp. 307-314). Mahwah, NJ: Erlbaum.

CHAPTER 7

PLAY AND EARLY DEVELOPMENT AND EDUCATION
The Instantiation of Parental Belief Systems

**Jaipaul L. Roopnarine, Meera Shin,
Kwanghee Jung, and Ziarat Hossain**

This paper examines parental beliefs about the significance of play for childhood development and the early childhood curriculum. After laying down some theoretical propositions on how parental belief systems are formulated, an overview of research on parental cultural models about play is provided. This literature points to the tremendous intra-cultural and inter-cultural variations in belief models about the value of play for both childhood development and early childhood education practices. Parental beliefs seem to fall along a continuum: parents in some societies embrace play as the sin qua non of early childhood socialization experiences, while in others they seem less impressed by its possibility for contributing to childhood development. The implications of the diverse parental belief models are discussed within the classic didactic instruction versus play-based constructivist model of early

Contemporary Perspectives on Play in Early Childhood Education
A Volume in: Contemporary Perspectives in Early Childhood Education, pages 115–132
Copyright © 2003 by Information Age Publishing, Inc.
All rights of reproduction in any form reserved.
ISBN: 1-930608-31-4 (cloth), 1-930608-30-6 (paper)

childhood education. A plea is made to examine parental beliefs about play in early childhood education using the *trajectory principle*.

Across societies, parents hold culturally constituted beliefs about parenting and childhood development (Goodnow & Collins, 1990; Super & Harkness, 1997). For example, they have specific ideas or ethnotheories about "independence training" (Harkness, Super, & Keefer, 1992), when children should enter school and the content of early childhood curricula (Stipek, Clements, & Daniels, 1992; Roopnarine, 1999), modes of disciplining children (Leo-Rhynie, 1997), degree of children's compliance to adult caregivers (Katgicabasi, 1996), and the value of different parent-child activities (e.g., playful interactions) for the development of social and cognitive skills during the childhood years (Gaskins, 2001). While some parental belief systems are readily apparent in everyday socialization practices, others are tacit surfacing when there are discrepancies between existing cultural schemas and the demands brought about by new childrearing experiences or institutional practices (Goodnow & Collins, 1990; Holloway, Rambaud, Fuller, & Eggers-Peirola, 1995).

A key aspect of parental belief systems is the nature of their variation within and across cultures (see Knight & Goodnow, 1988). Noteworthy differences have been observed at different educational levels (Bowman, 1992), in different socioeconomic groups (Zinsser, 1991), and by ethnicity (Goodnow, Cashmore, Cotton, and Knight, 1984; Cashmore & Goodnow, 1986). Analyzing such variations is informative in that it helps us interpret the virtue parents from different cultural milieus place on particular modes of socialization and the expectations they have for childhood development and education. In this paper, we first discuss broadly parental belief systems in the context of psycho-cultural theories of child development (Super & Harkness, 1997; Weisner, 1998; Whiting & Whiting, 1963) before turning to an overview of parents' ideas about the value of play for childhood development and early childhood education across cultures. This is followed by a discussion of the implications of these belief systems for early childhood education practices.

PREAMBLE

In early childhood education systems around the world, there has been noticeable movement toward child-centered approaches in educating young children or education that is sensitive to children's needs (Johnson, 2001). Yet in many societies and in different ethnic groups (see Bowman, 1991; Holloway, et al, 1995), there are major disagreements about what constitutes appropriate education (e.g., didactic instruction versus constructivist views on learning) for young children and on the importance placed on play activities for childhood development. While different organizations (e.g., National Association for the Education of Young Children (NAEYC); Bredekamp & Copple, 1997) and distinguished bodies (e.g., National Academy of Sciences Early Childhood Education Group) within the United States have addressed different aspects of culture and developmentally-appropriate practices, much confusion remains regarding the role of parental belief systems in designing and implementing early education programs.

Early childhood education professional groups (e.g., NAEYC) and play researchers in North America (see Johnson, Christie & Yawkey, 1999; Roskos & Christie, 2000) and Europe (see Trageton, Hagesaeter, & Helming, 1999, on play in Norwegian children) have consistently pointed to the value of play in the acquisition of cognitive and social skills during early childhood, and have maintained that play, rather than more direct instructional techniques, should be at the heart of the early childhood curriculum. But this belief may not be universally accepted because it fails to underscore that some groups of families (e.g., East Indian, Caribbean, Korean, Thai) place a high premium on educational systems that emphasize a strong push for learning the basics early in life, and subscribe to the premise that there is a critical window during the preschool years that not only prepares children for academic success but makes it easier for them to learn fundamental academic skills that are required for later school success (Parmar, Harkness, Super, & Johnson, 2001; Roopnarine, 1999). Furthermore, in a few societies (e.g., Hadza, Mayan children), play may be replaced by subsistence-type activities (Bock, 2001; Lancy, in press), and in the minds of parents relegated as secondary to childhood development.

As will become apparent, beliefs about the importance of play in childhood development is not uniform across cultures (see Bloch & Wichaidat, 1986; Pan, 1994; Hess, Price, Dickson, & Conroy, 1981; Lancy, in press). A difficulty that arises is that parental belief systems that center around the acquisition of academic skills early in childhood have the potential of colliding with the highly recommended developmentally appropriate practices approach embedded in constructivst principles (Bredekamp & Copple, 1997). Quite possibly, parents who are informed by the belief that play is incidental or frivolous to childhood development may show more reluctance to adopt play-based developmentally appropriate practices at home and at school. The most obvious outcome of codifying parents' ideas about the value of play in early childhood development is discerning the connection between childrearing and play. A provocative question that remains largely unanswered is: What developmental characteristics do parents from diverse cultural backgrounds assign to play, and what implications might these belief systems have for educating children from these diverse backgrounds?

THEORETICAL FRAMEWORKS ON
PARENTAL BELIEFS

Psycho-cultural theorists and researchers (e.g., Harkness & Super, 1996; Weisner, 1998; Whiting & Whiting, 1963) maintain that parental beliefs about growth and development influence practices and routines that are a part of children's everyday lives. An appreciation for the beliefs-practices interface is reflected in efforts to document ways to help children learn to read (Sonnenschein, Baker, Serpell, Scher, Truitt, & Munsterman, 1997), appropriate early education practices (Campbell, Goldstein, Schaefer, & Ramey, 1991; Harris & Lindauer, 1988; Rescorla, 1991; Stipek et al, 1995), parental input into children's creativity (Runco, Johnson, & Bear, 1993), parental influence over their children's social and cognitive development (Knight & Goodnow, 1988), the patterning of appropriate socialization goals for preschool-aged children from low-income households (Holloway, et al, 1995), and developmental expectations of children across cultures (for a good review see Super & Harkness, 1997).

How do parental beliefs systems or cultural models come into being? In other words, how do parents develop an interpretative framework for understanding their children's developmental needs, and how do their beliefs influence their behaviors in planning a course of action for meeting those needs? According to Super and Harkness (1997), "Parents' belief systems are related both to more general cultural belief systems and to the particular experiences of raising individual children in a specific time and place; they represent a convergence of the public and the private, the shared and the personal" (p. 17). To the "constructivist" influenced researchers (e.g., McGillicuddy-DeLisi, 1982), parents seem to modify their beliefs as a function of their daily experiences with their children. That is, parents' "internal representations" about parenting are constantly changing relative to the childrearing demands and experiences within a particular culture. As these internal representations or constructs become "reorganized" or altered, they may contain congruent as well as discongruent elements-a scenario that is more likely to occur in cultures that are witnessing dramatic social and economic changes (Super & Harkness, 1997). A competing theoretical view (Schweder, 1982) is that parental beliefs emanate from the incorporation of cultural norms that have been passed down by other generations. In a way, they are "pre-packaged" rather than "self-constructed." Allowing for the fact that there is a good deal of ambiguity surrounding parental beliefs, for the most part, early childhood researchers have stuck to the didactic-instructional (environmental) and the constructivist frameworks in assessing adults' beliefs about the socially and intellectually productive nature of play and parenting (e.g., Johnson, 1986; McGiilicuddy-DeLisi, 1985; Sameroff & Feil, 1985)).

PARENTAL BELIEFS ABOUT THE VALUE OF PLAY FOR CHILDHOOD DEVELOPMENT

Undoubtedly, the impressive array of discussions and studies within developmental and cultural psychology about parental belief systems (see Harkness & Super, 1996; Ogbu, 1991; Schweder, 1999; Weisner, 1998) have led contemporary play researchers to pay greater attention to parental concepts about the value of play in childhood development and in early childhood curricula. Central to this quest, is teasing out how parental cultural beliefs or cognitions about play influence parental encouragement of and involvement in play activities with children, and their acceptance of play as a viable component of the preschool curriculum (see Rescorla, et al, 1991). What is relevant is how beliefs about play may assist parents in shaping developmental goals and expectations for their children and whether they feature prominently in their decision-making regarding the type of early education program they eventually select (Stipek et al, 1992).

Attempts at understanding parental beliefs about play have not kept pace with research in other areas of children's play or parental concepts about childhood development. In comparison to the vast literature on the importance of play for social and cognitive development in children, the developmental sequences of different play forms, parent-child activities, and the diverse theoretical propositions on play and development (see Johnson et al, 1999; MacDonald, 1993; Roopnarine, in press; Roskos & Christie, 2000), there is correspondingly less information on parental beliefs about the value of play in young children's lives. After a few promising studies in the 1970s and 1980s, today parental beliefs about play are more systematically chronicled. We now turn to a review of this scattered and contradictory literature.

One of the earliest studies (Bishop & Chase, 1971) conducted on parents' conceptual frameworks and the home as play environment examined the link between children's creativity and favorable parental attitudes toward play. Parents' socioeconomic status, educational levels, and different dimensions of their cognitive style and personality traits (e.g., open-mindedness, adaptability, and spontaneity) were cataloged. It appears that mothers of creative children were more flexible in their conceptual style and had more favorable attitudes toward play than mothers of less creative children. Stated differently, children who were determined more "playful" during specified tasks had mothers but not fathers who displayed more differentiated belief systems. A subsequent study by Barnett and Kleiber (1984) basically found a similar relationship.

Administering primarily questionnaires, Johnson (1986) assessed European-American mothers' and teachers' beliefs about the nature of young children, general attitudes about school and play activities, and attitudes toward specific play modes for preschoolers. In this sample of mothers, there was a gap between contemporary knowledge about childrearing and development and attitudes about play. Teachers and parents from two different educational backgrounds ranked interactionist and environmental views about child development as their top choices. These similarities aside, mothers who were college-educated ranked divergent play and process learning as their preferred activities for children. By comparison, non-college-educated mothers rated convergent play and content skills as preferred activities for children. Rankings of specific activities that fall under expressive, convergent, divergent, physical, and game play revealed a similar trend: mothers with more education ranked divergent (e.g., pretending to be a favorite character) and expressive play (e.g., singing children's songs, and dance and movement) and mothers with less education ranked convergent play as preferred activities for their children. However, a closer examination of the mean rankings revealed that both groups of mothers had difficulty discriminating among the five major categories of play assessed. The preference for self-directed activities among better-educated parents has been recorded in previous work on European-American parents and teachers (Winetsky, 1981).

Using a framework similar to that of Johnson (1986) and Bloch and Wichaidat (1986), Pan (1994) explored maternal beliefs about play among a group of well-educated Taiwanese mothers with kindergarten-age children. In addition, children's free play behaviors were observed. A primary goal was to address whether mothers thought play contributed to their children's cognitive, physical, mental, or social development. From responses on a modified version of the *Maternal Attitudes Towards Children's Play Questionnaire* (Bishop & Chase, 1971), it was determined that mothers awarded the highest value to the cognitive development area, followed by the social, physical, and mental domains. The belief that play was entirely useless for development ranked far below the other areas surveyed. In as much as these mothers arranged diverse play activities for their children, the most predominant activity was constructive play, which usually involved academic pursuits such as arithmetic and alphabet play. This latter emphasis is clearly present in traditional preschools and kindergartens in Taiwan today (Johnson, 2001).

In extending the use of the play attitudes questionnaires employed in previous work (e.g., Bishop & Chase, 1971; Johnson, 1986; Pan, 1994), Soto and Negron (1994) provided data on maternal beliefs about play in migrant and non-migrant Puerto Rican families from low-income backgrounds. Both migrant and non-migrant mothers expressed confidence in the value of different domains of play for childhood development: convergent, divergent, game play, physical play, and expressive play. This notwithstanding, distinctions between the two groups did emerge. When general attitudes about school and play activities for preschool children were evaluated (i.e., divergent play, convergent play, content skills, and process learning) migrant mothers selected convergent play, while non-migrant mothers selected content skills as the most preferred activity for preschool children. Although migrant Puerto Rican mothers ranked convergent play as their first choice in preferred activities for children, their children participated in physical play activities the most-a preference observed for children in non-migrant homes also.

In a more comprehensive study of Dutch mothers and their 2- and 3-year-olds, van der Kooj and Slatts-van den Hurk (1991) examined the personal characteristics of parents, their childrearing orientation, the family climate, the play concepts of parents, the degree to which and reasons offered about why play is important, and possible ways of stimulating play in their children. Of 40 childhood activities presented, a majority of mothers considered 32 as play modes (activities ranged from sleeping to coloring). In accordance with their broad designations of what constitutes play, mothers believed that play contributed in important ways to different dimensions of childhood development: cognitive, social, personality, creativity, exploration, and socio-emotional. There were few domain-specific associations between mothers' opinions about play and the way parents intended to stimulate play.

By observing mother-child and father-child activities and their beliefs about the value of play to toddlers' development in European-American families residing in a town in central Illinois, Haight, Parke, and Black (1997) were able to demonstrate that middle-class adults attribute different developmental significance to everyday activities. Ninety-six percent of mothers and 92% of fathers reported that pretend play activities assisted children's development, 100% of mothers and fathers reported that book reading did, and 76% of mothers and 55% of fathers suggested that rough-and-tumble play did. However, book reading was judged to be more important for childhood development than pretend play, whereas pretend play was seen as more significant to childhood development than rough-and-tumble play. In accord with their responses, parents thought that book reading contributed to cognitive development and future success in school more than pretending, but that pretending was instrumental for the learning of social roles.

A comparative study (Holmes, 2001) of older children (between 8.9 and 10.6 years) and parents (mostly mothers) from Hong Kong and New Jersey allows an analysis of mothers' attitudes towards play in a culture that prizes individualism and in another in which there is an interesting mix of individualism and collectivism. The most frequent response in both societies to the question—"Why is play important to children?" was "socialization" (35.1% from Hong Kong, 45% from US). Additionally, parents from Hong Kong saw play as an avenue for self-expression (24.3%) and as educationally beneficial to children (19.6%), but no parent in the New Jersey sample viewed play as significant for the development of either construct. A more thorough interpretation of these data is hampered by the small number of respondents in each of the 11 categories of play benefit discerned.

Research on immigrant families in the United States permits some speculation on the stability of parental belief structures regarding the value of play. We asserted earlier that belief structures are modified as the demands on childrearing change due to migration to a new society or when a society is undergoing sharp socio-political and economic changes (see Super & Harkness, 1997). Accepting this line of reasoning, parents who emigrate from developing to post-industrialized societies may revise the health care and educational goals and expectations for their children post-migration. If so, there might be a drift in the more discrepant aspects of their natal cultural models of childrearing toward those that predominate in their new communities.

In an effort to explore this latter possibility, Roopnarine (1999) interviewed English-speaking Caribbean immigrant mothers and fathers (e.g., Guyanese, Trinidadian, Antiguian) on the importance of play in children's lives and interpreted their responses in terms of the matrix of beliefs commonly held in the Caribbean. The families were from middle-to lower-middle income backgrounds and had immigrated to the New York City area on average about 13 years ago. All families had a pre-kindergarten or kindergarten age child who was enrolled in an early childhood program. With the exception of one father, all parents affirmed that play was important for childhood development. Similar to Taiwanese, Dutch, and White mothers in the United States (Pan, 1994; van der Kooj & Slaats-van den Hurk, 1991; Parmar et al, 2001), Caribbean immigrant mothers and fathers acknowledged that children accrue social (opportunities to interact with other children, building friendships, cooperating and sharing in social activities with children, feeling good about self/self confidence) and cognitive benefits (learning academic skills, stimulate mind/imagination, problem solving, creativity) from play (50% of mothers and 43% of fathers gave as their first choice cognitive or social benefits). Unlike their counterparts in the aforementioned societies, though, 27% of Caribbean immigrant mothers conceptualized play as an avenue for children to relax from taxing school activities (identical to those who chose the cognitive domain), while 21% of fathers thought play offered physical benefits to children. There were no gender-of-parent differences.

This mixed pattern of results in belief systems is in stark contrast to those held by parents in the English-speaking Caribbean. Parents and early childhood teachers in the Caribbean seem largely unaware of the possibility of play as being beneficial to childhood development or to the early childhood curricula for that matter (Leo-Rhynie, 1997). Young, low-income Caribbean parents, who constitute a majority of parents in the region, rarely support their children's intellectual curiosity through play or supply them with play materials (Brown & Wint, 1988; LeoRhynie, 1997), and the aim of most childcare workers is to provide a warm and secure environment for children with very little attention paid to play and stimulation activities (Scott-Mcdonald, 1997). Emphasis is on rote memory, recitation, and learning to read.

Do the divergent attitudes toward play as an important activity among Caribbean immigrant families mean that they are reframing their childrearing belief systems? In the absence of longitudinal or comparative data, there is no way of knowing precisely what parents' pre-immigration beliefs about childrearing and development were. If we accept the theoretical proposition that parents are constantly modifying their cultural models about childrearing, then, they very well may be altering their beliefs about early academic training as their children become fully immersed in the diverse preschool and kindergarten programs in the New York City area. Given their demands on homework for preschoolers and views on what children should learn in preschool (Roopnarine, 1999), at the very least, these parents are struggling to balance their firmly entrenched beliefs about early academic training with that of constructivist principles of early education.

So far we have limited our discussion to cultures/groups in which parents share overlapping frameworks on the benefits of play for childhood development. In a few cultures, parents' beliefs about play and development favor maturational rather than interactionist interpretations (see Gaskins, 2001). Consequently, play is not interpreted as seminal to the acquisition of childhood skills as portrayed by child development experts. In these cultures, play is viewed as an intrinsic part of childhood, a belief that is best exemplified in the socialization goals of Yucatec Mayan families. In describing their beliefs about play, Gaskins (2001) notes that

> Mayan parents usually tolerate their children's play, unless it is potentially dangerous or destructive or it interferes with adult work or other adult activities. But they rarely mediate their children's play, either passively (by providing play materials or locations) or actively (by making suggestions or interfering in their children's ongoing play). And almost never do they participate in their children's play as a play partner.

Play concepts in these families are mirrored best in two socialization practices: (a) children's involvement in play provides room for uninterrupted adult activity, and (b) energy devoted to play signals that children are healthy.

The marginalization of play in early childhood development by parents is evident in the research findings of studies conducted in other industrialized and non-industrialized parts of the world as well: India, Thailand, Italy, and in the United States. Starting with work on Italian families, New (1994) observed that during infancy and toddlerhood, mothers and fathers rarely played with their children. No mother indicated that play was important for infant development and these beliefs remained stable over the toddler years. Like Mayan parents, Italian mothers saw play as occurring naturally, and as not requiring any meaningful participation by adults. Accordingly, mothers suggested that play was not integral to the maternal role. Instead, they abrogated this responsibility to siblings and extended family members.

In India (Roopnarine, Hossain, Gill, & Brophy, 1994) and Thailand (Bloch & Wichaidat, 1986) parents were also less certain about the cognitive and social value of play during the early childhood period. East Indian parents from different socioeconomic backgrounds engaged in elaborate games with children. However, this was done for the benefit of the child's enjoyment, not to increase the child's repertoire of social and cognitive skills (Roopnarine, Hooper, Ahmeduzzaman, & Pollack, 1993). Thai parents in Bangkok, too, express less optimism about the value of play in learning. They had less favorable attitudes toward play activities than teachers did, with parents whose children were enrolled in public schools reporting that play was more beneficial than those whose children were enrolled in private schools. Parents with higher levels of educational attainment had more positive views of play in the early childhood curriculum than those with lesser educational attainment (Bloch & Wichaidit, 1986). The low reliance on play for the socialization of childhood skills in Thailand was confirmed in a recent observational study of parent-child interactions in Chaing Mai Provence (Tulananda & Roopnarine, 2001). Exceedingly low rates of paternal and maternal engagement in fantasy and constructive play and in games with rules with preschool-age children were documented.

Asian immigrant mothers in the United States are equally dubious about the developmental significance of play. Parmar et al. (2001) examined Asian immigrant and European-American mothers' beliefs about play and development. Overall, European-American mothers attributed far higher significance to play for childhood development than Asian immigrant mothers did. More detailed analysis of the value attributed to different domains of play showed that Asian immigrant mothers held significantly stronger beliefs about the role of play in physical and social development, while European-American mothers held stronger beliefs about the role of play for children's individual and cognitive development. Asian immigrant mothers saw academic and social skills as more important for childhood development than play *per se*. Not surprisingly, pre-academic activities such as learning the alphabet, mathematics, and reading books were more likely to be encouraged in Asian immigrant than European-American homes. Again, a popular belief that resonates among some recent immigrants (e.g., Asian and Caribbean) is that an early start in educating children is crucial for future school success (see Farver et al, 1995; Parmar et al, 2001; Roopnarine, 1999).

To summarize: parental beliefs about the inherent intellectual, socioemotional, and physical benefits of play fall along a continuum. At the very extremes, in some societies play is the *sin qua non* of early childhood experiences, in others it remains peripheral to parental concerns about child-hood social and cognitive growth. In the middle range are societies/groups (e.g., immigrants to the US) who are now entertaining the underly-ing belief that play can contribute to childhood development other than in a physical manner. As might be expected, there were within and between culture/ethnic group differences. Nested within these were educational and socioeconomic differences.

PARENTAL BELIEFS ABOUT PLAY IN THE EARLY CHILDHOOD CURRICULUM: A PARADOX

The classic debate on the merits of constructivist play-based early child-hood education programs rooted in the "child development" philosophy of Rosseau versus more formal academic instruction based on the views of Locke has been revived once again in the national media (see Steinberg, 2001). Predictably, the same old passions have been stirred. Taking a strong stand, some caution that early academic pressures can cause anxi-eties for children that could negatively influence later schooling (Elkind, 1981, 1987), while others have found that parents expect academic skills of young children (Hess, Price, Dickson, & Conroy, 1981; Knudsen-Lindauer & Harris, 1989; Pan, 1994; Parmar et al, 2001: Roopnarine, 1999).

Regardless on which side of the intellectual debate one falls (see Res-corla, et al, 1991), there is scientific agreement that parents' involvement in children's academic pursuits at home and at school, the pervasive emphasis on the importance of education, parents' monitoring of school progress, frequent parent-teacher contacts, and parental involvement in school management and governance and input in school curricula are all linked to successful schooling (Comer, 1988; Roopnarine, 1999; Stevenson, Chen & Uttal, 1990). Having said that, parents from diverse cultural back-grounds seem to hold different beliefs about the nature and content of early childhood education and there may be more variability in parental preference for early academic training than has been previously acknowl-edged. This begs the question: Are parents so passionately divided about early academic training that they stand at different ends of the didactic instruction versus play-based education debate?

To answer this question more fully, we take a look at some of the research findings on beliefs and attitudes about the academic expectations of young children. This is because direct assessments of parental beliefs about play in early childhood education often emerge as an offshoot of investigations on views about preschool or kindergarten education (see Tobin, Wu, & Davidson, 1989). A case in point is a series of papers in *New Directions in Child Development* written by Rescorla (1991) and her col-leagues (Hirsh-Pasek, 1991; Hyson, 1991; Stipek, 1991). Drawing from the findings discussed in this volume, it can be said that early childhood programs are dispersed along a continuum and do not necessarily cluster at either end of the didactic instruction-constructivist dichotomy (Stipek, 1991).

Turning to studies that have solicited adult responses about play in the early childhood curricula, we again witness strong cross-cultural and within culture variability. Using multivocal ethnographic techniques, Tobin et al. (1989) compared children in early childhood settings in the United States, Japan, and China. It was reported that the United States fell between Japan and China on dimensions of play and academic values for young children. In responding to the question "Why should a society have preschool?" 70% of the Japanese, 42% of the United States, and only 25% of the Chinese sample gave 'opportunities for playing with other children' in their top three reasons. Academic goals were within the top three choices of 67% of the Chinese sample, 51% of the United States sample, and only 2% of the Japanese sample. The Japanese, it seems, are concerned about educational burn-out before the educational 'rat race' is over and prefer to stress kodomo rashii kodomo ("child-like children") during the early preschool years, while the Chinese favor preschool as a place for serious learning. Rather than 'play is the child's work', 'work (academics) is a form of child's play'.

To add to this confusion are the findings of three other research projects. In one (Carlson, & Stenmalm-Sjoblom, 1989), parents' perceptions of early education programs were compared in a county in Samaland, Sweden and St. Louis county in Minnesota. Parents in Sweden were more likely to rate creative materials (props, puppets, and musical instruments) and high-mobility materials (riding toys, woodworking equipment, and climbing structures) and creative dramatics (role playing in daily tasks of life) as important in early education than parents in the US. Parents in the US were more likely to value coloring books, lined paper, and technological equipment, rote counting, a stimulating physical environment, and field trips as important for early education than parents in Sweden. In line with the preceding, Latina, White, and Black mothers from low-income backgrounds residing in the Boston area preferred didactic caregiver-directed activities that stressed numeracy and literacy skills and music, reading, cooking, and field trips. Play was not seen as important for learning but parents did recognize the contributions of play to physical and emotional development (Holloway et al., 1995). Likewise, parents of Anglo-American children living in the Los Angeles area saw play, especially pretend play, as a tool for cognitive and language growth and school readiness. By contrast, Korean-American parents did not share these beliefs (Farver, Kim, & Lee, 1995; Farver & Shin, 1997). They favored a stronger orientation toward an academic program for preschoolers.

THE IMPLICATIONS FOR UNDERSTANDING PARENTAL BELIEFS IN EARLY CHILDHOOD EDUCATION

Policymakers, educators, and practitioners are increasingly realizing that the theorizing and research behind the child development knowledge that forms the foundation for education practices for diverse groups of children must be informed by other disciplines such as anthropology, ethnic studies, and cultural psychology (see Meacham, 1996; Ogbu, 1991; Schweder, 1999; Super & Harkness, 1997; Weisner, 1998). The theoretical and empirical evidence reviewed herein concerning parental beliefs about the value of play points to the importance of understanding the developmental niche—parental psychology, the eco-cultural setting, and customs—of children and their families before defining and articulating guidelines for practices and policies in early childhood education. The testimonials of parents in diverse cultures about their beliefs about the professed benefits of play suggest that the debate regarding didactic instruction versus play-based early education is not that polarized (see Stipek, 1991). Irrespective of the variations in parental beliefs about play, children in all of the societies mentioned above found time to play or to weave work and play together (e.g., Children in Botswana, Bock, 2001). It is likely that parental beliefs about didactic instruction and play-based education overlap to some degree.

In discussing the implications of cultural belief systems or cultural models about the importance of play, we build on the *trajectory principle* outlined by Sigel (1991) in a very thoughtful commentary on educational programs for preschool children from different economic and cultural backgrounds. This principle states that "what is done to children during these formative years leaves some impression on the quality and quantity of their growth in social, emotional, and cognitive domains." In keeping with Sigel's proposition, it is argued that discussions of play in the early childhood curriculum could profit from a consideration of the immediate and long-term educational goals and expectations for children within diverse cultural groups (see Super & Harkness, 1997; Valsiner, 1987). Indeed research (see Super & Harkness, 1997) has demonstrated that parents not only have different goals and expectations and developmental timetables for the acquisition of childhood skills, they also appear to express distinct beliefs about what aspects of behavior and development should be influenced by early childhood education (Roopnarine, 1999). To successfully design early childhood programs that meet the needs of diverse learners, it is important that parent's cultural beliefs about education and achievement be placed at the center of the "appropriate" early childhood practices crusade. Such a stance acknowledges that parents prioritize the educational and social goals for their children based on their interpretation of the opportunities and hazards of the immediate physical and cultural environment. For example, in less economically privileged groups, families may efficiently prioritize their child development and educational goals to include the molding of behaviors for schooling (e.g., behaviors, staying out of trouble) (Sigel, 1991) and/or focusing on early academic skills that will give their children an "even or head start" when formal schooling begins (Roopnarine, 1999). In both cases, play may be placed toward the bottom of the hierarchy of educational and social activities that serve as the nexus to early academic success. Simply put, some parents do not have the luxury of embracing the social skills enhancement approach as others from more advantaged backgrounds do.

So where does this leave us? It is highly unlikely that the didactic instruction-play-based controversy will end any time soon. Because of the diversity of educational and social needs among children from different cultural backgrounds, we call attention to the same question raised by Sigel (1991) about a decade ago. Taking cultural beliefs into consideration, what are the educational expectations and goals for different groups of children and how do we tailor educational practices to best meet those needs? Prudent answers to this question may lie along a continuum that is neither totally play-based nor academically inclined. Early childhood teachers already use conjoined approaches that include academic and play-based activities (Pan, 1994; Smith & Shepard, 1988) which are driven, in part, by parental beliefs about the salubrious effects of specific cognitive and social activities that constitute the early childhood curriculum. There is a good chance that high quality early childhood programs use the "balloon" rather than the "piston" model in meeting children's needs. Instead of frowning upon the adequacy of particular programs, it may be wise to highlight how each could better meet the educational needs of different groups of children taking into account parental beliefs and goals about early childhood education.

NOTE

Portions of this paper were presented at the Association for the Study of Play Meetings in San Diego, California, February 2001.

REFERENCES

Barnett, L. A., & Kleiber, D. A. (1984). Playfulness and the play environment. *The Journal of Genetic Psychology, 144,* 153-164.
Bereiter, C., & Engelmann, S. (1966). *Teaching disadvantaged children in the preschool.* Englewood Cliffs, NJ: Prentice Hall.

Bishop, D. W., & Chase, C. A. (1971). Parental conceptual systems, home play environment, and potential creativity in children. *Journal of Experimental Child Psychology, 12*, 318-338.

Bloch, M., & Adler, L. (1994). African children's play and the emergence of the sexual division of labor. In J. Roopnarine, J. Johnson, & F. Hooper (eds.), *Children's play in diverse cultures.* (pp. 148-178) Albany: SUNY Press.

Bloch, M., & Wichaidat, W. (1986). Play and school work in the kindergarten curriculum: Attitudes of parents and teachers in Thailand. *Early Child Development and Care, 24*, 197-218.

Bock, J. (2001). Forms of play and preparation for future work. Paper presented at the Association for the Study of Play Meetings, San Diego, CA.

Bowman, B. T. (1992). Reaching potentials of minority children through developmentally and culturally appropriate programs. In S. Bredekamp & R. Rosegrant (Eds.), *Reaching potentials: Appropriate curriculum and assessment for young children* (pp. 128-136). Washington, DC: NAEYC.

Campbell, F., Goldstein, S., Schaefer, E. S., & Ramey, C. T. (1991). Parental beliefs and values related to family risks, educational intervention, and child academic competence. *Early Childhood Research Quarterly, 6*, 167-182.

Carlson, H., & Stenmalm-Sjoblom, L. (1989). A cross-cultural study of parents' perceptions of early childhood programs. *Early Childhood Research Quarterly, 4*, 505-522.

Cashmore, J. A., & Goodnow, J. J. (1986). Influences on Australian parents' values: Ethnicity versus socioeconomic status. *Journal of Cross-Cultural Psychology, 17*, 441-454.

Bredekamp, S., & Copple, C. (Eds.). (1997). *Developmentally appropriate practice in early childhood programs* (Rev. ed.). Washington, DC: NAEYC.

Comer, J. P. (1988). Educating poor minority children. *Scientific American, 259 (5)*, 42-48.

Elkind, D. (1981). *The hurried child.* Reading, MA: Addison-Wesley.

Elkind, D. (1987). *Miseducation: Preschoolers at risk.* New York: Knopf.

Farver, J. A. M., Kim, Y. K., & Lee, Y. (1995). Cultural difference in Korean- and Anglo-American preschoolers' social interaction and play behaviors. *Child Development, 66*, 1088-1099.

Farver, J. A. M. & Shin, Y. L. (1997). Social pretend play in Korean- and Anglo-American preschoolers. *Child Development, 68*, 544-556.

Gaskins, S. (2001). Ignoring play: Will it survive?: A Mayan case study of beliefs and behavior. Paper presented at the Association for the Study of Play Meetings, San Diego, CA.

Goodnow, J. J., & Collins, W. A. (1991). *Development according to parents: The nature, sources, and consequences of parents' ideas.* Hillsdale, NJ: Erlbaum.

Haight, W. L., Parke, R. D., & Black, J. E. (1997). Mothers' and fathers' beliefs about and spontaneous participation in their toddlers' pretend play. *Merrill-Palmer Quarterly, 43*, 271-291.

Harkness, S., & Super, C. (Eds.) (1996). *Parents' cultural belief systems: Their origins, expressions, and consequences.* New York: Guilford.

Harkness, S., Super, C., & Keefer, C. (1992). Learning to be an American parent: How cultural models gain directive force. In R. G. D'Andrade & C. Strauss (Eds.), *Human motives and cultural models* (pp. 163-178). New York: Cambridge University Press.

Harris, K., & Lindauer, S. L. K. (1988). Parental and teacher priorities for kindergarten preparation. *Child Study Journal, 18*, 61-73.

Hess, R. D., Kashiwagi, K., Azuma, H., Price, G. G., & Dickson, W. P. (1980). Maternal expectations of mastery of developmental tasks in Japan and the United States. *International Journal of Psychology, 15*, 259-271.

Hess, R. D., Price, G. G., Dickson, W. P., & Conroy, M. (1981). Different roles of mothers and teachers: Contrasting styles of child care. In S. Kilmer (Ed.), *Advances in early education and day care*. Vol. 2. Greenwich, CT: JAI.

Hirsh-Pasek, K. (1991). Pressure or challenge in preschool? How academic environments affect children. In L. Rescorla, M. C. Hyson, & K. Hirscsh-Pasek (Eds.), *Instruction in early childhood: Challenge or pressure. New Directions for Child Development, 53*, 39-46.

Holloway, S. D., Rambaud, M. F., Fuller, B., & Eggers-Pierola, C. (1995). What is "appropriate practice" at home and in child care?: Low-income mothers' view on preparing their children for school. *Early Childhood Research Quarterly, 10*, 451-473.

Holmes, R. (2001). Parental notions about their children's playfulness and children's notions of play in the United States and Hong Kong. In S. Reifel (Ed.), *Theory in context and out: Play and culture studies*, Vol. 3. (pp. 291-314). Westport, CT: Ablex.

Hyson, M. (1991). The characteristics and origings of the academic preschool. In L. Rescorla, M. C. Hyson, & K. Hirssh-Pasek (Eds.), *Instruction in early childhood: Challenge or pressure. New Directions for Child Development, 53*, 21-29.

Kagitcibasi, C. (1996). *Family and human development across cultures: A view from the other side*. Mawah, NJ: Earlbaum

Knight, R. A., & Goodnow, J. J. (1988). Parents' beliefs about influence over cognitive and social development. *International Journal of Behavioral Development, 11*, 517-527.

Knudsen-Lindauer, S., & Harris, K. (1989). Priorities for kindergarten curricula: Views of parents and teachers. *Journal of Research on Childhood Education, 4*, 51-61.

Johnson, J. (2001). Taiwanese teacher educators', teachers', and parents' views on play. Paper presented at the Association for the Study of Play Meetings, San Diego, CA.

Johnson, J. (1986). Attitudes toward play and beliefs about development. In B. Mergen (Ed.), *Cultural dimensions of play, games, and sport. The Association for the Study of Play*, Volume 10. (pp. 98-102), Champaign, IL: Human Kinetic Publishers

Johnson, J. E., Christie, J., Yawkey, T. (1999). *Play and early childhood development*. New York: Longman.

Lancy, D. (in press). Cultural constraints on children's play. In J. L. Roopnarine (Ed.), *Play and culture studies: Conceptual, contextual, and social-cognitive connections*. Vol. 4,. Stamford, CT: Greenwood.

Leo-Rhynie, E. (1997). Class, race, and gender issues in child rearing in the Caribbean. In J. L. Roopnarine & Brown, J. (Eds.), *Caribbean families: Diversity among ethnic groups*. (pp. 25-55). Norwood, NJ: Ablex.

McGillicuddy-DeLisi, A. V. (1982). Parental beliefs about developmental processes. *Human Development, 25*, 192-200.

Meacham, J. (1996). Mind, society, and racism. *Human Development, 39*, 301-306

Ogbu, J. (1991). Immigrant and involuntary minorities in comparative perspective. In M. Gibson & J. Ogbu, (Eds.). *Minority status and schooling: A comparative study of immigrant and involuntary minorities.* (pp. 3-33). New York: Garland Publishing.

New, R. (1994). Children's play–una cosa naturale: An Italian perspective. In J.L. Roopnarine, J. E. Johnson, F. H. Hooper (Eds.), *Children's play in diverse cultures.* (pp. 123-147).Albany NY: SUNY Press.

Pan, H. W. (1994). Children's play in Taiwan. In J.L. Roopnarine, J. E. Johnson, F. H. Hooper (Eds.), *Children's play in diverse cultures.* (pp. 31-50). Albany NY: SUNY Press.

Parmar, P., Harkness, S., Super, C. M., & Johnson, J. E. (2001). Cross-cultural study of parents' ethnotheories of play and learning: Effects on home routines and children's behavior in preschool. Paper presented at the Society for Cross-Cultural Meetings, San Diego, CA.

Rescorla, L. (1991). Parent and teacher attitudes about early academics. In L. Rescorla, M. C. Hyson, & K. Hirssh-Pasek (Eds.), *Instruction in early childhood: Challenge or pressure. New Directions for Child Development, 53,* 13-19.

Roopnarine, J. L., Hossain, Z., Gill, P., & Brophy, H. (1994). Play in the East Indian context. In J.L. Roopnarine, J. E. Johnson, F. H. Hooper (Eds.), *Children's play in diverse cultures.* (pp. 9-30).Albany NY: SUNY Press.

Roopnarine, J. L., Hopper, F. H., Ahmeduzzaman, M., & Pollack, B. (1993). Gentle play partners: Mother-child and father-child play in New Delhi, India. In K. MacDonald (Ed.), *Parents and children playing* (pp. 287-304). Albany, NY: SUNY Press.

Roopnarine, J. L. (2000). Parental involvement, ethnotheories about development, parenting styles, and early academic achievement in Caribbean-American children. Paper presented in the Department of Applied Psychology, New York University.

Roskos, K. A., & Christie, J. F. (Eds.). (2000). *Play and literacy in early childhood: Research from multiple perspectives.* Mahwah, NJ: Erlbaum.

Runco, M. A., Johnson, D. J., & Bear, P. K. (1993). Parents' and teachers' implicit theories of children's creativity. *Child Study Journal, 23,* 91-113.

Sameroff, A., J., & Feil, L. A. (1985). Parental concepts of development. In I. Sigel (Ed.), *Parental belief systems* (pp. 83-105). Hillsdale, NJ: Erlbaum.

Schweder, R. A. (1999). Culture and development in our poststructural age. In A. Masten (Ed.), *Cultural processes in child development.* The Minnesota Symposia on Child Psychology, Vol. 29 (pp.137-148). Mahwah, NJ: Earlbaum.

Schweder, R. A. (1982).Beyond self-constructed knowledge: The study of culture and morality. *Merrill-Palmer Quarterly, 28,* 41-69.

Scott-Macdonald, K. (1997). The status of child care supports for Jamaican families. In J. L. Roopnarine & Brown, J. (Eds.), *Caribbean families: Diversity among ethnic groups.* (pp. 147-176). Norwood, NJ: Ablex.

Sigel, I. (1991). Preschool education: For whom and why? In L. Rescorla, M. C. Hyson, & K. Hirssh-Pasek (Eds.), *Instruction in early childhood: Challenge or pressure. New Directions for Child Development, 53,* 83-91.

Smith, M. L., & Shepard, L. A. (1988). Kindergarten readiness and retention: A qualitative study of teachers' beliefs and practices. *American Educational Research Journal, 25,* 307-333.

Sonnenschein, S., Baker, L., Serpell, R., Scher, D., Truitt, V. G., & Munsterman, K. (1997). Parental beliefs about ways to help children learn to read: The impact of entertainment or a skills perspective. *Early Child Development and Care, 127-128*, 111-118.

Soto, L. D., & Negron, L. (1994). Mainland Puerto Rican children. In J.L. Roopnarine, J. E. Johnson, F. H. Hooper (Eds.), *Children's play in diverse cultures.* (pp. 104-122).Albany NY: SUNY Press.

Steinberg, J. (2001). Bush's plan to push reading in "Head Start" stirs debate. *New York Times*, February 10.

Stevenson, H. W., Chen, C., & Uttal, D. H. (1990). Beliefs and achievement: A study of Black, White, and Hispanic children. *Child Development, 61*, 518-523.

Stipek, D. (1991). Characterizing early childhood programs. In L. Rescorla, M. C. Hyson, & K. Hirssh-Pasek (Eds.), *Instruction in early childhood: Challenge or pressure. New Directions for Child Development, 53*, 47-55.

Stipek, D., Milburn, S., Clements, D., & Daniels, D. H. (1992). Parents' beleifs about appropriate education for young children. *Journal of Applied Developmental Psychology,* 13, 293-210.

Super, C., & S. Harkness (1997). The cultural structuring of child development. In J Berry, P. Dasen, & T. Saraswathi (Eds.), *Handbook of cross-cultural psychology: Basic processes and human development* (pp.1-39). Needham, MA: Allyn & Bacon.

Tobin, J. J., Wu, D. Y., & Davidson, D. H. (1989). *Preschool in three cultures: Japan, China, and the United States.* New Haven, CT: Yale University Press.

Trageton, A., Hagesaeter, A., Helming, S. (1999). Theme-organised learning, play and physical environment in lower primary school. Paper presented at the 21st ICCP-World Play Conference, Oslo, Norway.

Tulananda, O., & Roopnarine, J. (in press). Mothers' and fathers' interactions with preschoolers in the home in Northern Thailand: Relationships to Teachers' assessments of children's social skills. *Journal of Family Psychology.*

Valsiner, J. (1987). *Culture and the development of children's action.* New York: Wiley.

van der Kooj, R., & Slaats-van den Hurk, W. (1991). Relations between parental opinions and attitudes about play and childrearing. *Play and Culture, 4*, 108-123.

Weisner, T. (1998). Human development, child well-being, and the cultural project of development. In D. Sharma & K. Fischer (Eds.), Socioemotional development across cultures. *New Directions in Child Development* (pp. 69-85). San Francisco, CA: Jossey-Bass Publishers.

Winetsky, C. S. (1978). Comparison of the expectation of parents and teachers for the behavior of preschool children. *Child Development, 49*, 1146-1154.

Whiting, B. B., & Whiting, J. (1963). *Six cultures.* New York: Wiley.

Wint, E., & Brown, J. (1987). Promoting effective parenting: A study of two methods in Kingston, Jamaica. *Child Welfare, 66*, 507-516.

Zinser, C. (1991). *Raised in East Urban: Child care changes in a working class community.* New York: Teachers College Press.

CHAPTER 8

PLAY IN CHILDREN
An Attachment Perspective

Gary Creasey and Patricia Jarvis

Many theorists view play activity as a major ability that reflects and promotes both cognitive and social competence in children (Erikson, 1950; Piaget, 1951). Young children and toddlers who engage in sophisticated pretend play (e.g., using a crayon as a phone) are often brighter than children who engage in less complex forms of play (Bond, Creasey, & Abrahms, 1990). In addition, preschoolers who engage in play that involves elaborate sociodramatic themes (e.g., "Let's play Star Wars!") are more socially competent and better liked than their counterparts that do not initiate such behavior (Creasey, Jarvis, & Berk, 1998). Because of these findings, a number of professionals have incorporated play as a central theme to their intervention work. For example, some specialists suggest that training children to play in more competent ways may encourage more acceptance within the peer group (Smilansky, 1968). Other experts stipulate that encouraging parents and children to play together may serve as a vehicle to improve relationships in the family system (Jernberg & Booth, 1999).

Because play is such a central theme to children's behavior across many societies, it is critical to better understand social and cognitive variables

Contemporary Perspectives on Play in Early Childhood Education
A Volume in: Contemporary Perspectives in Early Childhood Education, pages 133–151.
Copyright © 2003 by Information Age Publishing, Inc.
All rights of reproduction in any form reserved.
ISBN: 1-930608-31-4 (cloth), 1-930608-30-6 (paper)

that may facilitate its development. While a number of theories exist out-lining the developmental progress and social/cognitive consequences of play, a major goal of the present chapter is to examine why ethological attachment theory (Bowlby, 1982) provides an important perspective to consider for professionals interested in children's play. It is our position that integrating this perspective with other popular theories on children's play (e.g., Vygotsky, 1978) may encourage more diverse thinking about potential antecedents and consequences of this important activity.

This chapter is divided into a number of sections. First, we overview ethological attachment theory and highlight the role of play within this perspective. Next, we discuss why consideration of attachment theory may have important implications for theoretical approaches to children's play. Following this discussion, we turn to research that support's Bowlby's (1988) contention that attachment relationships form a major foundation for the development of exploration and play in children. Finally, we con-sider why such theory and research might have important implications for intervention efforts involving children's play.

BOWLBY'S ETHOLOGICAL ATTACHMENT THEORY

While a number of theories specify factors that underlie the development of infant-caregiver attachment, John Bowlby's (1982) ethological attach-ment theory is one of the most contemporary and heavily embraced per-spectives. The gradual development of close, affectional bonds between infants and caregivers is theorized as one major reason for why our species (as well as other animal species) has become successful (Bowlby, 1988). In some sense, this premise would suggest that if contact between the infant and caregiver is simply allowed then attachments between parents and chil-dren are guaranteed by our biology, and not simply an artifact of primary drive reduction or pleasurable feelings that arise from contact with par-ents. Indeed, this theory would account for why children of abusive par-ents, in the absence of pleasurable parenting behavior, become attached to their parents (Cassidy, 1999).

In the spirit of ethological theory, attachment bonds (like children's play) are a phenomenon that should be witnessed across all cultures across the world. Indeed, Bowlby's colleague, Mary Ainsworth, provided dramatic support for this premise by documenting that classic signs of infant-care-giver attachment (e.g., proximity seeking; stranger distress; separation anx-iety) can be witnessed in other societies (Ainsworth, 1967). However, while Ainsworth's work suggested that almost all infants eventually become attached to primary caregivers, the caregiving environment has been theo-rized to also produce striking differences in the quality of this attachment. To better capture this diversity, Ainsworth and colleagues developed the

Strange Situation procedure (Ainsworth, Blehar, Waters, & Wall, 1978). In this methodology, infants are paired with, and separated from, their primary caregiver, as well as a "stranger" over the course of brief observational segments. Using this method, Ainsworth identified three organized patterns of attachment that can be witnessed in infants across all cultures (e.g., Sagi, 1990). *Secure* infants often actively explore their environment when not distressed, yet seek comfort and proximity from caregivers when upset. *Avoidant* infants tend to distance themselves from caregivers and rely on themselves (or focus on the environment) for comfort during times of potential distress. *Ambivalent* or *resistant* infants tend to have great difficulty with exploration, often seek contact with caregivers during times of duress in an angry manner, and can not be comforted by caregivers (Ainsworth et al., 1978). The latter two attachment classifications are often viewed as signs of attachment insecurity.

It should be pointed out that in Ainsworth's original 3-way attachment classification scheme (secure, avoidant, resistant), a percentage of infants could not be classified into one of these traditional categories. Upon reexamining these infants, Main and Solomon (1990) concluded that these infants did not appear to have an organized attachment system and classified these cases as *disorganized/disoriented.* Such infants seem to dramatically oscillate between approach and avoidant behavior, and often display bizarre and contradictory behavior towards their caregivers. For example, the infant, upon seeing the parent return to the room, may begin to approach the caregiver and suddenly freeze or put their hands over their eyes (Jacobvitz & Lyons-Ruth, 1999).

While most of the empirical attachment research has concentrated on the development of infant attachment, it is quite incorrect to view Bowlby's approach as solely focusing on the development of infant-caregiver attachment. Perhaps one of the greatest contributions of this theorist was his perspective on the role of attachment relationships after the period of attachment dependence normally associated with infancy. It was Bowlby's position that early infant and childhood experiences with parents gradually become internalized in the form of cognitive working models of attachment (Bowlby, 1988). These working models are conceptualized as both conscious and unconscious schemas and expectancies regarding past and future attachment relationships, and are thought to guide affect, thinking, and behavior in relationships across the life-span (Bretherton, 1985).

It has been documented that during adulthood, individuals develop different working models of attachment that closely parallel the infant patterns of attachment (Main, Kaplan, & Cassidy, 1985). For example, adults with *secure/autonomous* working models of attachment view attachment as an open topic, value close relationships, and are able to process attachment relevant information in a timely and efficient manner (e.g., Main et al., 1985; Main, 1996). *Dismissing* adults tend to rely heavily on themselves when distressed, view attachment relationships as relatively unnecessary, and have great difficulties processing information relevant to attachment. *Preoccupied* individuals often display angry feelings towards attachment figures, harbor deep fears of rejection and abandonment, and appear "confused, unobjective and preoccupied with past relationships within the family and/or past experiences" (Main & Goldwyn, 1994, p. 140). Finally, *unresolved/ disorganized* adults possess poorly integrated attachment representations regarding previous loss or trauma, and often display startling lapses in the monitoring of reasoning and thinking during such discussions. For example, the individual may begin speaking of a deceased parent in the present tense, or, incorrectly assume responsibility for the onset of abuse during childhood (Main & Goldwyn, 1994).

In support of this aforementioned theory, attachment researchers have posted an impressive array of reliability and validity work on both the Strange Situation, as well as methodologies designed to capture working models of attachment in older populations (e.g., Adult Attachment Interview; George, Kaplan, & Main, 1996). Infant attachment classifications are relatively stable over time, and predict many important outcomes during childhood and adolescence, such as social competence in the peer group, the ability to cope with stress, psychological health, and school adjustment (see Thompson, 1999 for a comprehensive review). In addition, parent working models of attachment assessed prenatally forecast eventual infant-parent attachment (e.g., Benoit & Parker, 1994). Finally, infant attachment classifications, as assessed via the Strange Situation, have been shown to longitudinally predict adult working models of attachment (Waters, Weinfield, & Hamilton, 2000). Having briefly outlined the major tenets of attachment theory, we next turn to theory suggesting important connections between the development of attachment, infant exploration, and the development of early object play.

ATTACHMENT PERSPECTIVES ON EXPLORATION AND PLAY

Bowlby remarks in a number of works that children's play, like attachment, is a universal phenomenon that can be witnessed across both human and nonhuman species. His perspective on the development of children's play was quite clear and unidirectional in nature. It was Bowlby's (1988) premise that exploration, competent play, and mastery of the environment—major fundamental milestones during early childhood (Erikson, 1950; Mahler, Pine, & Bergman, 1975)—only can occur when the child feels secure in relationships with caregivers. Additionally, attachment insecurity can only dampen these activities (cf. Ainsworth et al., 1978).

Thus, on theoretical grounds, attachment theory would suggest that children's play might be dramatically influenced by attachment difficulties in several critical ways. First, insecure attachment relationships should significantly reduce the quality of exploratory behavior (Bowlby, 1982; 1988). Thus, a child with an insecure attachment relationship with a parent may feel less inclined to explore their environment. A poverty in exploration could lead to less interest in play materials, less competent play with objects (cf. Ainsworth et al., 1978; Mahler et al., 1975; Werner & Kaplan, 1963), and less initiation of social play with peers. In addition, the social competence difficulties (e.g., negative affect; low frustration tolerance) associated with attachment problems may inhibit the inclination of others to engage in play bouts with insecure children. While all of these ideas make theoretical sense, and in parts, are incorporated in existing theories of child play, it is important to underscore the fact that Bowlby (1988) seemed to view exploration and play (particularly social play) as an outcome, rather than antecedent, of secure attachment relationships.

ATTACHMENT, EXPLORATION, AND SYMBOLIC PLAY: EMPIRICAL FINDINGS

The premise that secure attachment relationships should facilitate the development of exploratory behavior in infants has been documented in numerous empirical investigations. For example, lack of exploration (e.g., failure to leave caregiver's presence, as well as low involvement with play materials) during the Strange Situation procedure is a specific attachment behavior difficulty that may lead to an insecure attachment classification rating. Ainsworth, in her early validation work, documented that the exploratory behavior of ambivalent/resistant infants in the presence of caregivers was more suppressed than that of avoidant and secure infants (Ainsworth et al., 1978). Since this initial work, a number of researchers have documented less exploratory behavior in insecure infants, particularly infants who have been assigned an ambivalent/resistant attachment classification (Belsky, Garduque, & Hrncir, 1984; Matas, Arend, Sroufe, 1978; Main, 1983; Sroufe & Egeland, 1991).

These aforementioned findings have a number of implications. The simple exploration of objects and toys is viewed as a fundamental prerequisite to more advanced types of play behavior (Belsky et al., 1984). Thus, the finding that the exploratory behavior of ambivalent/resistant infants is actually suppressed *in the presence of caregivers* might have important implications for later play and/or learning environments, and, may contradict the notion that the presence of a caregiver automatically translates into more positive learning experiences. For example, a fundamental difficulty with ambivalent/resistant children is their tendency to focus solely on the caregiver, as opposed to the learning or play context. This finding is directly relevant to theoretical positions on children's play that stipulate that the supportive presence of caregivers is a necessary component to the development of more sophisticated abilities, including play, during later child-hood (e.g., Vygotsky, 1978).

While active exploration of one's environment is often viewed as an important skill that develops during the first two years of life (e.g., Mahler et al., 1975), it becomes apparent from observing infants and toddlers that the simple exploration and manipulation of toys gradually evolves into more functional play with objects (e.g., turning a handle on a toy), fol-lowed by increasingly more sophisticated pretend or symbolic play after the second year of life (e.g., Bretherton, 1984; Piaget, 1951). The idea that positive relationships between caregivers and infants encourage the devel-opment of symbolic processes has its origins in traditional psychoanalytic (Mahler et al., 1975) and sociocultural (Vygotsky, 1978) theories, as well as attachment theory (e.g., Ainsworth et al., 1978; Bowlby, 1982). The evolu-tion of sophisticated play behavior in young secure children is due to their ability to actively explore new and interesting objects, as well as their recep-tivity to sophisticated pretend play bouts initiated by significant others, according to attachment theory.

Available research suggests a connection between attachment security and the tendency for toddlers and young children to spontaneously exhibit more pretend play (e.g., using a block as a phone) than insecure children (Bretherton et al., 1979; Matas et al., 1978; Slade, 1987) (however, see Main, 1983, for somewhat contradictory findings). In addition, Belsky et al. (1984) documented that a major difference between secure and inse-cure children rests with their executive capacity, or ultimate potential for achieving high levels of pretend play. In this study, Belsky and colleagues observed the spontaneous play of 12-13 month secure and insecure infants, and then had research assistants attempt to encourage more sophisticated pretend play (e.g., "the doll is thirsty, give the doll a drink"). The results of the study suggested that secure infants, in general, per-formed very close to their executive capacity (or top potential) during spontaneous play bouts, while insecure infants showed a greater gap between their actual performance during free play and their eventual executive capacity. These interesting findings have also been recently repli-cated in a sample of British toddlers (Meins & Russell, 1997), leading both research teams to conclude that secure infants, because of their ability to freely explore in and out of the presence of caregivers, are able to more spontaneously display their best cognitive and social competence in play environments.

It is also interesting to note that the differences in exploratory behavior that are witnessed between ambivalent-resistant infants and their counter-parts with alternative attachment classifications (i.e., secure and avoidant) are not as well replicated when contrasting secure and insecure children on symbolic play abilities (e.g., Belsky et al., 1984; Cassidy & Berlin, 1994). For example, while ambivalent-resistant toddlers display less pretend play than secure children, the differences between the former group of children and avoidant toddlers are not as strong. What may account for this finding? Sociocultural theories of play (e.g., Vygotsky, 1978) postulate that advances in cognitive development (as well as play sophistication) come largely about through interactions with older, competent individuals. Thus, ambivalent-resistant infants may handicap themselves through failures to explore new and interesting learning and play opportunities (due to an excessive preoccupation with caregivers), while avoidant infants, in spite of their inclination to readily explore their environment, play materials, etc., are simply less receptive to mentoring due to their particular form of attachment organization.

In summary, much of the early attachment work has concentrated on establishing connections between attachment classifications, infant exploration, and the emergence of symbolic play in toddlers. This line of inquiry makes sense, because theoretically, each construct is expected to form the foundation for the development of the next capacity (i.e., attachment begets exploration, and exploration, in turn, predicts the emergence of more sophisticated play). The bulk of the research would suggest that ambivalent infants are the most at risk for exploratory problems during infancy, and that play difficulties associated with toddlerhood (deficits in pretend play and executive competence) are slower to emerge (and perhaps less pronounced) in avoidant than ambivalent children. Because play increasingly becomes more sophisticated and social over the course of early childhood, a logical next step would be to turn to research documenting associations between social play and attachment. We will first examine how attachment influences play with parents, followed by a discussion of how this construct influences play interactions with peers.

ATTACHMENT AND THE DEVELOPMENT OF SOCIAL PLAY WITH PARENTS

When conducting our own attachment and play studies (e.g., Creasey & Jarvis, 1994; Jarvis & Creasey, 1991), we noted that it became increasingly difficulty to conduct naturalistic observations of "free play" with 18- to 24-month-old toddlers in the presence of caregivers. Even when caregivers were specifically instructed not to elicit more competent play, or respond to the play bids of their children, these imposed rules were often quickly violated. In order to decrease the likelihood of parental encouragement (or even interference) during these free play bouts, we quickly realized that we needed to keep parents busy during these procedures. Thus, parents were asked to complete questionnaires and complex attachment Q-sorts—not surprisingly, for many toddlers, our distraction of parents actually seemed to *increase* toddler bids for attention and instruction during these free play bouts! We speculated that such behavior was not only highly indicative of the power of the attachment system during this time period, but also why such mentoring behavior and parental encouragement is important to toddlers in these early play/learning environments (cf. Vygotsky, 1978).

Although relations between assessments of infant attachment and the quality of later parent-child play somewhat dissipates as the child progresses through the later preschool years (e.g., Youngblade & Belsky, 1992), research supports the contention that there are close connections between the development of attachment during infancy and parent-child social play during toddlerhood. Early research on this issue supports the suggestion that securely attached infants make better "play partners" with parents than insecurely attached children (Ainsworth et al., 1978; Londerville & Main, 1981; Matas et al., 1978). For example, the data from these early studies, as well as more recent work (e.g., Teti, Nakagawa, Das, & Wirth, 1991), strongly suggest that securely attached infants display more positive affect, are more cooperative, and are more likely to seek assistance from their parents when "stuck" on play materials than their insecure counterparts. In addition, children classified as ambivalent during infancy display more negative behaviors (e.g., block throwing) in play bouts with parents during toddlerhood than their avoidant counterparts (e.g., Pastor, 1981).

Just as importantly, attachment research supports the notion that the infant-caregiver attachment relationship is not just based on issues pertaining to the infant (e.g., Ainsworth et al., 1978; Bowlby, 1982). Parents of securely attached infants are more attentive and responsive to the bids of children than parents of insecurely attached infants (NICHD Early Child Care Research Network, 1997). In terms of relating these ideas to theories on play, a number of researchers (e.g., Meins and Russell, 1997; Pastor, 1981) have concluded that parents of secure infants and children possess an ability to coordinate their behavior to the needs of their children, which in learning and play theories, is frequently referred to as scaffolding (e.g., Bruner, 1983).

Conversely, the play environments that parents construct with insecure children seem to be quite different. For example, mothers of avoidant infants are frequently described as cold and insensitive to the needs of their children and shun close contact with their infants (e.g., Egeland & Farber, 1984). In addition, Isabella & Belsky (1991) noted that mothers of ambivalent infants appeared to have difficulty paying attention to the bids of their children (cf. Pastor, 1981). In perhaps one of the best studies documenting relations between attachment security and the quality of children's play, Slade (1987) documented that toddlers classified as securely attached at approximately 18 months of age displayed the most competent social pretend play at the encouragement of their mothers, and, that these mothers *maintained* more involvement with their toddler's play while engaged in a conversation with an experimenter than the mothers of insecure toddlers (who often were very passive in their orientation toward the child). This research further highlights the need to consider attachment issues when conducting play research (or interventions). While Belsky et al. (1984) found that *experimenters* could not elicit higher levels of play in secure children, Slade (1987) documented that higher levels of social play could be elicited in secure children—*in the presence of an attachment figure* (i.e., mothers). Conversely, the presence of an experimenter appears to elicit more competent forms of play in insecure children than what one would ordinarily observe in free play, yet, the presence of a parent seems to inhibit this executive capacity!

This research has major implications for contemporary theories of children's play. For example, Vygotsky (1978) stipulated that in play and learning environments, the presence of parents and other older attachment figures in the community should directly benefit the ultimate welfare of the child. Similar to the idea of executive capacity (Belsky et al., 1984), Vygotsky theorized that the play and learning potential of children could be better mastered in the presence of older, wiser collaborators. The fact that some children actually seem to perform worse in the presence of caregivers suggests that we should better examine psychological factors that explain why some adult "mentors" display behaviors (e.g., inattentiveness; rejection) that actually undermine the performance of their children. We will address this important issue in a later section.

ATTACHMENT AND THE DEVELOPMENT OF SOCIAL PLAY WITH PEERS

Attachment theory would predict that relationship difficulties with caregivers should also influence the child's ability to engage in social play with non-familial attachment figures. Because children become increasingly involved in the peer group during the preschool years, examining relations between parent-infant attachment and the development of social play in the peer group is an important issue. In some of the best-controlled work on this issue, researchers traditionally pair focal children who had received either secure or insecure attachment classifications during infancy with peers who had received secure attachment ratings. These interactions are frequently observed in the early preschool years (e.g., ages 3-4). The researchers subsequently observe how the target child interacts with a secure, unfamiliar peer during play bouts

As one might predict, secure children tend to readily engage other peers in play and are often better "play partners" than insecure children. For example, Pastor (1981) found that the exploration problems of ambivalent children continue during the early preschool years. These children less readily initiated play interactions with peers and were more likely to ignore the play bids of other children. While avoidant children were as likely to approach peers during play than secure youth, their play bouts were more negative and frequently marked by less cooperative play. In addition, the social play of secure children is frequently more interesting than that of insecure youth. For example, Rose-Krasnor, Rubin, Booth, & Coplan (1996) classified toddlers as secure or insecure at 20 months of age and paired them with secure children at 4 years in a laboratory context. Children's social play was coded using Rubin's (1989) Play Observation Scale, which assessed the focal child's likelihood to participate in social play (as opposed to solitary or onlooker play), and their engagement in positive or negative behaviors during such interactive play. The study results suggested that during social play, secure children engaged in play themes that were more interesting than their insecure peers. For example, secure children were more likely than insecure youth to engage in more cooperative play, as well as more play that involved elaborate sociodramatic themes (e.g., "You be Batman and I'll be Wonder Woman!").

Because children who engage in play with more interesting themes are more likely to attract other peers as play partners (Creasey et al., 1998), it is not surprising that peers readily seek and accept secure children as play partners. Jacobson and Wille (1986) documented that children rated as securely attached at 18 months elicited more positive responses from peers during play bouts at 3-years of age than avoidant children. In addition, children classified as ambivalent were more likely to receive negative behaviors (e.g., "You can't play with that, it's mine!", or, "I'm going to tear your building down!") by peers than children with alternative attachment classifications. Thus, the available research would suggest that secure children not only initiate high levels of social play, but also serve as a magnet for other children because of their sophisticated play themes.

While the target children in the aforementioned studies were all paired with peers who had received secure attachment classifications, Troy and Sroufe (1987) found that insecure children were more often mistreated and victimized during peer play when paired with other peers who had received insecure attachment classifications. It has been also suggested by Sroufe (1983) that avoidant children may be more likely to victimize others during play while ambivalent-resistant children may more likely be the targets of such treatment. Because the development of bully-victim relationships is an important concern for intervention specialists, more work is needed to ascertain the role of attachment in these relationships.

While much of the early research documenting associations between attachment and the development of peer play was conducted in laboratory settings, more recent work has concentrated on examining these connections in more naturalistic contexts. For example, conducting peer play research in child care centers allows social scientists to study children in a more "real world" context, and enhances the validity of research findings because children are allowed to play with more familiar peers. Supporting the findings of laboratory researchers, a number of studies indicate that secure children are more likely to initiate and maintain interesting play themes, and display less negative behavior during these play interactions than insecure children (Cassibba, Van IJzendoorn, & D'Odorico, 2000; Suess, Grossman, & Sroufe, 1992; Turner, 1991).

In conclusion, previous laboratory and naturalistic research contrasting secure and insecure infants and children on social play in the peer group during the early preschool years has yielded somewhat consistent data. It general, the play of more secure children is more sociable and sophisticated, and their level of engagement may serve as a "magnet" for the attention of other peers. Because high levels of sociodramatic play are thought to further bolster social competence in children (Creasey et al., 1998), this may be a clear case where the socially "rich" actually become richer. Also, a number of studies suggest that insecure children may be at more risk for difficulties in social play with peers, and may actually engage in behaviors more likely to elicit problematic interactions with peers (Jacobson & Wille, 1986).

CONTROVERSIES, EMERGING DIRECTIONS, AND INTERVENTION AVENUES

While attachment theory may hold considerable promise as a viable approach to explain the development of infant exploration, as well as the emergence of symbolic and social play during the preschool years, we would like to point out (or perhaps create!) a number of important debates and controversies. First and foremost, it should be pointed out that research findings documenting associations between attachment and play are not always consistent. For example, while a number of experts have documented relations between attachment classifications and the emergence of symbolic play, some research has yielded weak or nonsignificant findings (e.g., Main, 1983). In addition, while securely attached infants make better "play partners" with parents and peers during infancy and toddlerhood (e.g., Matas et al., 1978), other investigators have found that infant attachment classifications do not strongly predict future play interactions with parents and peers during the late preschool years (e.g., Youngblade & Belsky, 1992). Finally, while some studies highlight startling differences between avoidant and ambivalent children and the quality of play with peers (e.g., Sroufe, 1983), other research has documented less consistent findings.

What may account for these contradictory findings? First, it is quite possible that *infant* attachment does not automatically forecast the competencies of youth across childhood. It is interesting to us that the magnitude of research results are greater in cases when attachment assessments are garnered concurrently with observations of exploration, symbolic play, or social play with parents and peers, or in cases when the data collection for these potential outcome measures are collected shortly after attachment assessments. Bowlby suggested that as attachment experiences become internalized over time, children's representations of these experiences become incorporated into working models of attachment that may change as the child begins to interact with other viable attachment figures (e.g., siblings, peers, teachers). A six-year-old with a secure working model of attachment of a parent may not have necessarily had a secure relationship with that parent at age 12 months—this would seem to be particularly true in cases when child and family life circumstance change for the better or worse (cf. Thompson, 1999). Thus, this idea could explain why concurrent assessment of child-parent attachment during the preschool years are more strongly related to socially competent play in the peer group (e.g., Park & Waters, 1989) than longitudinal assessments involving infant-parent attachment observations (e.g., Youngblade & Belsky, 1992).

Another concern is more methodological in nature. Because most investigators associating attachment and play have relied on Ainsworth's traditional 3-way classification system (i.e., "forcing" unclassifiable or potentially disorganized children into secure, avoidant, or ambivalent classifications), a major concern might be that using such a strategy confounds the results of previous investigations. This concern is magnified in light of more current findings on infant attachment and the emergence of social behavior during the preschool years. While few studies have examined associations between infant disorganization and play competency, the available data would suggest that attachment disorganization might have unique input to play environments. For example, Wartner, Grossman, Freemmer-Bombik, and Suess (1994) examined the play behavior of 5-year-old secure, insecure (i.e., avoidant or ambivalent-resistant), and disorganized preschoolers. Children were rated as competent players with peers if they readily initiated play themes, and demonstrated high levels of sustained enthusiasm in social play environments. In general, the results demonstrated that secure children were rarely rated as incompetent in social play, while the majority of disorganized children displayed extremely poor play competence. Using more qualitative data, Jacobvitz and Hazen (1999), provide striking examples of how the behavior of disorganized children may create major obstacles for the development of social play during childhood. Unlike children with fundamental security problems (i.e., avoidant or ambivalent), disorganized children seem to engage in peer play that is either overly controlling or simply downright bizarre. Note the play behavior of Sam (age 32 months), who was classified as disorganized during infancy in the Strange Situation:

Sam played for several minutes with a toy bus and ignored Greg's repeated requests for a turn with it. When Greg took the bus from him, Sam became extremely distressed, jumping around aimlessly and screaming in a panicked voice, "My car! My car!". The screaming did not seem to be directed to Greg or anyone else. Later, when Greg's back was turned, Sam quickly ran up to grab the bus, pushed Greg away, and ran to the other side of the room with it (Jacobvitz & Hazen, 1999, p. 148).

Perhaps the most disturbing aspect of attachment disorganization is that unlike the organized behavior of children rated as secure, avoidant, or ambivalent, disorganized children may play in less predictable and organized ways. Thus, their behavior may seem more chaotic and not tied to any logical play theme, which in turn, reinforces more problematic attributions from peers. For example, while peers may label the behavior of insecure children as "uncaring" or "mean", they may view the behavior of disorganized children as strange or "weird" (cf. Jacobvitz & Hazen, 1999). Because play, particularly social play, is closely tied to the development of social competence (Creasey et al., 1998), more research is needed to determine the unique role disorganized attachment status may have on the development of play in children. Also, it might be impossible to ascertain firm conclusions from previous research involving attachment and play in cases where disorganized children have been grouped with other children in alternative attachment categories—this issue might represent a major drawback regarding a majority of the previous research involving attachment and play.

Another consideration rests with specifying ways to better integrate attachment theory with theoretical perspectives on play. Perhaps the play theories most ripe for such integration would be perspectives that stress collaborative relationships between children and others as a central ingredient for the development of competent play (e.g., Vygotsky, 1978). While contemporary attachment theorists would endorse this premise, current thinking on this matter would suggest that successful interactive play can only occur through competent, reciprocal interactions between the child and a play partner (e.g., Sroufe, Egeland, & Carlson, 1999). When considering the research presented in this chapter, it would seem that successful collaboration is not always guaranteed by the presence of a mentor or play partner. Let us consider the mother of Sam, the little boy portrayed in the aforementioned example of disorganized attachment status and play:

Sam's mother appeared dreamily absorbed with the toys herself, paying little attention to Sam or Sam's interests. Sam still did not play with his mother but he watched her much more and was more attentive to her moods and interests. Near the end of the play session, his mother became inexplicably still, staring into space with a dazed expression for over 30 seconds. Sam looked concerned, and tried to snap her out of this state by going up to her face and saying, "Hi!". This was the only utterance during the entire interaction session and his mother could not respond (Jacobvitz & Hazen, 1999, p. 135).

It is important to consider this parent's behavior in light of current theories on the development of children's play. For example, perhaps one of the most important components of sociocultural theories of play rests with ascertaining the role/development of mentoring relationships in play and learning contexts. One of the most glaring concerns regarding the previous research on attachment and play has been too heavy a focus on the input of the infant or child in the play process, and not enough attention to the other side of the equation—that is, the mentor or play partner. The play behavior of the partner (whether it be a parent or peer) is often viewed by attachment researchers as something that is simply "elicited" by the attachment security of a focal child.

Play theorists would view the role of a mentor/partner as much more important in the play context. In Vygotskian (1978) theory, this individual has a huge task in the process, and is charged with the role of constructing stimulating play and learning environments that will allow children to reach their ultimate potential for development. If something were amiss regarding this individual then the play context would be severely compromised. In terms of integrating attachment theory into this process, a logical next step would be to examine how the attachment status of the play partner facilitates or corrodes the development of play in children. It would be our opinion that the most exciting research involving these issues would be to better examine the role more experienced mentors (parents, teachers, and older siblings) have in this process. While the attachment status of peers could be argued as important for the development of social play, we have a more difficult time viewing the peers of preschooler children as central attachment figures (e.g., Bowlby defined attachment figures as "*older and wiser*"), preschoolers may not play with any one child on a highly consistent basis, and a 4-year-old may not have as much experience "mentoring" another 4-year-old preschooler as a parent, teacher, or older sibling.

In terms of examining psychological issues that might influence the development of mentoring behavior in play environments, perhaps one of the most exciting trends in child development research is the examination of how attachment processes in adults influences expectancies and behaviors towards their own children. This work is especially compelling in light of recent research suggesting strong connections between parental working models of attachment and the subsequent development of infant attachment (see Hesse, 1999, for a review). Thus, with the development of adult attachment methodologies, such as the Adult Attachment Interview (George, Kaplan, & Main, 1996), we can now examine how internal working models of attachment in adults influence play and learning environments in children. Such an association would seem likely, because it has been theorized that adult working models of attachment may predict the types of behaviors (e.g., attentiveness, sensitivity, responsiveness to children's bids for attention) that may be necessary for a mentoring relationship (cf. Main et al., 1985).

Initial research (e.g., Crowell & Feldman, 1988; Grossmann et al., 1988; Ward & Carlson, 1995) supports this contention. In challenging play and learning environments, parents who were rated as secure in terms of attachment were more responsive to the needs of children and more likely to provide assistance that encouraged executive competence and mastery than caregivers with alternative attachment representations. In contrast, dismissing parents were often portrayed as cooler and aloof, more controlling, and provided less instrumental assistance to their children than secure parents. According to Crowell and Feldman (1988), the focus of the dismissing parent in play sessions was more often on basic task completion than a learning process. Preoccupied parents often displayed oscillations in affect (e.g., sometimes warm, other times angry and frustrated), had difficulties articulating suggestions, and engaged in behaviors that overwhelm and confuse their children (Crowell & Feldman, 1988). Finally, new research on unresolved or disorganized parents would suggest that these adults often engage in bizarre, strange behavior that may frighten, overwhelm, or confuse young children (Main & Hesse, 1990). For example, the parent may suddenly begin stalking the child, utter frightening verbal expressions ("Don't play with the little car that way, you'll kill everyone!"), or display symptoms of dissociation (see aforementioned example of Sam's mother).

In light of these concerns, when considering the role of adult attachment in terms of influencing mentoring behavior in play environments, a number of points should be considered. First, while emerging research suggests important connections between adult thinking regarding attachment and parental responsiveness in the play context, we should keep in mind that there may also be present temporal factors (e.g., marital distress) that influence parental inattentiveness or insensitivity that have less to do with attachment. On the other hand, adults with certain attachment representations may actually show less responsiveness and attentiveness in play and learning environments if they are also adversely affected by these proximal variables. For example, a parent suffering from occupational stress who also possesses an insecure working model of attachment may be less attentive or display more hostility during play bouts than a stressed parent with a secure attachment representation.

Secondly, while initial research has documented relations between adult attachment and parent and child behavior in play environments, for the most part, this research has concentrated on mother-infant interactions. While the extension of this theory and research to fathers and siblings makes theoretical sense, the role attachment may play in relationships between teachers and children may be the most important next step in this area of study. In the spirit of findings suggesting connections between the attachment status of clinicians and client responsiveness to the therapeutic process (see Slade,1999), it is quite possible that the sensitivity and respon-

siveness of teachers in child care and future school settings may be influenced by adult attachment issues.

On a final point, the numerous educational contexts that children experience during early childhood may serve as a major intervention setting for
children with attachment problems. For example, educating early childhood teachers on how attachment processes influence child-child and
child-teacher interactions in educational settings may constitute one
important educational direction. In addition, peer play and play between
children and teachers may serve as a major focal point for intervention
efforts. For example, teaching children to become better play partners
through the use of scaffolding and play scripts may help insecure children
serve as more attractive partners to other peers in the classroom environment. In addition, encouraging play interactions between insecure children and more socially competent children may serve as a powerful model
for appropriate behavior and affect during play interchanges.

In conclusion, perhaps one reason that the early childhood education
context represents such an exciting setting for intervention efforts rests
with a central premise of Bowlby's attachment theory. Because internal
working models of attachment are thought to become increasingly resistant to change over time, the preschool years may represent a time period
when these representations are more malleable. Teachers, peers, and
other play partners that demonstrate affect and behavior that contradicts
the working model of attachment for an insecure child may serve as an
important vehicle for modification of these schemata.

REFERENCES

Ainsworth, M. (1967). *Infancy in Uganda: Infant care and the growth of attachment.* Baltimore: Johns Hopkins University Press.

Ainsworth, M., Blehar, M., Waters, E., & Wall, S. (1978). *Patterns of attachment: A psychological study of the strange situation.* Hillsdale, NJ: Erlbaum.

Belsky, J., Garduque, & Hrncir, E. (1984). Assessing performance, competence, and
executive capacity in infant play: Relations to home environment and security
of attachment. *Developmental Psychology, 20,* 406-417.

Benoit, D., & Parker, K. (1994). Stability and transmission of attachment across
three generations. *Child Development, 65,* 1444-1456.

Bond, L., Creasey, G., & Abrams, C. (1990). Play assessments: Reflecting and promoting cognitive competence. In E. Gibbs & D. Teti (Eds.), *Interdisciplinary
assessment of infants* (pp. 113-128). Baltimore, MD: Brookes.

Bowlby, J. (1982). *Attachment and loss: Vol. 1: Attachment* (2nd ed.). New York: Basic.

Bowlby, J. (1988). *A secure base: Clinical applications of attachment theory.* London: Routledge.

Bretherton, I. (1984). *Symbolic play.* New York: Academic Press.

Bretherton, I. (1985). Attachment theory: Retrospect and prospect. In I. Bretherton & E. Waters (Eds.), Growing points of attachment theory and research. *Monographs of the Society for Research in Child Development, 50,* (1-2, Serial No. 209), 3-35.

Bretherton, I., et al. (1979) Relationships between cognition, communication, and quality of attachment. In E. Bates et al. (Eds.), *The emergence of symbols.* New York: Academic Press.

Cassiba, R., van IJzendoorn, D'Odorico, L. (2000). Attachment and play in child care centers: Reliability and validity of the attachment Q-sort for mothers and professional caregivers in Italy. *International Journal of Behavioral Development, 24,* 241-255.

Cassidy, J. (1999). The nature of the child's ties. In J. Cassidy & P. Shaver (Eds.), *Handbook of attachment: Theory, research, and clinical applications* (pp. 3-20). New York: Guilford Press.

Cassidy, J., & Berlin, L. (1994). The insecure/ambivalent pattern of attachment: Theory and research. *Child Development, 65,* 971-991.

Creasey, G., & Jarvis, P. (1994). Relationships between parenting stress and developmental functioning in 2-year-olds. *Infant Behavior and Development, 17,* 423-429.

Creasey, G., Jarvis, P., & Berk, L. (1998). Play and social competence. In O. Saracho & B. Spodek (Eds.), *Multiple perspectives on play in early childhood education (pp. 116-143).* New York: SUNY Press.

Crowell, J., & Feldman, S. (1988). Mothers' internal models of relationships and children's behavioral and developmental status: A study of mother-infant interaction. *Child Development, 59,* 1273-1285.

Egeland, B., & Farber, E. (1984). Infant-mother attachment: Factors related to its development and changes over time. *Child Development, 55,* 753-771.

Erikson, E. (1950). *Childhood and society.* New York: Norton.

George, C., Kaplan, N., & Main, M. (1996). *Adult Attachment Interview.* Unpublished manuscript, Department of Psychology, University of California, Berkeley (3rd ed.).

Hesse, E. (1999). The Adult Attachment Interview. In J. Cassidy & P. Shaver (Eds.), *Handbook of attachment: Theory, research, and clinical applications* (pp. 395-433). New York: Guilford.

Isabella, R., & Belsky, J. (1991). Interactional synchrony and the origins of infant-mother attachment: A replication study. *Child Development, 62,* 373-384.

Jacobson, J., & Wille, D. (1986). The influence of attachment pattern on developmental changes in peer interaction from the toddler to the preschool period. *Child Development, 57,* 338-347.

Jacobvitz, D., & Hazen, C. (1999). Developmental pathways from infant disorganization to childhood peer relationships. In J. Solomon & C. George (Eds.), *Attachment disorganization* (pp. 127-159). New York: Guilford Press.

Jacobvitz, D., & Lyons-Ruth, K. (1999). Attachment disorganization. In J. Cassidy & P. Shaver (Eds.), *Handbook of attachment: Theory, research, and clinical applications* (pp. 520-554). New York: Guilford.

Jarvis, P., & Creasey, G. (1991). Parental stress, coping, and attachment in families with an 18-month-old. *Infant Behavior and Development, 14,* 383-395.

Jernberg, A., & Booth, P. (1999). *Theraplay: Helping parents and children build better relationships through attachment-based play* (2nd Ed.). San Francisco: Jossey-Bass.

Londerville, S., & Main, M. (1981). Security of attachment, compliance, and maternal training methods in the second year of life. *Developmental Psychology, 17,* 298-299.

Mahler, M., Pine, F., & Bergman, A. (1975). *The psychological birth of the human infant.* New York: Basic Books.

Main, M. (1983). Exploration, play, and cognitive functioning related to infant-mother attachment. *Infant Behavior and Development, 6,* 167-174.

Main, M. (1996). Introduction to the special section on attachment and psychopathology: 2. Overview of the field of attachment. *Journal of Consulting and Clinical Psychology, 64,* 237-243.

Main, M., & Goldwyn, R. (1994). *Adult attachment interview scoring and classification system.* Unpublished manuscript, University of California at Berkeley.

Main, M., & Hesse, E. (1990). Parents' unresolved traumatic experiences are related to infant disorganization attachment status: Is frightened and/or frightening parental behavior the linking mechanism? In M. Greenberg, D. Cicchetti, & E. Cummings (Eds.), *Attachment in the preschool years: Theory, research, and intervention* (pp. 161-182). Chicago: University of Chicago Press.

Main, M., Kaplan, N., & Cassidy, J. (1985). Security in infancy, childhood, and adulthood: A move to the level of representation. In I. Bretherton & E. Waters (Eds.), Growing points of attachment theory and research. *Monographs of the Society for Research in Child Development, 50,* (1-2, Serial No. 209), 66-106.

Main, M., & J. Solomon, J. (1990). Procedures for identifying infants as disorganized/disoriented during the Ainsworth strange situation. In M. Greenberg, D. Cicchetti, & E. Cummings (Eds.), *Attachment in the preschool years: Theory, research, and intervention (pp. 121-160).* Chicago: University of Chicago Press.

Matas, L., Arend, R.., & Sroufe, L. (1978). Continuity of adaptation in the second year: The relationship between quality of attachment and later competence. *Child Development, 49,* 547-556.

Meins, E., & Russell, J. (1997). Security and symbolic play: The relation between security of attachment and executive capacity. *British Journal of Developmental Psychology, 15,* 63-76.

NICHD Early Child Care Network (1997). The effects of infant child care on infant-mother attachment security: Results of the NICHD study of early child care. *Child Development, 68,* 860-879.

Pastor, D. (1981). The quality of mother-infant attachment and its relationship to toddlers' initial sociability with peers. *Developmental Psychology, 17,* 326-335.

Piaget, J. (1951). *Play, dreams, and imitation in childhood.* New York: Norton.

Rose-Krasnor, Rubin, K., Booth, C., & Coplan, R. (1996). The relation of maternal directiveness and child attachment security to social competence in preschoolers. *International Journal of Behavioral Development, 19,* 309-325.

Rubin, K. (1989). *The play observation scale (POS).* Unpublished coding manual, University of Waterloo.

Sagi, A. (1990). Attachment theory and research from a cross-cultural perspective. *Human Development, 33,* 10-22.

Slade, A. (1987). Quality of attachment and early symbolic play. *Developmental Psychology, 23,* 78-85.

Smilansky, S. (1968). *The effects of sociodramatic play on disadvantaged children. Preschool children.* New York: Wiley.

Sroufe, L. (1983). Infant-caregiver attachment and patterns of adaptation in pre-school: The roots of maladaption and competence. In M. Perlmutter (Ed.), *Minnesota Symposia on Child Psychology: Vol 16. Development and Policy concerning children with special needs* (pp. 41-83). Hillsdale, NJ:Erlbaum.

Sroufe, L., & Egeland, B. (1991). Illustrations of person-environment interaction from a longitudinal study. In T. Wachs & R. Plomin (Eds.), *Conceptualization and measurement of organism-environment interaction* (pp. 68-84). Washington, DC: American Psychological Association.

Sroufe, L., Egeland, B., & Carlson, E. (1999). *Our social world: The integrated development of parent-child and peer relationships*. In W. Collins & B. Laursen (Eds.), Relationships as developmental contexts: The 30th Minnesota Symposium on Child Psychology. Hillsdale, NJ: Elbaum.

Suess, G., Grossman, K., & Sroufe, L. (1992). Effects of infant attachment to mother and father on quality of adaptation in preschool: From dyadic to individual organization of self. *International Journal of Behavioral Development, 15*, 43-65.

Teti, D., Nakagawa, M., Das, R., & Wirth, O. (1991). Security of attachment between preschoolers and mothers: Relations among social interaction, parenting stress, and mothers' sorts of the attachment Q-set. *Developmental Psychology, 27*, 440-447.

Thompson, R. (1999). Early attachment and later development. In J. Cassidy & P. Shaver (Eds.), *Handbook of attachment: Theory, research, and clinical applications* (pp. 265-286). New York: Guilford.

Troy, M., & Sroufe, L. (1987). Victimization among preschoolers: Role of attachment relationship history. *Journal of the American Academy of Child and Adolescent Psychiatry, 26*, 166-172.

Turner, P. (1991). Relations between attachment, gender, and behavior with peers in preschool. *Child Development, 62*, 1475-1488.

Vygotsky, L. (1978). The role of play in development. In M. Cole, V. John-Stiener, S. Scribner, & E. Souberman (Eds.), *Mind in society* (pp. 92-104). Cambridge, MA: Harvard University Press.

Ward, M., & Carlson, E. (1995). Associations among adult attachment representations, maternal sensitivity, and infant-mother attachment in a sample of adolescent mothers. *Child Development, 66*, 69-79.

Wartner, U., Grossmann, K., Fremmer-Bombik, E., & Suess, G. (1994). Attachment patterns at age six in south Germany: Predictability from infancy and implications for preschool behavior. *Child Development, 65*, 1014-1027.

Waters, E., Weinfield, N., & Hamilton, C. (2000). The stability of attachment security from infancy to adolescence and early adulthood: General discussion. *Child Development, 71*, 703-706.

Werner, H., & Kaplan, B. (1963). *Symbol formation*. New York: Wiley.

Youngblade, L., & Belsky, J. (1992). Parent-child antecedents of 5-year-olds' close friendships: A longitudinal analysis. *Developmental Psychology, 28*, 700-713.

CHAPTER 9

THE TEENING OF PRESCHOOL PLAY

Francine Smolucha

Since when have Barbie Dolls become a toy for three year old kids? What happened to baby dolls? (a preschool teacher for thirty years)

I want to take a gun and blow up those houses across the street (comment in 1998 by a white middle-class three year old boy who has been enacting scenes from the British science fiction series *Dr. Who*)

While academics continue to debate whether caregivers can actually guide children's pretend play, the media and merchandisers have already changed pretend play in dramatic ways. The term *media culture* refers to the widespread corporate use of educational and entertainment programs as promotions for products (in addition to commercial advertising). This is the first publication to specifically address *the teening of preschoolers*. During the past twenty years, teen clothing and music have been marketed for preschoolers. Four-year-old girls have adopted the bare midriff look associated with Rock Stars like Britany Spears, Christine Aguilera, and the Spice Girls. Boys as young as two years of age wear Harley-Davidson biker jackets and

Contemporary Perspectives on Play in Early Childhood Education
A Volume in: Contemporary Perspectives in Early Childhood Education, pages 153–170.
Copyright © 2003 by Information Age Publishing, Inc.
All rights of reproduction in any form reserved.
ISBN: 1-930608-31-4 (cloth), 1-930608-30-6 (paper)

Pro-Wrestling T-shirts. Toys representing media personalities are marketed for preschoolers along with teen clothing, music, and videotapes.

A related topic, the *teening of childhood,* has been discussed in the popular press for several years. In the common vernacular, children aged 8-to 12-years are now called *tweens,* a term coined by marketing researchers (Hymowitz, 1999). Merchandisers see tweens as a consumer group that is eager to acquire the fashions and entertainment media previously marketed for teenagers (Kantrowitz & Wingert, 1999).

For the most part, academic researchers appear to have overlooked the teening of childhood. There are several books written for the general public that have discussed this trend, notably Winn (1981) *Children Without Childhood,* Postman (1982) *The Disappearance of Childhood,* Elkind (1998) *All Grown Up and No Place to Go,* Hymowitz (1999) *Ready or Not ,* Medved & Medved (1999) *Saving Childhood,* and Giroux (2000) *Stealing Childhood.*

Some authors use the term *postmodern* childhood to describe this state of affairs (Steinberg & Kincheloe, 1998). The word *modern* derives from a late 17th century French term *moderne* referring to the latest trends in the mode of the *industrial revolution.* Postmodern society, in contrast, is *de-industrialized* with an economy based on computer technology rather than factory machinery. While some people equate the postmodern era with the *computer revolution,* contemporary postmodern culture has really become a *media culture* based on the use of technology by the entertainment business. For example, most children's experience with the world of high technology consists almost entirely of cable television, CD-rom players, videogames, and Internet chat rooms.

The marriage between computer technology and the media is also evident in the organizational structure of the media corporations. At the time this chapter was written, there were five major media corporations: Viacom, AOL Time-Warner, Disney, General Electric, and Universal Vivendi (*The Nation,* March 17, 1997; *Frontline: Merchants of Cool,* 2001). A few of the subsidiaries owned by these corporations are listed here. Viacom owned CBS News, the Infinity all news radio network, MTV (cable TV Rock videos), Nickelodeon (cable TV cartoons), Paramount motion pictures, Simon & Schuster Publishing, The Free Press, and Allyn & Bacon and Prentice-Hall (college textbook publishers). AOL Time-Warner owned America Online, Time Magazine, Warner Brothers motion pictures, Warner music, CNN (the cable news station), and *Parenting* magazine. Disney owned ABC Network News, ABC Radio Networks and Radio Disney, and several motion pictures companies. General Electric owned NBC and Newsweek magazine. These corporations also profit from the marketing of products that include character toys such as Mickey Mouse and Britany Spears.

A child's daily life is also affected by the contracts and gentleman's agreements between corporations. For example, in the summer of 2001, both of my neighborhood Kid's Choice child-care centers were showing films like Disney's *Life Size* (about a Barbie doll that comes to life), Rugrats, and Mary Kate and Ashley to groups of boys and girls aged 5 to 8 years. At one center, on two consecutive days, I observed children *sitting in the dark* watching a big screen TV (some of the children were trying to play board games and some boys were mock fighting.) I was told by the director of one Kid's Choice child-care center that *they have to* show Disney films because their mother company, Kindercare, has a verbal agreement to show Disney films in return for a contract to run child-care centers at Disney World. The Kindercare customer's relations representative from the corporate headquarters in Portland, Oregon told me *this was not true* but the regional manager has never returned my call.

The emergence of *media monopolies* is a recent development related to the deregulation of the broadcast industries in the USA in the 1980s (Kline, 1993; Bagdikian, 1997). According to Bagdikian (1997), in 1983 there were fifty corporations that dominated the mass media and in 1997 there were ten.

The media culture conflicts with parental attempts to shelter preschoolers from sordid realities of life. In my surveys and interviews, many parents and preschool teachers voiced concerns about children growing up too fast. However, it should be noted that the very concept of a sheltered childhood is now regarded by some authors as an antiquated Victorian concept. According to Giroux (2000), what people are really lamenting is the loss of a white middle-class affectation that poor children had *never* been privy to. There had never been a sheltered childhood for impoverished ghetto children whose plight was described by authors such as Charles Dickens, Upton Sinclair, and more recently Alex Kotlowitz (1991).

Now because of the pervasiveness of television, children from all social classes witness sexual vulgarity, fighting and killing, natural disasters, war and terrorism *on a daily basis*. In my surveys and interviews, parents expressed concerned about how sex and violence viewed on television effected their children; they also lamented that there was little they could do to limit their children's exposure (see Hymowitz, 2001). A few parents would say that children should be "exposed to everything" and not be sheltered from the realities of life.

Sesame Parent Magazine (September, 2000) reported the results of a survey that asked "Are Kids Growing Up Too Soon?" The research revealed that this was a hot-issue among parents today, with attitudes breaking down into two camps—the *Sooner* moms (43%) who embraced pop culture and the *Later* moms (57%) who did not want their child to be influenced by the latest crazes (Connor,September 2000, pp. 62-63).

The collapse of the World Trade Center in New York City on September 11, 2001 provided the most poignant example of how postmodern children are *deliberately* being exposed to traumatic news *as it happens...* In some classrooms, television sets were turned on just in time for the children and their teachers to see the buildings collapse after a terrorist attack. The teachers did not know what was going to happen next and they were not prepared to help children deal with such shocking images. Psychologists need to offer adults some guidelines about the *age appropriate exposure* of children to disturbing news and images. Note, however, that this very statement is representative of the *modern* view that children need to be sheltered from disturbing realities.

From my surveys and interviews, I found that it was preschool teachers who *consistently* tried to discourage sexist and violent themes in play activities (see Kaiser, Snyder, & Rogers; 1995). Preschool classes might be the only place where children are *relatively* free of the media culture. Network and cable television, along with videotapes, are deliberately excluded from many preschools. Many preschools have no Barbie dolls or Superhero action figures, and no weapons to play with. Preschool teachers' activism in restricting media culture from their classrooms can be linked to a position statement issued by NAEYC in April 1990. The National *Association for the Education of Young Children's Position Statement on Media Violence in Children's Lives* calls for teachers and care givers to limit children's exposure to sexism and violence in the media, "Of great concern to early childhood educators is the negative effect of viewing violent programs on children's play" (NAEYC Position Statement reprinted in Levin, 1998, p. 175).

Play activities related to news events like the attack on the World Trade Center are a special case because play activities could also be therapeutic. Teachers and care givers should know how to help children use pretend play to cope with emotional crises. The first step towards this would be for adults to realize that pretend play is important. Adults also need to realize that they can intervene in play in positive ways.

The social commentary that has comprised the introduction to this paper provided a necessary background for the discussion to follow. It no longer makes sense to talk about the pretend play of American children from an *ahistorical* perspective. History shows that there have been major changes in concept of childhood in Eurocentric cultures before.

According to Philippe Aries (1963), the concept of childhood as a separate stage of the lifespan had existed for the ancient Romans, was lost during the Middle Ages, and was reintroduced in the 19th century. The mid-1800's also saw the introduction of adolescence as a transitional stage between childhood and adulthood. This *late modern* concept of adolescence was distinctly different from the ancient Roman concept of adolescence as the first stage of young adulthood. In his book, Aries described the 20th century as the *Age of Adolescence* because little children want to be like teenagers and adults do not want to grow up.

> Thus our society has passed from a period that was ignorant of adolescence to a period in which adolescence is the favorite age. We now want to come to it early and linger in it as long as possible (Aries, 1963, p. 28).

It is also important to note that *postmodern adolescence* is distinctly different from the *late modern* concept of adolescence described by G. Stanley Hall (1904), L.S. Vygotsky (1931/1996), and E. Erikson (1959/1980). The teen culture of the late 20th century is a media culture. According to Elkind (1998), the postmodern adolescent has a *patchwork* identity derived from shifting identifications with media role models and no coherent sense of self. This contrasts with the *late modern* concept of the adolescent identity crisis, in which the adolescent tried to achieve a hierarchically organized personality structure (Elkind, 1998), and a coherent world view (Vygotsky, 1931/1984, 1991; Smolucha 1992). This means that the media culture is socializing preschoolers to act like *postmodern teens* rather than the adolescents of the late-modern era. Postmodern adolescence centers on hedonistic consumerism not identity achievement.

Social scientists need to determine how pervasive these new social trends are and how they affect development. Play researchers need to consider that a change in cultural paradigms might have occurred that has repercussions for children's play. Baby dolls, doll houses, cars, and trucks might not be the most popular preschool toys. Teachers and care givers need strategies that guide children's play in positive directions. Caregivers need to make *informed* decisions when buying toys and clothing, and about the types of play and entertainment to encourage.

This paper will examine the theoretical significance of these changes in children's play culture and review the research literature as it relates to this topic.

THE DISAPPEARANCE OF LATENCY IN GIRLS

For those psychologists who still think that there is some value to Freud's stages of psychosexual development, the disappearance of the latency stage would have devastating implications. Socializing three-year-olds to embark upon a premature adolescence would mean that phallic stage issues went unresolved and that there was no longer a latency stage.

The phallic stage (approximately age 3 to 5 years) is characterized by sexual curiosity, voyeurism, exhibitionism, and the Oedipal complex Freud (1962). Sexualizing preschool girls means that girls as young as 3 years of age want to dress sexy, dance sexy, and watch sex scenes in movies. Phallic sexuality is a self serving exhibitionism, not the shared intimacy of mature genital sexuality.

This sexual exhibitionism is obvious in the performances of the female Rock Stars that the preschool girls are imitating. For example, two white middle-class 3-year-old girls (who do not play together) told me that their favorite movie was *Grease*. By the time they were 4 years old they could sing the lyrics to Spice Girl Songs, *dress-up* play for them meant dressing up like the Spice Girls, and they danced like the Spice Girls too. These preschoolers would complement other girls for "looking hot." By age 6 years, one of the girls was flirting with guys in cars, oblivious to the obvious stranger danger inherent in such a situation.

This is not an isolated or recent phenomenon. For example, back in 1987, at my local *Chuckie Cheese* Restaurant *(Where a Kid Can Be A Kid)* three- and four-year-olds were dancing to Bruce Springsteen's song *Born to be Wild* with lyrics such as "I want to die with you baby on the street tonight in an everlasting kiss." Eventually *Chuckie Cheese* restaurants replaced rock music with videotapes featuring their own trademark characters singing restyled lyrics to popular songs. My local *Chuckie Cheese* restaurant now broadcasts songs from *Veggie Tales* (featuring singing vegetables) with prosocial lyrics proclaiming "I can be your friend."

However, not all organizations are sensitive to the *age-inappropriateness* of teen entertainment for young children. For example, in the year 2000, my local park district was offering hip hop dancing for a mixed group of boys and girls aged 6 to 15.

The tween years (age 8- to 12) present a particular challenge for girls who were teened as preschoolers,because it will still be several years before they can do the things that teenagers do (Corwin, 1999; Manz, 1995). Specifically, sixteen-year-olds can work and earn their own money, drive cars, and party unsupervised with friends. David Elkind (1998) has described the contemporary teenager as being *all grown up with no place to go,* however this crisis is even more acute for *tweens.* We can expect increases in eating disorders, depression, and adolescent rebellion in middle childhood. A recent survey by the *Girls Scouts of America* (2000) found that eating disorders have become more common during middle childhood. Precocious sexual behavior might also be on the increase. Staff members from a local crisis center for domestic violence claim that oral sex has become a fad for tweens. One white middle-class mother told me that her 6-year old daughter told how girls on her school bus were talking about kissing boys penises (her daughter rides the school bus with girls and boys from age 6 to 8 years).

By the time, many girls reach ten years of age and enter puberty, they have already been trying to act like *cool* teenagers for six years, but, it will still be another six years before they reach age sixteen. The clash between expectation and reality breeds frustration. The *tween* still has years of schooling ahead and tons of homework, is not supposed to date older boys or have sex, she can not drive a car, and she is financially dependent on the generosity of adults.

A ten-year-old girl in Victorian times, or even a Baby Boomer in the 1950's, could get wish-fulfillment from pretend play but not the post-modern girl. By the time many girls reach seven years of age, they have begun to think that pretend play is for babies. Baby dolls, toy kitchen sets, and even Barbie dolls are sold off at garage sales. Mothers lamenting that their daughters are growing up too fast, encourage sports activities. Sports activities are seen as a way to build self-confidence in one's abilities, rather than being preoccupied with one's *looks*. Notice, however, that the growing popularity of competitive sports for little children is also part of the teening of childhood.

Pretend play could be prolonged by developing an interest in collectibles such as American Girl Dolls, Madeline, or even Barbie Dolls. The Victorian era girl could extend her pretend play by writing stories, participating in reader's theater, or acting in plays. These activities could be revived for contemporary girls.

The sexualizing of preschool girls is further complicated by the earlier onset of puberty for girls in industrialized nations during the last one hundred years (called the *secular trend*). A recent cover story in Newsweek magazine (October 1999) brought this phenomena to the attention of the general public. While the secular trend is news to the general public, it has been discussed in college textbooks for the last twenty-five years.

A hundred years ago the average age for an American girl to reach menarche was fifteen; by the 1960's it had become twelve and a half. Since secondary sex characteristics appear about two years before menarche this means that the average American girl begins to show an increase in height and breast development at age ten and a half, Girls aged 8 to 10 years are pre-pubescent (tweens). This is in sharp contrast to past centuries when girls experienced the adolescent growth spurt at age 13 and reached menarche at 15 years of age.

Even if some girls are reaching menarche at 9 years of age this does not mean that they have to automatically dress sexy. There are many cultures throughout history where *modesty* accompanies sexual maturation in women. The veils and robes of contemporary Muslim women are an example of concealing sexuality rather than flaunting it. Fashion is not dictated by sex hormones.

The current situation is further complicated by the number of girls in the USA experiencing an early onset of puberty. Sixteen percent of white girls and fifty percent of African-American girls enter puberty at eight years of age, reaching menarche by age ten (Lemonick, 2000). These early maturing girls were pre-pubescent at age six.

The earlier onset of puberty in girls, combined with the media's sexualizing of preschool girls, surely affects their play activities during the preschool years and middle childhood.

THE DISAPPEARANCE OF LATENCY IN BOYS

The teening of a preschool boy to be a tough guy increases phallo-sadistic tendencies. The phallic symbolism of guns, knives, swords, light sabers, rockets, and racing cars is obvious, the obsession with pyrotechnics and fiery explosions is another expression of phallic aggression. *Mighty Morphin Power Rangers* is one example of a phallo-militartisic television series (McLaren and Morris, 1998).

The two deaths during children's play re-enactments of *Power Rangers* (Kline, 1993) and the four recent deaths during re-enactments of World Championship Wrestling, mean that play researchers have to re-examine the contention that play aggression is not real aggression (Goldsetin, 1995; Hellendoom & Harick, 1997; Pelligrini, 1995;Watson & Peng, 1992; Wegener-Spoering, 1994).

For example, one white middle class mother told me how she came to regret having a Power Rangers theme party for her son's second birthday. By age three years, he had become so aggressive in his imitation of Power Rangers that she had to restrict Power Rangers from his television viewing and play activities.

It is important to note that there is no scientific evidence supporting the claim that preschool boys are aggressive because of male sex hormones. Keenan's (1996) review of the research literature found that boys are not more aggressive than girls until 4 to 5 years of age. Also, testosterone is not produced during the preschool years. There is a release of testosterone at eight months prenatal, that dissipates by two months postnatal. The next time testosterone is produced is at 6 years of age. Testosterone production slowly increases from 6 to 11 years of age, the sudden increase at age eleven is the beginning of puberty. Since there is no clear link between testosterone and aggression in humans, testosterone production at puberty does not even mean that *violence* is normal among adolescent males.

There is also a basic fact of neurochemistry that many people overlook, that is *testosterone can not reach the brain until it has been converted into estrogen (estradiol)*. There is no reason to expect that a female sex hormone would masculinize the male brain to be become aggressive. Claims of gender differences in the human brain are unfounded. My recent review of the research literature showed that studies claiming to have found gender differences in the human brain lack replicability and do not control for ethnicity or age (Smolucha, 1998).

The media has a vested interest in popularizing the idea that boys are naturally aggressive because of sex hormones and gender differences in the brain. In 1996 and again in the year 2000, U.S. Senate hearings have been held on violence in the entertainment industry. The media wants to avoid legislation that would censor the level of violence in the entertainment industry. However, the court ruling against the tobacco industry set a precedent for seeking punitive damages for advertising products to children that are detrimental to the health of children.

THE PATCHWORK SUPEREGO

According to psychoanalytic theory, at the end of the phalllic stage (age 3 to 6 years), the preschool child's identification and rivalry with parental authority figures should result in the formation of the *Superego*. Pretend play during the preschool years is an important means of identifying with adult role models, imitating their behavior, and internalizing their speech. At approximately 6 years of age, latency begins when the child internalizes an adult role model as the Superego.

During the latency stage (age 7 to 11 years) the Superego functions both as a conscience and ego ideal. In order for the Superego to form, the preschool child's primary identification must be with adult role models. Preschoolers whose main identification is with teenagers and teenage media celebrities would not form a superego. They do not have a mature role model to guide their own quest for identity achievement (ego ideal), have no clear sense of right and wrong (no conscience), and would be unable to delay gratification (no work ethic). Although David Elkind did not use psychoanalytic terms, this is essentially the postmodem patchwork identity that he has described in his book (Elkind, 1998).

According to Elkind (1998), many contemporary teenagers do not resolve their adolescent identity crisis by forming a centralized ego, instead they have shifting identifications with various media role models. Such a *patchwork* personality finds identifications with role models that fit the demands of particular situations. There are *situational identities* rather than a centralized identity that transcends situations. Any new situation would be compared to scenes from a movie, and the dialogue and actions would follow from the *script*. The patchwork personality as described by Elkind is reminiscent of Harry Stack Sullivan's concept of the personality multiplex.

In the Victorian era and early 20th century, pretend play prepared girls for their mothers' roles (homemaker, hostess, and mother). By the 1980's the media's image of the hip teenage girl had become the predominant role model for many preschool girls. The Barbie doll had been transformed into a hip teenager; and, was fast becoming *a doll for babies* (for preschoolers). By age seven, many girls consider themselves *too cool* to play with dolls; they are ready to start dating.

In the Victorian era and early 20th century, pretend play prepared boys for an occupation—soldier (knight), train engineer, cowboy, or farmer. In the 1970's , megalomaniacal Superhero action figures flooded the airwaves and toy stores. These new role models were not heroic,because there was no clear difference between the bully who was the bad guy and the bully who was the good guy. Even the G.I. Joe doll which originated as a heroic soldier of World War II had been transformed into some kind of *soldier of fortune*. The ultimate culmination of the superhero as *bully without a cause* can be seen in the violent theatrics of world championship wrestling.

ONE LAST LOOK AT VICTORIAN KINDERCULTURE

It should be noted that Freud's psychoanalytic theory is critical of Victorian culture and does not champion it. Neither Freud nor Erikson idealized childhood; from Freud's perspective, the infant is polymorphously perverse—a creature of the Id. Early childhood is characterized by constant demands for instant gratification of desires and temper tantrums. Caregivers must socialize and civilize the child, conformity to social norms does not come easy, the developmental gain is the internalization of a parental role model that acts as a conscience, the cost is an continual frustration of desires through denied or delayed gratification. From a psychoanalytic perspective, pretend play satisfies desires in a disguised and socially acceptable form. Ludic symbols convey multiple levels of meaning through metaphor and analogy. Like dreams, play is a product of the primary process thought of the ID.

The Victorian ideal of childhood is the basis for 20th century nostalgia about the ideal childhood. While Victorian toys and play themes came to be regarded as the form of *generic*-pretend play, from a historical/cultural perspective it is only the *play culture* of the Victorian era. Play culture in the Victorian era (late-modern or late-industrialized) served the economic conditions of the times, just as postmodern play culture does today. Play in the late-modern era was highly genderized; girls were socialized with baby dolls, tea parties, playing house, and dressing up like *mommy,* boys were socialized with military paraphernalia such as toy soldiers, bugles and drums, guns and swords, ships and airplanes, hobby horses, rocking horses, and trains. These are the toys pictured on Christmas cards around a Victorian Christmas tree, in Santa 's Toy Shop, and in the Toy Store window.

In the 1950's the emergent middle class in the USA appropriated the Victorian ideal of childhood. Parents who typically had little or no childhood of their own, due to the economic devastation of the Great Depression of 1929, now had an opportunity to indulge their children. The new found economic affluence in America after WWII enabled parents to purchase the types of toys that they themselves had longed for as children. A new coalition of television, advertising, and toy industry responded to the increased demand for toys, fueled the demand for toys, and began to create a preference for certain toys (Kline, 1995).

The generic toys for girls changed very little until Barbie came out. When Barbies first came out they were the toy of preference for preteen girls (girls aged 8 to 13 years)—girls who fantasied through their play about being a young woman, going out on dates, getting married, and having a career as a flight attendant or nurse. By the 1970's Barbie had gone mod and was a hip teenager. By the 1990's Barbie had become the toy of preference for preschool girls, who were deluged with Barbies at their third birthday parties.

In the 1950's, World War II era toy soldiers for boys were the plastic equivalent of the old lead toy soldiers of the 1800's. In the 1970's, in the aftermath of Vietnam the popularity of toy soldiers declined and Superhero *science fantasy* toys were widely promoted by television series such as

He-Man and Transformers. The fiftieth anniversary of WWII brought a revival of interest in toy soldiers from WWII (examples: the G.I. Joe commemorating Pearl Harbor, the Normandy Invasion, the Battle of the Bulge, etc.). The marketability of these WWII commemorative figures might be extended in the aftermath of the attack on the World Trade Center, as the USA, prepares to fight another "good war" this time against the evil of terrorism. In the aftermath of September 11, 2001, Fisher-Price's Rescue Heroes (firemen and policemen) were moved up to the front shelves at toy stores. Toys like Spawn (decomposing mutants), and violent films and videogames featuring terrorist attacks, might wain in popularity, as the public's tolerance for such images changes.

WHAT CAN WE LEARN FROM RESEARCH ON PRETEND PLAY?

During the last twenty years, American play researchers have been re-evaluating Piaget's (1945/1984) theory of the solitary origins of pretend play (Smolucha & Smolucha, 1998). In the 1980's, American play researchers took an interest in the writings of Russian psychologists whose work had been marginalized in the USA during the Cold War era. According to Vygotsky, play interactions with a more experienced play partner could lead to the development of higher cognitive processes. Pretend play creates a zone of proximal development and is the highest level of preschool functioning.

Vygotsky's concept of *zone of proximal development* resolved the nature-nurture controversy, by acknowledging that children can learn unassisted, but they could learn even more under the verbal guidance of a more knowledgeable person. Children can play alone but they learn to function at a higher level through pretend play interactions with a more experienced play partner. Piagetians would not assume that care givers or the media had any great influence on pretend play; Vygotskians would see pretend play as the vehicle for the social construction of the child's mind.

Which theory has the most empirical support? My review of the research literature would conclude that Piaget's general theoretical framework as well as his play theory have not held up under scientific scrutiny (Smolucha & Smolucha, 1998). Nevertheless, there still are prominent play researchers who argue that children's play styles are natural and not learned (Fein & Fryer, 1995a,b). The evolutionary psychology movement also continues to champion this position (Pelligrini, 1995). The Piagetian and evolutionary psychology perspectives are deeply entrenched in American play research, constituting the *old guard*. Their rhetoric would support the claim that children's play is natural and not influenced by interactions with mothers or the culture in general. This is illustrated in the concluding statements by Fein & Fryer (1995a, p. 379), "The early evolution of pretense may simply not be tied to environmental or cultural influences" and "If pretense reflects a crucial human competence, its early development will not depend on the whims or values of parents, families, or societies (p. 380)." Although Fein & Fryer (1995a,b) are really talking about abstract levels of symbolic representation in children's play, their statement is so general that it could refer to play themes and semiotics as well. After all, if the culture in general does not affect children's pretend play, then the sexism and violence of children's television, videogames, and toys would not affect play.

Researchers advocating the Vygotskian approach see the research literature as demonstrating that care givers *can* influence children's pretend play in important ways (Bodrova & Leong, 1996; Slade, 1987; Smolucha, 1991, 1992; Smolucha & Smolucha, 1998; Zupancic et al. 1999). Ecological psychology is another approach similar to Vygotsky's theory in its focus on environmental influences on pretend play (Bretherton, 1982; Bornstein & Tamis-IeMonda, 1995). However, neither Vygotskian nor ecological play researchers have payed much attention to the influence of the media on children's play.

For decades, both experimental and correlational studies have shown that television violence increases aggression in viewers and desensitizes them to violence in real life (Aidman, 1997; Bushman & Anderson, 2000; Gressen, 1998; Levine, 1999; McCain, 1998; Seawall, 1997). There are even a few studies that specifically look at the effects of television on pretend play (Molitor & Hirsch, 1994; Sanson & di Muccio, 1993; see van Der Voort & Valkenburg's review, 1994). Observations from preschool teachers also provide evidence of the link between violent children's cartoons and increased antisocial behavior in the classroom (Bauer & Dettore, 1997; Boyatzis, Matillo, & Nesbitt, 1995; Crosser, 1995; Dyson, 1994; French, 1991; Kostelnik, 1986; Reglin, 1996; Silva, 1996; Watson & Peng, 1992) .

Stephen Kline's book *Out of the Garden* presented the results of a Canadian study of how children's television is used to market toys. Kline described how corporations actively use television to influence children's play preferences in order to sell toys, clothes, music, videos, videogames, etc. (Kline, 1993; 1995). The absence of a similar study in the USA is a glaring omission. It was only recently (June 2000) that the American Psychological Association convened a task force to study advertising's impact on children (following a letter of complaint about psychologists conducting advertising research on children) (Clay, 2000).

Educational television can also bring in revenues, when its licensed trademark characters are used to market products. Teachers and care givers can offset compulsive shopping by encouraging children to work on arts and crafts projects and make their own playthings. Lacking a playset for *Magic School Bus*, I suggested to my three-year-old son that we make the characters out of clay. Discovering that we had no beige colored clay for their skin tones (Caucasian), my son suggested that we use black clay, we did and he was happy with his new toys.

The *merchants of cool* (see Goodman & Dretzin, 2001) have been aggressively marketing to preschoolers. And, some parents like myself, are willing to spend money on *cool* educational toys and products that can direct the child's attention away from the vile products that are also being marketed for children. Television shows like Sesame Street, Barney, and Mr. Rogers Neighborhood are designed to guide pretend play in a positive directions. During the last ten years there has been a proliferation of other high quality educational programming for children (examples: *Magic School Bus, Thomas the Tank Engine, Blues Clues, Little Bear, Dragon Tales, Oomafoo*). These programs have demonstrated that educational television for children is highly profitable when accompanied by sales of videotapes, videogames, toys, clothing, bedding, etc.

Vygotskian theory does not assume that *how* caregivers guide children's play is going to be consistent across cultures, within cultures, or over time (Vygotsky's cultural/historical perspective). As Vygotsky's theory gained popularity in the USA, cross-cultural studies began to proliferate that showed cultural differences in mother-child interactions during play (Farver et ai,1993, 1997 , 2000; Haight, 1994; Haight, Wang, & Fung, 1999). There is no reason to assume that any particular group of mothers will be adept at guiding pretend play. This is why descriptive studies such as those cited by Fein & Fryer (1995a,b) do not disprove Vygotskian theory.

Vygotskian theory raises the disquieting possibility that the media industry has been misguiding the development of children's play during the last half century. While most research on Vygotsky's theory has focused on interactions with caregivers and peers, Vygotsky himself was also interested in movies as a medium of cultural transmission. Vygotsky actually participated in brainstorming sessions with Sergei Eisenstein during the production of Eisenstein's film *October.*

A Vygotskian theoretical framework could very well include the influence of movies, television, music, literature, and videogames, in addition to social interactions with peers, caregivers, and teachers.

PLAYING IN A MEDIA CULTURE

Academics need to address historical change, as well as cultural differences in the way children play. Preschool teachers and parents interacting directly with children need to hear an informed discussion of this topic. It is also important that thorough scientific investigations be conducted and that scholarly information be readily available to educators and care givers.

Adults who believe that pretend play follows a natural path have little reason to intervene in play activities unless the play becomes destructive or dangerous. This is a reactive model rather than a proactive model.

Care givers can be proactive in guiding children's play in directions that lead to cognitive growth, prosocial skills, and even character development. For example, even when my son was a toddler, I discouraged him from building a tower out of blocks just to knock it down. When we would build a tower, our goal was to see how high we could build it. If a tower fell over we would rework the base so it had greater stability the next time.

On September 16, 2001 as we visited his grandparents, I suggested (out of habit) that he build some skyscrapers with Grandpa. Building skyscrapers (towers) out of Megablocks had become one of their favorite play activities. However, in the days immediately following the terrorist attack and collapse of the World Trade Center in New York City, this activity took on a new meaning. Realizing that recent events might change the play script, I still let my son initiate his own play scenario. He built a long wall (something he had never done before) and said "this is the wall for the fort, to keep the bad guys out." I stacked some blocks up in a vertical column and he said "that's the tower," "now let's go get the planes." He brought out a box of his grandmother's wooden clothespins and assembled them into airplanes (Grandmother used to play that way as a child in the 1920's). He gave me one airplane and said "you have the bad guy's plane, now try to attack the tower." Everytime my plane approached the tower he would knock it out of my hand with the good guys' planes, saying "see you can't do it, you can't knock it down. "

What had once been a neutral example of constructive play had become play therapy to satisfy the wish that the terrorist attack could have been prevented. There were some details to the terrorist attack that he did not know, such as the fact that the bad guys had hijacked passenger planes full of civilians. Real life problems are rarely as simple or as easily solved as scenarios enacted in children's play.

This example raises a fundamental issue in play and in real life: "How do we know who the good guys are?" Is it just a matter of national or team loyalty? Are there no real heroes, just one bully taking on another bully?"

I had to address this issue when my son was 3 years old, when we watched Power Rangers for the first time and I turned the program off. I explained to him that the problem with this television show was that except for the color of their uniforms the Power Rangers acted too much like the bad guys (punching and kicking all the time). Good guys save someone, they—rescue mothers and babies, grandpas and grandmas, and even animals—just like the Star Trek movie where they rescue the humpback whales. My son was very impressed with the fictionalized Star Trek rescue of the humpback whales and it became the criterion we use to distinguish the good guys from the bad guys. It is not how many buildings you blow up, or how many people you kill, it is how many lives you save that makes you one of the good guys. By age five, my sons favorite play scenarios have become *marine biologist* (we build an aquarium out of quilts on a bed, stock it with stuffed toy whales, fish, octopus, etc., and my son teaches us about them), a *fire fighter* who rescues animals and people (modeled after the Fisher-Price Rescue Heroes computer game), and *a soldier* who rescues families. For Halloween 2001, he has decided to be a fire fighter. he said "Spiderman was last year..." The deaths of nearly 400 firefighters and policemen trying to rescue people at the World Trade Center, saddened him with the realization of something that I had told him long ago "Sometimes good guys get killed."

Teachers and care givers can use role models from the media can to help children formulate a healthy ego ideal. Both of these elements are critical to reclaiming pretend play as a family dynamic. Adult-child interactions during play are an opportunity for emotional bonding, as well as an opportunity for cognitive, social, and character development. The Victorian middle class isolated children in nurseries on the third floor of the home, the post-modern American family isolates children in basement playrooms. But, there are also families like ours where children play under foot, under the dining room table, in the living room, among the adults. Perhaps this is a pre-industrial model from families that were farmers, ranchers, herded flocks, tradesmen, etc. (not impoverished peasants but not extremely wealthy, either).

Freud (1900/1965) had the great insight that dreams are not concerned with trivia, and neither is pretend play. While play does imitates life, it also reconstructs the past with an eye to future possibilities.

Acknowledgments: I would like to thank the following individuals for contributing to this paper: my husband and colleague Larry Smolucha and my son Nathan. Sally Bala and Susan Novak of Rockinghorse preschool, Vita Bates and Annette Herbert of the Moraine Valley Children 's Learning Center, and Mrs. Dorsey of St. John's Lutheran preschool distributed surveys to parents and shared their professional observations. Angela Paterakis and the graduate students at the School of the Art Institute of Chicago introduced me to Giroux's writings. And, thank you to many friends who shared examples with me from their own professional and personal experience.

REFERENCES

Aidman, A. (1997). Television violence: Content, context, and consequences. ERIC Digest PS026088. Also, http://ericeece.org/pubs/digests/1997/aidman97.html.

Aries, P. (1954/1963). *Centuries of childhood.* Penguin Books.

Bagdikian, B. H. (1997). *Media monopoly*. Boston: Beacon Press.

Bauer, K. & Dettore, E. (Fall, 1997). Superhero play: What's a teacher to do?*Early Childhood Education, 25*(1), 17-21.

Bodrova, E., & Leong, D. (1996). *Tools of the mind*. Englewood Cliffs, Nj: Merrill.

Bornstein, M & C Tamis-LeMonda. (1995). Parent-child symbolic play: Three theories in search of an effect. *Developmental Review: 15*, 382-400.

Boyatzis, C., Matillo, G., & Nesbitt, K. (1995). Effects of "The Mighty Morphin Power Rangers" on children's aggression with peers. *Child Study Journal, 25*(1) 4555. ERIC 508796.

Bretherton, I. (Ed.). (1982). *Symbolic play*. New York: Academic Press.

Bushman, B. & Anderson, C. (June/July 2000). Meda violence and the American public: Scientific facts versus media misinformation. *American Psychologist, 56* (6n), 477-489.

Clay, R. (September, 2000). Advertising to children: Is it ethical?*APA Monitor.*

Connor, L. (September, 2000). Special Sesame research report: Are Kids growing up too soon? *Sesame Street Parents*, Section 2 of 2, 62-68.

Corwin, D. (1999). *The tween years: A parents guide for surviving those terrific, turbulent and trying times between childhood and adolescence*. Chicago: Contemporary Books.

Crosser, S. (May-Jun, 1995). Mighty Morphin Power Ranger Play: Research and reality, *Early Childhood News, 7*(3), 25-27.

Dyson, A. (Win, 1994). The Ninjas, the X-Men, and the Ladies: Playing with power and identity in an urban primary school. *Teachers College Record, 96*(2), 219-239.

Elkind, D. (1988). *The hurried child: Growing up too fast too soon*. Addison-Wesley. (first published 1981).

Elkind,D. (1998). *All grown up and no place to go*. Cambridge, Ma: Perseus Books.

Erikson, E. (1959/1980). *Identity and the life cycle*. New York: Norton.

Farver, J. & Shin, Y. Lee-Shin, Y. (Sep, 2000). Within cultural differences: Examining individual differences in Korean American and European American preschoolers' social pretend play. *Journal of Cross-Cultural Psychology, 31*(5), 583-602.

Farver, J. & Shin, Y. (Jun, 1997). Social pretend play in Korean- and Anglo-American preschoolers. *Child Development, 68*(3), 544-556.

Farver, J. & Howes, C. (Jul, 1993). Cultural differences in American and Mexican mother-child pretend play. *Merrill-Palmer Quarterly*, 39(3), 344-358.

Fein, G. & Fryer, M. (1995). Maternal contributions to early symbolic play competence. *Developmental Review: 15*, 367-381.

Fein, G. & Fryer, M. (1995). When theories don't work chuck'em or change'em. *Developmental Review: 15*, 401-403.

Freud. S. (1900/1965). The *interpretation of dreams*. New York: Avon Books.

Freud. S. (1975). *Three essays on the theory of sexuality*. New York: Basic Books.

French, J. & Penna, S. (1991).Children's hero play of the 20th century: Changes resulting from television's influence. *Child Study Journal*. *21*(2), 79-95.

Giroux. H. (2000). *Stealing innocence*. New York: St. Martin's Press.

Giroux, H. (1998). Are Disney movies good for your kids? In Steinberg, S. and Kincheloe, J. L. (Eds.). (1998). *Kinder-culture*. Boulder, Co: Westview Press.

Goldstein. J. (1995). Aggressive toy play. In Pelligrini, Anthony *(Ed.). The future of play theory: A multidisciplinary inquiry into the contributions of Brian Sutton-Smith.* New York: State University of New York Press.

Goodman. B. & Dretzin, R. (2001). *Merchants of cool.* Public Broadcast System: Frontline (www.pbs.org)

Gressen, A. D. III. (1998). Professional wrestling and youth culture: Teasing, taunting, and the containment of civility. In Steinberg, S. and Kincheloe, J. L. (Eds.). (1998). *Kinder-culture.* Boulder, CO: Westview Press.

Haight, W., Wang, X., & Fung, H. (Nov-Dec. 1999). Universal, developmental. and variable aspects of young children's play: A cross-cultural comparison of pretending at home. *Child Development, 70*(6), 1477-1488.

Haight, W. (1994). The everyday context and social functions of spontaneous mother-child pretend play in the home. *Merrill-Palmer Quarterly, 40*(4), 509-522.

Hall. G.S. (1904). *Adolescence.* New York: Appleton.

Hellendoorn, J. & Harinck, F. (Nov, 1997). War toy play and aggression in Dutch kindergarten children. *Social Development, 6*(3), 340-354.

Hymowitz. K. (1999). *Ready or not: Why treating children as small adults endangers their future and ours.* New York: The Free Press.

Hymowitz. K. (Spring 2001). Parenting: The lost art. *American Educator: 25*(1), 4-9.

Kaiser, J., Snyder, T., & Rogers, C. (Jul, 1995). Adult choice of toys affects children's prosocial and antisocial behavior. *Early Child Development & Care, 111*, 81-193.

Kantrowitz, B., & Wingert, P. (act 18, 1999). The Tween Years. *Newsweek, 134*(16), 62-72.

Keenan, K. & Shaw, D. (1996). Developmental and social influences on young girl's early problem behavior. *Psychological Bulletin, 121*(1), 95-113.

Kline, S. (1995). The promotion and marketing of toys: Time to rethink the paradox? In Pelligrini, A. (Ed.). *(1995). The future of play theory: A multidisciplinary inquiry into the contributions of Brian Sutton-Smith.* New York: State University of New York Press.

Kline, S. (1993). *Out of the garden: Toys, TV, and children's culture in the age of marketing.* London: Verso.

Kostelnik, M. (May, 1986). Living with He-Man: Managing superhero fantasy play. *Young Children, 41*(4), 3-9.

Kotlowitz, A. (1991). *There are no children here: The story of two boys growing up in the other America.* New York: Doubleday.

Lemonick, M. (Oct 30, 2000). Teens before their time. *Time, 156*(18), 66-74.

Levin, D. (1998). *Remote control childhood:Combating the hazards of media culture.* Washington, DC: National Association for the Education of Young Children.

Levine, M. (1996). *Viewing violence: How media violence affects your child and adolescents development.* New York: Doubleday.

McCain, R.S. (Dec. 21, 1998). Television's bloody hands. *Washington Times: Insight on the News, 14*(47) 37-39.

McLaren, P. & Morris, J. (1998). Might morphin power rangers: The aesthetics of phallo-miltaristic justice. In Steinberg, S. & Kincheloe, J. L. (Eds.). (1998). *Kinder-culture.* Boulder, Co: Westview Press.

Manz Simon, M. (1995). *How to parent your tweenager.* Nashville: Thomas Nelson Publisher. Medved, Michael and Diane Medved. *(1998). Saving childhood.* New York: HarperCollins.

Molitor, F., & Hirsch, K. (1994). Children's toleration of real-Life aggression after exposure to media violence: A replication of the Drabman and Thomas studies. *Child Study Journal, 24*(3), 191-207.

Piaget, J. (1945/1962). *Play, dreams, and imitation in childhood.* New York: Norton.

Pelligrini, A., (Ed.). *(1995). The future of play theory: A multidisciplinary inquiry into the contributions of Brian Sutton-Smith.* New York: State University of New York Press.

Postman, N. (1982/1994). *The disappearance of childhood.* New York: Vintage Books.

Reglin, G. (1996). Television and violent classroom behaviors. ERIC ED394687.ws

Rich-Harris, Judith. (1998). The *nurture assumption.* The Free Press.

Seawall, M. (Ed.). (1997). *National Television Violence Study.* Volumes 1, 2, and 3. ERIC PS026610, PS026611, PS026612.

Silva, D. (1996). Moving young children's play away from TV violence: A how-to guide for early childhood educators. ERI C ED 400052.

Sanson, A. & di Muccio, C. (1993). The influence of aggressive and neutral cartoons and toys on the behavior of preschool children. *Australian Psychologist, 28*(2), 93-99.

Slade, A. (Apr, 1987). A longitudinal study of maternal involvement and symbolic play during the toddler period. *Child Development, 58*(2), 367-375.

Smolucha, F. (1998). Alleged gender differences in the human brain. University of Illinois: Unpublished manuscript.

Smolucha, F. (1992). A reconstruction of Vygotsky's theory of creativity. *Creativity Research Journal, 5*(1), 49-68.

Smolucha, L. & Smolucha, F. (1998). The social origins of mind. In O. Saracho & B. Spodek (Ed.). *Multiple perspectives on play in early childhood education.* New York: State University of New York Press.

Steinberg, S., & Kincheloe, J, L. (Eds.). (1998). *Kinder-culture.* Boulder, Co: Westview Press.

The Nation (March 17, 1997). The national entertainment state.

van Der Voort, T., & Valkenburg, P. (1994). Television's Impact on fantasy play: A review of research. *Developmental Review, 14,* 27-51.

Vygotsky, L. (1931/1984). *Pedologiia podrostka* (The Pedalogy of the Adolescent). In Vygotsky's Collected Works, Vol.4. Moscow: Pedagogika.

Watson, M., & Peng, Y. (Oct 1992). The relation between toy gun play and children's aggressive behavior. *Early Education & Development, 3*(4), 370-389.

Wegener-Spoering, G. (1994). War toys and aggressive play scenes. In J. Goldstein (Ed.). *Toys, play, and child development.* New York: Cambridge University Press.

Winn, Marie. (1981). *Children without childhood.* New York: Pantheon Books.

Zupancic, Maria. (Jun-Sep, 1999). Zgodnji razvoj oitrokove igre z igracami: Struktura, predmetno obnasanje in vsebina. (Early development of child's play with toys: Structure, object-behaviors, and contents.) *Psiholoska Obzorja/Horizons of Psychology, 8* (2-3), 115-135.

Zupancic, M., Kavic, T. and Erpic, S. C. (Jun-Sep, 1999). Vzdolzna primerjava malckove igre z igracami v interakciji z mamo in s testatorko. (A follow-up comparisn of mother-toddler and experimenter-toddler interctive play with objects.) *Psiholoska Obzorja/Horizons of Psychology, 8* (2-3), 59-86.

CHAPTER 10

EARLY CHILDHOOD EDUCATIONAL PLAY

Bernard Spodek and Olivia N. Saracho

Play is a natural part of the behavior of all children. The play of children has been described in many cultures and in many periods of history, documenting its universality. It has been described in literature by such eminent authors as William Shakespeare, Leo Tolstoy, Mark Twain and William Wordsworth. It has also been illustrated in diverse pictures, such as those painted by Breugel in Europe and by the Sung Dynasty painters in China. Many of the games played by children centuries ago continue to be played by children today, although sometimes in modified form. Thus, we can see that play in children has occurred in many places over long periods of time. It continues today.

While play has long been considered an important element in the life of young children, it was only relatively recently that play was also been seen as an educative force. Some of the pioneer early childhood educators discounted play—as we know it—as an element in their educational curriculums. While Freidrich Froebel, used the term "play" to describe his kindergarten activities, these activities were so teacher-directed that few modern early educators would consider them play. Maria Montessori, on the other hand, discounted play completely in developing her educational

Contemporary Perspectives on Play in Early Childhood Education
A Volume in: Contemporary Perspectives in Early Childhood Education, pages 171–179.
Copyright © 2003 by Information Age Publishing, Inc.
All rights of reproduction in any form reserved.
ISBN: 1-930608-31-4 (cloth), 1-930608-30-6 (paper)

method. She saw children as more interested in work than they were in play and even suggested that some of young children's play might hinder their learning and development. She also felt that allowing children to engage in fantasy experiences would interfere with their understanding of reality.

It was only with the establishment of the nursery school by Margaret Macmillan in England and with the reform of the American kindergarten by progressive educators spearheaded by Patty Hill Smith, that play became a legitimate part of early childhood education programs. Since that time, however, there has been a continuing argument about the nature of play in early childhood education and especially about the role of the teacher in relation to that play. Often the discussion is posed in terms of an "either/ or" dichotomy. If play is to be considered "good", some have argued, then it must be free of teacher intervention. Thus, play in preschool should be "free play." On the other side, there are those who still argue that free play has little or no significant role to play in early childhood education. These educators feel that the teacher, who best understands the goals and purposes of educational program, should direct the activities of children, possibly only using play as a reward for valued work.

One must wonder, however, about whether play in early childhood schools is actually free. In some of the preschools in Iceland—which are called *playschools* in Icelandic—a room is set aside for children's play. The children go into the room and close the door behind them, not allowing the teacher to observe their play. This is probably as free as play gets in preschools. In most schools, however, teachers observe children's play even if they do not intervene in that play. Even those who value free play generally will intervene in children's play if there is the possibility of danger, if the children's play is unacceptable (aggressive, for example), or if unacceptable play materials are used (toy guns, for example). In these cases, teachers will often redirect children to more acceptable activities in the classroom.

But even in "free play," there is considerable teacher influence. Teachers create the play settings in the classroom and select the play materials. It might be best to call this type of play "choice play," rather than "free play" since children are actually given the choice of playing in relation to themes that are acceptable to the teacher and playing with materials that have been provided by the teacher. They also have a choice in how to use the materials within stated limits.

"FREE PLAY"

For a long time there has been controversy regarding the issue of child-initiated play in early childhood settings as opposed to teacher-directed play.

The position paper on developmentally appropriate practice in early childhood education, issued by the National Association for the Education of Young Children (Bredekamp, 1986), clearly established the association's position in support of child-initiated activities as being developmentally appropriate. This would suggest that teacher-initiated activities in classrooms would be developmentally inappropriate.

Actually, we can argue that few if any activities are actually child—initiated, because of the influence of the teacher in setting up activities and determining which activities to follow through on and which to suppress. Halliwell (1995) has used what we consider a more appropriate term, "child responsive activities," recognizing the power of the teacher in the classroom—whether that power is used directly or indirectly—as children and teachers negotiate activities.

Perhaps it is best not to think of play as an either/or phenomenon, judging that an activity is either play or work and that it is either child-initiated or teacher-initiated. Bergen (1998) views work and play as two extremes along a continuum. On one end there is placed "free play" while on the other end "work" is placed. In between she places "guided play," "directed play" and "work disguised as play," describing the various degrees of teacher guidance or intervention. While all of these types of activity can be found in most early childhood classes, "guided play" and "directed play" best characterizes the kind of play most often seen.

Nor is "free play" always free of academics, while work is always academically oriented,since free play can be used even in relation to academic study. David Hawkins (1965), for example, describes the importance of playing freely with materials—or "messing about"—in relationship to science learning. Hawkins suggests that such free exploratory play needs to be followed by activities that are more focused. The same has been said of the use of manipulative materials in the study of mathematics by young children. Such play is explored in the chapter in this volume by David Uttal.

Both guided play and directed play require that teachers do something to focus children's play in appropriate directions. The degree of teacher intervention differentiates between the two types of play. The intervention may be either direct or indirect. Direct interventions include play tutoring and joining in the play of children. Indirect interventions may consist of providing children with additional information about their play theme or modifying the variable that influence play to optimize its outcomes. These variables include the time, space, materials and people involved in play. If we want to understand the influence of these variables than we need additional research on their relationship to children's play and to the outcomes of children's play. Perhaps before we are able to launch such studies and seek suggestions from the relationship of these studies to practice, we will need to address the issues of teachers' ideologies in relation to play.

EARLY CHILDHOOD EDUCATIONAL PLAY

We can categorize educational play into *manipulative play, physical play, dramatic play,* and *games.* Games may actually be the least free type of play, since children, in playing games, must adhere to rules that they do not establish themselves, although they might modify these rules. While children determine the nature of activity to a greater degree in the other forms of play, there is always a degree of teacher guidance in these activities. At the minimum, teachers create the settings, furnish the materials and equipment, establish the physical and temporal framework, and set limits as to what the children may do. Teachers also guide the children's play to a greater or lesser extent.

Manipulative play is often heavily structured by the teacher. Many of the materials used in this type of play are less open-ended than those used in other forms of play. Manipulative play may be used to teach academics, as the mathematics materials found in many classrooms attest.

Physical play is usually limited by teachers in terms of protecting the safety of children, but teachers seldom have explicit educational objectives for this type of play, which may take place either indoors or in outdoor areas adjacent to the classroom.

The form of play that has received the most attention in research and is probably most valued by teachers of young children is dramatic or sociodramatic play. It is in relation to this type of play that the debate regarding teacher intervention rages. Many teachers feel that this type of play can best reflect the thoughts and feelings of young children and that these should be protected. Too much interference, the argument states, suppresses these and reflects the thoughts and feelings of teachers instead. Yet this type of play can be very supportive of children's understanding of the world, since children reflect their understandings in this play. Dramatic play allows children to reconstruct their understanding of the world. It can show children's misconceptions and allow teachers to correct these misconceptions. These corrections may be done indirectly, to allow the children's play to continue and still remain play.

Dramatic play reflects children's feelings and emotions as well as their ideas. It can serve a cathartic function, allowing children to rid themselves of negative feelings. It can also serve as a way for young children to learn to cope with their feelings, working through in play situations what they cannot work through in real-life situations (Murphy, 1964). Because children can express feelings in play that they cannot express in words, it served as a basis for psychotherapy. Play therapy became a mode that child psychologists use rather than trying to talk through problems as they might do with adults (Landreth, 2001).

It is the concern that teachers have had in allowing children to express their intimate thoughts and feelings through play that led early childhood teachers to recommend a "hands-off" approach to children's play. The belief was that the thoughts and feelings of children would be distorted if the teacher intervened in their play. Teachers, however, are not psycho-therapists and dramatic play in the early childhood classroom serves differ-ent purposes than does dramatic play in the therapist's office.

RESEARCH ON EDUCATIONAL PLAY

It was probably Sarah Smilansky who, in modern times, noted the impor-tance of dramatic play in early childhood educational programs and who tested ideas regarding the way that teachers can guide children's play to make it more educational. Smilansky (1968) noted that all children do not know how to play. She identified those ways that had been effective helping children learn to play and in guiding children's dramatic play in order that it become more educational. These included providing more information about the play themes, adding additional resources to the play, asking lead-ing questions of children and actually joining into the children's play for periods of time. Since that time there has been an increasing number of studies of children's play in early childhood settings.

The educational uses of play has been studies by many scholars and edu-cators (see, for example, Bergin, 1994; Saracho & Spodek, 1998). Some of this research has been used to provide teachers with guidelines for creat-ing play environments and selecting materials and equipment to support play in early childhood education. Frost, Shin and Jacobs (1998) raised concerns about the consequences of crowding when inadequate space is provided for children's play in centers. They also note the consequences of the lack of appropriate, constructive attention given by teachers. Not only should the space be adequate for children's play but, they suggest, it should also be well organized. Activity centers can be provided indoors and outdoor play areas can be zoned. Frost and his colleagues also suggest that there should be a variety of play materials available. They note that decreasing the quantity of play materials in an area can increase the num-ber of social interactions in both positive and negative ways. Thus, teachers need to be aware of the decisions they make regarding the physical and social characteristics of play environments for young children and the con-sequences of these characteristics on young children's play and the out-comes of that play.

Some of the research that has been done has been used to help teachers understand the way that play can be used to help support children's learn-ing in academic areas. Much of that research has looked into the relation-ship of children's play and their literacy development (Roskos & Newman, 1998). Research on play has provided useful descriptions of literacy activi-ties in play. The research has also suggested ways that teachers can function to support literacy activities within the children's play. Saracho (2002) studied the roles of teachers in promoting literacy-related play. The roles that teachers take include those of discussion leader, storyteller, examiner, instructional guide, informer, learning center monitor, and decision— maker. This research provides guidance to teachers in relation to how they can function to guide of children's play in support of literacy development.

Much of the research on play has also focused on understanding the cultural context of children's play. Children in different cultures use different forms of play, use different play materials, and have different styles of play (Roopnarine, Lasker, Sacks, & Stores, 1998). Some scholars see reflections of the culture in children's play. Smoluka, in this volume argues that childrens' play currently reflects a premature involvement in activities most often seen in older children. Such a concern is also voiced more generally by Elkind (1981) who argued that children are being prematurely introduced into the adult world.

In both the Roopnarine et al chapter and the chapter by Smolucha, play is seen as a reflection of the lives children lead within a particular culture. It may be that play is used by children to reconstruct their understandings of reality, as has been suggested by progressive educators. Thus, play reflects children's understandings, whether from some form of formal tuition or from assimilating understandings of what happens within childrens' environment. If this is the case, then, just as we can make judgements regarding what children have assimilated from their observations of the world around them as noted above, but that play might also be used as a way to assess what children have learned in an educational setting, as Pellegrini (1998) has suggested.

THE FUTURE OF RESEARCH RELATED TO EARLY CHILDHOOD EDUCATIONAL PLAY

Conducting research into the play of young children is difficult. Not only is the phenomenon itself hard to grasp, but the subjects of the study are not the best informants. While it is easy to observe young children at play, it is hard to interpret what is observed. Manipulations of objects can be relatively easily observed and recorded. But inferences must be made as to the meanings of these observations and of the children's purposes in making these manipulations, which may not be accurate.

Play therapists also make inferences regarding the play of the children they observe, but these inferences seldom meet the criteria of objectivity required of researcher. Dramatic play, by its very nature, is symbolic. That means that the actions and the objects of play stand for something else. Thus interpretations of what children are playing and what meanings they ascribe to such play must requires a degree of triangulation. More than one perspective is necessary to make appropriate inferences.

In addition, the purposes that children have for playing may be quite different than the purposes that teachers have for supporting their play. Children play to have fun while teachers support play because they consider it to be educational. This does not suggest that we not research children's play. Rather it suggests that we need to be careful in conducting our research and in interpreting the findings of our research.

One can assume there will continue to be research conducted about the nature of play itself. The more we learn about the nature of play, the better we will be able to use play to support the education of young children. Some of this research will be related to anthropological studies of play. We continue to look at play in different cultures and countries to help us understand the nature of the cultures in which the play is conducted.

We need to continue our studies of the relationship between young children's play and the various developmental processes. There have been studies of play related to cognitive development and there have been studies of the relationship between play and social and emotional development. As we begin to see development as a more comprehensive process (Seifert,2002), we will be able to conceptualize the relationship between play and development differently.

We certainly need more research related to the play of young children in educational settings. We need to further consider the consequences of different kinds of play on young children's learning. We have been interested in the relationship between children's play and their literacy development. While there is evidence to support a positive relationship here, the specific ways in which particular kinds of play might enhance literacy needs, to be further explored. Similar research still needs to be done on the relationship between children's play and other areas of learning—science, social studies, the arts, for example. Conversely, would be useful to see how the nature of children's play changes as they become more knowledgeable themselves.

We need additional research on how teachers can modify play situations in early childhood classes and what the consequences of these modifications are both in terms of the play itself as well as the outcomes of the play. We also need to develop and test strategies that parents can use to facilitate play in the home. While increasingly young children are spending time in out-of-home situations—child care services, preschools and kindergartens—we know the importance of home school cooperation. Helping parents facilitate play and having them learn of the strategies that teachers use to facilitate play in preschools can enhance this cooperation.

Generally we have considered the play of young children as taking place in "hands-on" situations. This may no longer be the case, however. Computers are increasingly being found in homes and schools, including preschools. Computers may be seen as a new kind of play environment. There are a number of computer programs available now that provide games for children. While many of these are closed-ended, a number are open-ended. These computer programs can be considered as providing a new form of play for young children. While no one considers that the use of computers will substitute for the "hand-on" play of young children, it certainly is supplementing it. The various parameters of this form of play, as well as its consequences have not yet been adequately studied. Certainly, this an important area of research in relation to the play of young children.

We can expect a continued interest in studying the play of young children and the educational consequences of this play. The more we know about the nature of young children's play, the better we will be able to support it in the context of early childhood education. In addition, as we understand the consequences of what we do to enhance young children's play, we will be able to make it increasingly educative. All of this will require a continued collaboration among early childhood practitioners and researchers in early childhood education. We would hope that this collaboration will increase in the future.

REFERENCES

Bergen, D. (1998). Using a schema for play and learning. In D. Bergen (ed.),*Play as a medium for learning and development* (pp. 109-122). Olney, MD: Association for Childhood Educational International.

Bredekamp, S. (Ed). (1987). *Developmentally appropriate practices in early childhood programs serving children from birth through age eight.* Washington, DC: National Association for the Education of Young Children.

Elkind, D. (1981). *The hurried child: Growing up too fast too soon.* Reading, MA: Addison-Wesley.

Frost, J., Shin, D., & Jacobs, P. J. (1998). Physical environments and children's play. In O. N. Saracho & B. Spodek (Eds.), *Multiple perspectives on play in early childhood education* (pp. 255-294). Albany, NY: SUNY Press.

Halliwell, G. (1995). Gaining acceptance for child-responsive practices: what do teachers know about it? *Journal of Curriculum Studies. 27,* 647-665.

Hawkins, D. (1965). Messing about in science.*Science and Children, 2*(5), 5-9.

Landreth, G. L. (Ed.). (2001). *Innovations in play therapy: issues, processes and special populations.* Philadelphia, PA: Brunner-Routledge.

Murphy, L. (1964). *The widening world of childhood.* New York: Basic Books.

Pellegrini, A. D. (1998). Play and the assessment of young children. In O. N. Saracho & B. Spodek (Eds.), *Multiple perspectives on play in early childhood education* (pp. 220-23 9). Albany, NY: SUNY Press.

Roopnarine, J. L., Lasker, J. Sacks, M., & Stores, M. (1998). The cultural context of children's play. In Saracho, O. N. & Spodek, B. (Eds.), *Multiple perspectives on play in early childhood education* (pp. 194-219). Albany, NY: SUNY Press.

Roskos, K. & Neuman, S. B. Play as an opportunity for literacy. In O. N. Saracho & B. Spodek (Eds.), *Multiple perspectives on play in early childhood education* (pp. 100-115). Albany, NY: SUNY Press.

Saracho, O. N. (2002). Roles of the teacher during literacy-related play. *International Journal of Early Childhood Education.*

Seifert, K. (2002). Sociable thinking: Cognitive development in early childhood education. In O. N. Saracho & B. Spodek (Eds.), *Contemporary perspectives on early childhood curriculum* (pp. 15-40). Greenwich, Ct: Information Age Publishers.

Smilansky, S. (1968). *The effects of sociodramatic play on disadvantaged young children.* New York: Wiley.

ABOUT THE AUTHORS

Doris Bergen is Professor of Educational Psychology at Miami University, where she also serves as Director of the Center for Human Development, Learning, and Teaching. She has written a number of books on the importance of play and on infant/toddler assessment and curriculum. Her most recent book is on the implications of brain research for educators. She has also written about her studies of children's humor development and has conducted cross-cultural research on Chinese early education. She is a past-president of the National Association of Early Childhood Teacher Educators and presently serves on their Foundation Board.

Gary Creasey is Professor of Psychology at Illinois State University. He received his Ph.D. from Virginia Commonwealth University. His research focuses on attachment and interpersonal relationships.

Ziarat Hossain was born in Bangladesh. He is currently an Associate Professor of Psychology in Fort Lewis College. His research focuses on fathering and parental involvement across cultures. He was a Fulbright Scholar to Malaysia.

Contemporary Perspectives on Play in Early Childhood Education
A Volume in: Contemporary Perspectives in Early Childhood Education, pages 181–183.
Copyright © 2003 by Information Age Publishing, Inc.
All rights of reproduction in any form reserved.
ISBN: 1-930608-31-4 (cloth), 1-930608-30-6 (paper)

Fergus Hughes is Professor of Human Development and Psychology at the University of Wisconsin-Green Bay. . His books include *Human Development: Across the Life Span* (1985, 1991), *Child Development,* (1988, 1996) and *Children, Play and Development.* His articles have been published in such journals as *Developmental Psychology,* the *Journal of Genetic Psychology,* and *Young Children.* He current research deals with college students' perceptions of their own learning experiences.

Patricia Jarvis is Professor of Psychology at Illinois State University. She received her Ph.D. from Virginia Commonwealth University. Her research focuses on stress and coping processes in children and adults.

Kwanghee Jung was born in South Korea. She is working on her doctorate at Syracuse University. Her research focuses on risk and resilience in families.

Ole Fredrik Lillemyr is Associate Professor of Early Childhood Education at Queen Maud's College in Trondheim, Norway. His research interests include curriculum development, student motivation and teacher education. He has written extensively in the area of play and learning.

Jaipaul L. Roopnarine was born in Guyana, South America. He is Professor of Child Studies and Early Childhood Education at Syracuse University. His research interests include father-child relationships in diverse cultures, peer relationships and play, Caribbean immigrant children and schooling. He has published extensively in developmental psychology and early childhood journals. He is the current editor of *Play and Culture Studies.*

Olivia N. Saracho is a Professor in the Department of Curriculum and Instruction, College of Education, at the University of Maryland at College Park. She has taught Head Start, preschool, kindergarten, and elementary classes as well as university students at the undergraduate and graduate levels (both master's and doctoral students). Her current research and writing is in the field of early childhood education. She has written several works in young children's play such as "The role of play in the early childhood curriculum," "What Is Stylish about Play?", "An historical overview of theories of play," "The challenge of educational play," "Play and young children's learning." Her research studies include factors in three- to five-year-old children's play, exploring young children literacy development through play, a factor analysis of preschool children's play strategies and cognitive style, socialization factors in the cognitive style and play of young children, preschool children's cognitive play: a factor analysis, some implications of cognitive style on young children's play, a play foundation for family literacy, literacy activities in a play environment, and many others. She is co-author of *Foundations of Early Childhood Education* (Allyn and

Bacon), Right from the Start (Allyn and Bacon), *Individual Differences* (Longman) and co-editor of *Play in Early Childhood Education* (State University of New York Press).

Meera Shin was born in South Korea. She is Assistant Professor of Early Childhood Education at Kean University. Her research focuses on parenting across cultures.

Francine Smolucha has published research on pretend play and her original translations of Vygotsky's works. She is a professor at Moraine Valley Community College in the southwest suburbs of Chicago for the last 25 years. She also taught educational psychology at the School of the Art Institute of Chicago.

Bernard Spodek is Professor Emeritus of Early Childhood Education at the University of Illinois. He received his doctorate from Teachers College, Columbia University. His research and scholarly interests are in the areas of curriculum, teaching, and teacher education in early childhood education. He has written and edited 31 books, 48 chapters in books, and 67 scholarly articles. Dr. Spodek's most recent books are *Multiple Perspectives on Play in Early Childhood Education*, with Olivia Saracho (SUNY Press), *Issues in Early Childhood Educational Research* (Teachers College Press), with Olivia Saracho and Anthony Pellegrini and the *Handbook of Research on the Education of Young Children* (Macmillan). Dr. Spodek has been president of the National Association for the Education of Young Children (1976-78) and is currently president of the Pacific Early Childhood Education Research Association.

David H. Uttal is Associate Professor of Psychology at Northwestern University in Evanston, IL. Uttal's research focuses on the development of symbolic reasoning and spatial cognition. He studies how young children come to understand basic symbolic relations, particularly those involved in maps, scale models, and mathematics manipulatives. Uttal's work has been published in *Child Development, Developmental Psychology*, and the *Journal of Applied Developmental Psychology*. He serves on the board of editors of the journal, *Spatial Cognition* and directs the interdisciplinary program in Language and Cognition at Northwestern University.